GW01157254

Palgrave Studies in Globalization, Culture and Society

Series Editors
Jeroen de Kloet
Centre for Globalisation Studies
University of Amsterdam
Amsterdam, The Netherlands

Esther Peeren
Centre for Globalisation Studies
University of Amsterdam
Amsterdam, The Netherlands

Palgrave Studies in Globalization, Culture and Society traverses the boundaries between the humanities and the social sciences to critically explore the cultural and social dimensions of contemporary globalization processes. This entails looking at the way globalization unfolds through and within cultural and social practices, and identifying and understanding how it effects cultural and social change across the world. The series asks what, in its different guises and unequal diffusion, globalization is taken to be and do in and across specific locations, and what social, political and cultural forms and imaginations this makes possible or renders obsolete. A particular focus is the vital contribution made by different forms of the imagination (social, cultural, popular) to the conception, experience and critique of contemporary globalization. Palgrave Studies in Globalization, Culture and Society is committed to addressing globalization across cultural contexts (western and non-western) through interdisciplinary, theoretically driven scholarship that is empirically grounded in detailed case studies and close analyses. Within the scope outlined above, we invite junior and senior scholars to submit proposals for monographs, edited volumes and the Palgrave Pivot format. Please contact the series editors for more information: b.j.dekloet@uva.nl / e.peeren@uva.nl

More information about this series at
http://www.springer.com/series/15109

Peter Hitchcock

Labor in Culture, Or, Worker of the World(s)

The book title should read "Labor in Culture, Or, Worker of the World(s)" which has been printed previously "Labor in Culture, Or, Workers of the World(s)" by mistake.

palgrave
macmillan

Peter Hitchcock
The Graduate Center and Baruch College
City University of New York (CUNY)
New York, New York, USA

Palgrave Studies in Globalization, Culture and Society
ISBN 978-3-319-45398-9   ISBN 978-3-319-45399-6 (eBook)
DOI 10.1007/978-3-319-45399-6

Library of Congress Control Number: 2017931693

© The Editor(s) (if applicable) and The Author(s) 2017
This book was advertised with a copyright holder in the name of the publisher in error, whereas the author holds the copyright.
This work is subject to copyright. All rights are solely and exclusively licensed by the Publisher, whether the whole or part of the material is concerned, specifically the rights of translation, reprinting, reuse of illustrations, recitation, broadcasting, reproduction on microfilms or in any other physical way, and transmission or information storage and retrieval, electronic adaptation, computer software, or by similar or dissimilar methodology now known or hereafter developed.
The use of general descriptive names, registered names, trademarks, service marks, etc. in this publication does not imply, even in the absence of a specific statement, that such names are exempt from the relevant protective laws and regulations and therefore free for general use.
The publisher, the authors and the editors are safe to assume that the advice and information in this book are believed to be true and accurate at the date of publication. Neither the publisher nor the authors or the editors give a warranty, express or implied, with respect to the material contained herein or for any errors or omissions that may have been made. The publisher remains neutral with regard to jurisdictional claims in published maps and institutional affiliations.

Cover illustration © Les LeVeque "Frequency and Redundancy" (Workers Leaving the Factory)

Printed on acid-free paper

This Palgrave Macmillan imprint is published by Springer Nature
The registered company is Springer International Publishing AG
The registered company address is: Gewerbestrasse 11, 6330 Cham, Switzerland

Preface

Writing a book on "Labor in Culture" is as daunting and difficult a prospect as the topic itself: a receding horizon directly mediated by the myriad forms of labor and culture in everyday life. From such a perspective, the project here is marked by a certain impossibility which I connect, theoretically, politically, and philosophically, to the general problem of worker representation in culture when measured by the abstractions of labor as a social relation (and processes of work).[1] This is primarily an aesthetic and historical critique rather than a description of phenomena or a sociological window on the hugely complex nature of labor in the present. Justifying the narrow and suspect confines of the former over the explanatory power of the latter may offer a false opposition; one indeed that has precisely led to some of the elisions in cultural representation this study traces.[2] Each time I have approached the problem of labor in culture in the past I have attempted to delineate provocative symptoms rather than a universalist grid of interpretation, to stress an open cultural materialism over a formalism that reduces the dynamism in play.[3] No doubt such a view falls into the cliché there is but one book in the making after all, split by wayward iterations or my own "long space" into which I have figured woefully partial paradigms of cultural expression and change. Given the vastness of the focus (a contradiction that takes the form of a material antinomy in how we understand the "the cultural representation of labor") these efforts are prompted more by Edward Said's *Beginnings*, a reflection on the nature of comprehension rather than the equally Sisyphean task of comprehensiveness itself.[4] Nevertheless, with three theoretical chapters on concepts of "worker inquiry," the "subject," and "value" followed by three cultural critiques on fiction, photography, and film, the study here would seem to be as guilty of absenting as those that parade cultural globalization without any sense of labor at all. Rather than attempt to explain away everything that is not here, the following will provide a brief commentary on the significance of this odd assembly and the promise of further work to which it inexorably bends.

If globalization is a way of both dividing and integrating the world economically, socially, and politically, then it is relatively easy to see how culture might come to facilitate or represent this process. Yet the fact that globalization is so contested and contestable is also symptomatic of culture's discrepant role in linking peoples, spaces, and places across the planet.[5] How is the cultural representation of labor part of this vexed dynamic? What interests me is the interrogative possibilities of two forms of problematic integration. The dreams and realities of global markets and labor unity are not false on their own terms but dubious as processes for each other. For instance, the intensification of globalization after the collapse of the Socialist Bloc, expressed initially as a form of neoliberal triumphalism, proceeds as if labor's role in capitalism no longer constitutes a bar on its will to accumulation on a world scale. Similarly, if the worker as subject had enjoyed an increasingly strained relation to putatively worker parties and states, their dissolution has not in fact cleared the path to Marx and Engels' justly famous exhortation "Working people of all countries, unite!" Instead, the selling of labor at a global scale has fragmented the logic of unity as workers anxiously compete against each other under the terms of a dispersed and disparate precariat. There is massive labor resistance to capital's demands but most of this is not premised on a fully-fledged global project of worker solidarity primed to smash capitalism tout court, but instead it attends to the political immediacy of understandably specific and local concerns. Lifting the burden of state authoritarianism may be deemed freedom enough, even with the deadening demands of the wage for sustenance. Yet, when it comes to labor this has not invalidated Marxism's critique of capitalism but it has dramatically changed the cultural logic in which it may be expressed. Thus, an alternative and prescient title for the project is its subtitle: "worker of the world(s)." What does the shifting of the mischievous "s" mean in this context?

If we once believed the concept of world was stable enough for workers to "win" it in Marx and Engels' sense at the end of the *Manifesto*, a plurality of possible worlds undoes that synergy. This does not abandon the project of worker solidarity and class struggle but it places a special demand on the forms of global integration currently posed. The singularity of world is globalization's promise; the plurality of worlds undoes globalization's claims. But surely, there is only one world and, as for the worker, she exists only, as Mario Tronti puts it, in the plural?[6] Indubitably. But what if this is also globalization's logic? Can we not think its negative, dialectically, to challenge globalization's concept of world and, simultaneously, open the figure of the worker to an alternative to subject reason, to a being in the world? The point would not be to make the singularity of the worker stand in for worker difference but would be to mark instead a form of non-identity in difference, just singular enough to question globalization's false inclusivity, a "whatever singularity" as Agamben terms it, but purposeful in terms of cultural logic (singular here, of course, does not mean individual).[7] Why should the worker work for the world according to globalization? Indeed, why work at all if that is socialization's primary pivot (growth, capital accumulation, gross inequality, etc.)?[8] If we need one world to save the planet ecologically from ourselves, is the worldliness of globalization the key to that redemption?

Another layer of contention signified in the roving "s," the other side of plurality, concerns the matter of multiplicity itself. Multiculturalism, whether as a state policy or as a liberal reflex (inclusionism as its own reward rather than as a question about the politics and power of inclusion), would seem to be globalization's cultural front, its mediation at every scale of identity and identification. Culture is always already multiple: "multi" only marks that some hegemony or homogeneity needs to be qualified, reformed, better equipped to be seen to represent the world's rich diversity. I do not doubt the good intentions of multipliers in this vein (without doubt such an approach has demystified the shibboleths of cultural canons, "great traditions," etc.) but the addition of an "s" has its own register of power, even as it appears to disavow it in its utility. Just keep adding "s's" and soon every identity will be covered, contained, niched. Moving the "s" in this instance does not confirm the multiplicity of worlds or their intersectional truth but points to the ambivalence of such possibility (hence the parentheses), just as removing it from the worker does not reduce her to some monadic consciousness but marks that a singularity may be at stake. What then is the relationship between my title and subtitle?

Labor is always "in" culture since it is coextensive with all of the work, makings, practices, expressions that constitute living. One could claim to have culture, as one would have a commodity, as a source of capital and esteem, but culture is more productively understood as immanent, or as a dynamic system of signs rather than something simply reducible to objecthood and its circulation. Labor, as I use it here, is that which relates through work, is that which has a definite relation to capital as a means of production. It is not work as such, nor is it that which represents workers in all of their difference but labor as that social relation adequate to capital itself. Adequate here is not equal to but sufficient to: clearly this draws from a Marxist tradition in which labor must be thought beyond "thingness." Culture, at this level, becomes a practice for thinking such a "beyond." Thus, labor in culture is not just the instance of cultural representation (of work, of workers, of the working class) but is a knot in the way social production and reproduction is understood. Ultimately, labor in culture is not about a catalog of instances but is closer to a cultural logic, a "way of seeing" to borrow from John Berger that is materially produced and constrained.[9] It is this sense of labor that moves the "s" from worker to world in the current conjuncture and signals a conceptual array at odds with globalization's studied accumulation of the world as a narrative of capitalist dispossession.

What are the themes of this project that elaborate the above and how might the chapters on theory relate to the case studies in the second half of the book? How do you represent a relation that is not in itself an object, a thing, an identity? When, at the beginning of *Capital*, Marx attempts to understand labor and value in terms of the commodity, he asks us to think back from the finished form to the conditions of its very possibility. Use value is unrepresentable because it is only in exchange that value can "appear." What he calls the "residue of the products of labor" can be considered, through a process of reduction, as "congealed quantities of homogenous human labor" rather than as "the form of their expenditure" (the commodity itself). What we thus "see" are values, commodity values, rather than the commodity or its price (this logic, by the way, can be applied to the work of services as much as commodity production even if Marx himself does not explore that possibility). Marx uses a process of subtraction to get us to understand extraction (the extraction of surplus value from labor, for instance, for any worker who must sell their labor to subsist). For the cultural critic, this is profoundly aesthetic, a negative sublime where excess, surplus, is glimpsed in its opposite as reduction and subtraction.[10] Several lessons may derive from such an approach. One is that even if labor as relation is not present in cultural surfaces it is at work in the ways in which culture is cognized. Surely, however, featuring the worker front and center as the focal point of a worker inquiry and as its producer is the best way to assess such cognitive possibility and the regimes of knowledge that may attend it? This study both confirms this tenet and simultaneously doubts the truth claims it produces. The material determinants of labor as relation can be calculated but are not simply culturally expressive. Similarly, showing the worker is at once an appreciative act but does not in itself undo the objectifying processes of labor that are vital to capitalism's rationalization of globalization. What the chapters on theory attempt to do, starting with the problem of the workers' inquiry, is track the dialectics of representation and its extraction/subtraction as a historical and by all means global critique. The aim is to encourage further analysis of the cultural representation of labor where it challenges both the platitudes of globalization's world order and the conventional ways in which the worker is ordered within it.

Some of the ideas addressed in this work include labor is about its relation; the worker is about its singularity in the plural; in the realm of labor, being is about work not the individual identity of the worker. In addition, I am interested in why forms of labor do not comport with representational claims; why the reality of workers in social production and reproduction confounds all cultural and critical equivalence; and why the figure of the worker always stands in for labor/capital as figura. To begin with mimesis, as I do, and especially with Erich Auerbach's elaboration of mimesis in the book of the same name, may be read as equally a banalization and anachronism of the cultural representation of labor as globalization's interest in bringing workers of the world together, but the project is to expand our keywords of cultural analysis, a lexicon of labor if you will, to fathom more critically the ways in which work and workers are expressed. The limits of globalization place special burdens on such an undertaking and on the legacies of labor representation in modernity. Auerbach, for instance, thinks of this in terms of high/low distinctions in the European tradition, yet globalization is not simply an export of such cultural difference, even if it speaks to a certain homogenization in the circulation of differentiation itself. Processes of value extraction and capital accumulation are regularized to promote a world of exchange but when and where these processes take place and who is engaged in them have only problematic cultural correlatives with European modernity. The entangled histories of civilization and barbarism, of rights and the right to conquer, enslave, and exploit, for instance, have been resisted and recomposed so that mimesis means more than reality enforced from abroad. In truth, of course, labor was simultaneously being recomposed in the West from the high point of the workers' inquiry on via post-Fordism and neoliberal prerogatives, but also as a result of examining the fabric of capitalism as fundamentally racial and gendered in addition to the primacy given its divisions of class. Thus, if we now have a radically different perspective on labor difference at a global scale, it is both because of Europe's fading primary axis (which would nevertheless depend on the precise metric) and because of modernity's exploded globality, fragments of a singular key transformed by capital's attempts to make itself over and labor's ability to make it otherwise. Whether we think of sweatshop workers, domestic and service workers, line workers, knowledge workers, care workers, autonomous workers, gig or precarious workers (including zero hours contractors), workers who have barely had the chance to work at all or who have been made redundant (the reserve army), or unwaged workers (including women, in particular, who centrally reproduce the social relations of production), modernity's project lies scattered across the worlds of labor. If I trace more than a little conceptual oscillation in Jacques Rancière's use of labor, laborer, work, worker, proletarian, proletariat, working class, poor, people, and plebs, it is both to acknowledge the seriousness of such vacillation and to suggest these are veritable "parts of no part" that have a significant cultural valence. We are in a massively enmeshed world of workers in which the worker makes, among all the other things she makes, vital cultural worlds.

But if I suggest in the workers' inquiry, the problem of the subject, and the question of value, that the cultural representation of labor necessitates a theoretical and historical reflexivity rather than only a description of global difference in the present, it is to accentuate how the former grounds the knowledge of the latter as a positive resource of change. The brief examples I provide in later chapters, on Berger's novels, Salgado's photographs, and Jia's films, are more about the possibilities of such resources rather than about making any absolute claims for their individual and exemplary prominence in representing workers of the world. Although I do explain the importance of the forms of their expression, it is clear the argument is also about the limits of such engagement (What about other forms? Why individual artists? Doesn't the pervasiveness of labor mean the worker is everywhere where culture is ordinary? Is not the politics of selection as suspect as it is polemical?[11]). Regarding artists we could say they are themselves workers of the world, but they are not the workers they represent and, while they may speak *to* questions of alterity in their art, they do not speak *for* worker difference, whether in terms of gender, race, class, sexuality, age, ability, or place, to mark at least some of that difference politically and economically. To that extent, the case studies do not in fact solve the theoretical knot of labor in culture but attempt to explain why such a desire must necessarily exceed the confines, like the world according to globalization, in which the worker is generally posed.

Labor in culture is as immeasurable as value whose metrics, defined by production, no longer fully constitute labor's contribution to it. Yet part of the polemic of this book is that the absenting of labor is part of a more general fault-line in subject reason, one that says, in the West in particular, that if one cannot see the factory the factory does not exist (the assumption that "working class" only means manual labor also contributes to this metaphysical conundrum), except around the ethics of disaster perhaps, like the mediated horror that was the collapse of Rana Plaza in April 2013, an eight-story commercial building in Savar, close to Dhaka, Bangladesh, that killed 1,129 and injured at least 2,500 garment workers who labored there. The export of labor-intensive factory work to the global South is a key feature of globalization in the last fifty years and is as much a reason for the oddly elegiac in invocations of the working class as those outpourings directly linked to the end of socialist states. Andre Gorz's *Farewell to the Working Class* (1983) comes to mind, as does more recent work by Jodi Dean (*The Horizon of Communism* [2012]). Class composition is always on the move but now assumes forms in which the working class itself no longer seems discernible (the aforementioned conceptual oscillation is also a part of this), or it must be hunted down as if it has gone to ground. Stephen Hasting-King's important book (to be discussed in Chapter 1) is titled *Looking for the Proletariat*, and John Kirk claims to be "on the trail of the working class," and so on. It does not take a catastrophe like Rana Plaza (or, for instance, the Marikana massacre of platinum miners in South Africa in August, 2012) to figure workers into narratives of class, but clearly changing articulations of class in worker narrative mean that, theoretically, workers are as likely to be a "multitude" (Hardt/Negri) or a "people" (Rancière) as they are to constitute a class that, in its specific relation to capital, occupies a pivotal role in the future of globalization. Again, the cultural representation of labor does not fill in this absenting or metonymy: it is, rather, constitutive of globalization's contemporary meaning. On one level, Berger's parables of European peasantry, Salgado's paeans to a dying industrialism, and even Jia's intimations of post-socialist migrancy are out of step with the real of labor across globalization (again signaled by the roving "s" in my subtitle); on another level, discrepancies of space (the "multiplication of labor" as Mezzadra and Neilson provocatively put it[12]) and disjunct temporalities (the worker of the world[s] has a history despite our presentist obsessions) are the very scene of globalization's most acute dialectical contradictions. Salgado notes that "Globalization is presented to us as a reality, but not as a solution."[13] If the world as abstraction is a bar on such knowledge, a cultural critique of labor offers other worlds of possibility. It is to such labor, a labor of labor, that this book is dedicated.

NOTES

1. I have attempted to answer this question in a number of ways, but here I concentrate on how globalization complicates the effulgence of the worker in particular cultural forms. On the general difficulty of "representation" regarding labor as relation and the working class, see Peter Hitchcock, "They Must Be Represented?: Problems in Theories of Working-Class Representation," *PMLA* 115 (1) (January, 2000): 20–32.
2. I do not believe this to be necessarily the case. Trenchant examples of creative methodology within very specific bounds are still highly recommended. See, for instance, Roberto del Valle Alcalá, *British Working-Class Fiction*. London: Bloomsbury, 2016. Among other things, del Valle Alcalá's transforms what has always seemed the safest option in linking class and fiction by re-purposing Deleuze and Agamben. It is interesting, nevertheless, that this "line of flight" eschews the scalar challenge of globalization. For a book that shares the polemical interest in confronting globalization on the cultural terrain of worker representation, see Sonali Perera, *No Country: Working-Class Writing in the Age of Globalization*. New York: Columbia University Press, 2014. While I take a very different methodological tack from Perera, her project elicits a keen understanding of how working-class literature currently comes to mean.
3. See, for instance, Peter Hitchcock, *Oscillate Wildly: Space, Body, and Spirit of Millennial Materialism*. Minneapolis: University of Minnesota Press, 1999; *Dialogics of the Oppressed*. Minneapolis: University of Minnesota Press, 1993; *Working-Class Fiction in Theory and Practice: A Reading of Alan Sillitoe*. Ann Arbor: UMI Research Press, 1989.
4. Edward Said, *Beginnings: Intention and Method*. New York: Columbia University Press, 1985.

5. I will not attempt to summarize the literature on globalization either for or against but its volume and availability is symptomatic of its subject (as quantity and circulation). Pertinent texts on the culture/globalization connection include: Jan Nederveen Pieterse, *Globalization and Culture*. London: Rowman and Littlefield, 2008; John Tomlinson, *Globalization and Culture*. Chicago: University of Chicago Press, 1999; Roland Robertson, *Globalization*. London: Sage, 1992; Arjun Appadurai, *Modernity at Large*. Minneapolis: University of Minnesota Press, 1996; Ulf Hannerz, *Transnational Connections*. London: Routledge, 1996; Radical critiques of globalization abound. I highly recommend the work of Neil Smith in this regard: *The Endgame of Globalization*. New York: Routledge, 2004; and that of another colleague, David Harvey, *A Brief History of Neoliberalism*. Oxford: Oxford University Press, 2007. Globalization can be thought without neoliberalism, but neoliberalism cannot be thought without globalization. Both, of course, have transmogrified labor over the last half century.
6. Mario Tronti: "Fin da principio gli operai, come i valori di scambio del capitalista, vengono avanti al plurale: l'operaio al singolare non esiste." ("From the beginning the workers, as exchange values of the capitalist, come forth in the plural: the worker in the singular does not exist"). Mario Tronti, *Operai e Capitale*. Roma: DeriveApprodi, 2006: 234. I would add: "especially for the capitalist." I will say more about operaismo in relation to the workers' inquiry in Chapter 1.
7. See Giorgio Agamben, *The Coming Community*. Trans. Michael Hardt. Minneapolis: University of Minnesota, 1993: 2. It may seem odd to invoke a philosopher who explains the idea of communism using pornography (his point is actually about class markers) but the question of substantiality in labor as other than substance as commodity (or value *qua* commodity) is what I interpret as a useful singularity in deconstructing labor's meaning for capitalist globalization.
8. This critique also harks back to the autonomist movements of the Fifties and Sixties but is easily misinterpreted as yet one more decentering of the worker, this time from within the Left itself. In fact, of course, it emphasizes how the focus on the wage and wage labor has mystified worker solidarity by excluding unwaged work, including reproductive labor, from critiques of capitalism. See, for instance, Kathi Weeks, *The Problem with Work*. Durham: Duke University Press, 2011.
9. See, John Berger et al., *Ways of Seeing*. London: Penguin, 1972.
10. This is not quite the "Marxist sublime" in Terry Eagleton's delicious formulation but it does draw on the long tradition of materialist analysis for and against Kant's Third Critique. It should be noted, however, that even Marxist aesthetics often falls silent at the point when the cultural

representation of labor is at stake. See Terry Eagleton, *The Ideology of the Aesthetic*. Oxford: Blackwell, 1990.
11. Each time one starts such a project the figures and works are different. "In each time," as John Berger puts it, one figures labor into globalization as a cultural problematic the conjunction seems only to mark the paucity of one's own imagination and political perspicacity. And what of translation and translatability? If the "found object" of labor in culture is primarily English or Anglophone how can the worker of the world(s) possibly meet the demands of scale and difference in globalization, despite its often Anglocentric and preternaturally parochial concerns? The answer to the "what if?" of the cultural representation of labor necessarily changes according to the choices made, and obviously not necessarily for the better. In the main I wish to stress the significance of the problem of labor in culture and how these selections may help in addressing it rather than take the position they might overcome all of the absences they indicate. In effect, I find this approach also points to the cultural logic of exclusion whenever labor as relation is invoked and the compromised politics of representing it, including in cultural critique itself.
12. See Sandro Mezzadro and Brett Neilson, *Border as Method, or, The Multiplication of Labor*. Durham: Duke University Press, 2013. Rather than begin within cultural signification, the authors examine labor's transformations as a problem of spatial method and of the border as a topos of epistemic frisson. Whether the present study also complicates what they call "the pattern of the world" others must decide.
13. Sebastião Salgado, *Migrations: Humanity in Transition*. New York: Aperture, 2000: 15.

Acknowledgments

To the extent a work of this kind imagines a collective author a list of names by itself might not capture that sensibility. Certainly, however, over the course of elaborating this project there are people and institutions that have facilitated in its construction and I am grateful for their support in various ways. Some of the impetus for this book began with earlier research on Henry Green and Pat Barker and I thank Youngstown State University and Pat Barker herself for encouraging my studies on working-class representation. That elements of Bakhtinian thinking permeate this text owes much to my interactions with Bakhtinians more capable than me over the years including David Shepherd, Craig Brandist, Galin Tihanov, and Clive Thomson. Individual events, like the Bakhtin conferences in Cocoyoc and Moscow, shaped my worldview on workers in more ways than I can say. Other portions of the text inevitably began as conference papers and keynote lectures. I thank the University of Pennsylvania, Simon Fraser University, University of Sheffield, Beijing University, Hong Kong University, University of Western Ontario, University of Massachusetts, Shanghai University, and Pasadena City College for hosting relevant work, and the Modern Language Association, American Studies Association, and American Comparative Literature Association for the conference opportunities. I especially thank Tim Corrigan and Brian Kennedy in this regard, whose invitations allowed me to think through key aspects of this project. I would like to express my deep gratitude to Jeff Derksen, poet, thinker, teacher and all around good guy, for facilitating the event on "expenditure" and "value" in Vancouver, and to his great students for contributing appreciable value in their own ways. Many of my own current and former students have also been teaching me about theory and practice over the years and I thank in particular Jamie Skye Bianco, Roger Rawlings, Fiona Lee, Lily Saint, Ajay Gehlawat, Joon Lee, Hyewon Shin, Nikolina Nedeljkov, Tom Davies, and Kate Moss. Without doubt this work could not have proceeded without the vibrant conversations in a theory reading group I help to run and the special contributions of Jesse Schwartz, Justin Rogers-Cooper, James Arnett, and the irrepressible Sean Grattan. Labor is difficult but their theoretical ardor has been inspirational.

The major institutional support for this endeavor has come from the Center for Place, Culture, and Politics (CPCP) at the Graduate Center of the City University of New York. The Center was founded at the turn of the century by Neil Smith, a brilliant scholar of geography, Marxism, and all things liberatory whose untimely death was a great loss to many, including those of us at the CPCP. As Associate Director I have had the privilege of working with some amazing people, including Padmini Biswas, Mary Taylor, Ruthie Gilmore, and David Harvey. Ruthie in particular has been a sustaining presence in recent years and has never been averse to me thinking out loud about theorizing the cultural representation of labor. Many of the events at the Center have opened up avenues for me on the subject of workers and worker culture. This is as much a work of the CPCP as it is mine, although the Center is not responsible for any of my shortcomings.

I want to thank the good people over at *Modern Fiction Studies* and *Cultural Critique* for allowing me to work from earlier versions of the chapters on Berger and worker subjects respectively (the latter benefitting from the editorial expertise of Sean Grattan and Christian Haines). Although I would have liked to include images by Sebastiao Salgado, I thank Amazonas for at least considering that possibility. Much of what I say about labor rests on the powers of imagination, a faculty intensified by the absence of Salgado's photos among these pages. Gratitude is extended to the Center for the Humanities at the CUNY Graduate Center where I was a Mellon Fellow for part of my initial research on Salgado. I extend comradely gratitude to the video artist Les LeVeque for allowing me to use a screen shot from his work "Frequency and Redundancy," a project developed from an old worn-out 16-mm print of the Lumière brothers' famous film of 1895, "Workers Leaving the Factory." For those who reach Chapter 6, the significance of this will become more deeply resonant. A special thank you to Esther Peeren and Jeroen de Kloet, the series editors, for believing in this project and to the professional support staff of Palgrave Macmillan for their inestimable help, including Felicity Plester, Sophie Auld, Eva Hodgkin, and Heloise Harding. Esther in particular has been a key interlocutor in the development of this book, and although we both could have wished for more it is thanks to Esther that it is not considerably less. As this book was being prepared for publication I learned of the passing of John Berger. Although this book is not focused on his considerable oeuvre I do hope it underlines why his work is worthy of further study.

This book is dedicated to my mother, Joyce Pamela Hitchcock, whose working life began at 14 and continued until her retirement at the age of 78. For the working class such a life is not unusual and while we are supposed to wait upon the robots and the end of work it remains very much the norm for billions of people across the planet. Although my working life began in factories and on a farm, the fact that I now do this is testimony to the hard work of my mother and her lessons on how labor is my foundation.

Finally, a special shout out to Molly, Sam, and my dearest Amy. Every family believes they are special and you know we really are! Thanks.

Contents

Part I Worker

1 An Inquiry of Labor 3
   Notes 36

2 The Worker Subjects 47
   Notes 69

3 On the Cultural Representation of Labor (Value) 75
   Notes 95

Part II World(s)

4 Sensing Class in John Berger's "Into Their Labors" Trilogy 103
   Notes 130

5 A Gift: Workers to Sebastião Salgado 133
   Notes 184

6 The Paradox of Moving Labor: Workers in the Films of Jia Zhangke 191
   Notes 219

Bibliography 225

Index 239

PART I

Worker

CHAPTER 1

An Inquiry of Labor

In what Allan Bloom calls a "permanent book" (Plato's *Republic*),[1] Socrates rationalizes social division in some very provocative ways by using hierarchies that have the appeal of universality. Gods mixed gold in the souls of rulers so that gold is somewhat literally the substance of their command. Farmers and other laborers, we are told, are subject to an admixture of bronze and iron and live that reality according to appropriate subjection. These soulful combinations are not absolute, and occasionally workers will reveal a little gold and will be encouraged to become guardians instead. Yet a pall hangs over this anomaly, since the oracle says, "the city will be destroyed when an iron or bronze man is its guardian" (94—the prospect of an iron lady, of course, was not even imagined, still less divisions of labor in general as gendered and raced). Jacques Rancière seizes on the *Republic's* reason to argue for "countermyths, tales that muddy this difference of natures."[2] In Rancière's *Proletarian Nights*, artisans dream of so much more than their allotted place and Rancière underlines, in detailed examples, why this is proof enough "the equality of intelligences" must continue to be articulated. Of course, artisanal reverie is not quite or not always proletarian reality but nevertheless, and in contradistinction to the persistence of some kind of gold standard (which includes the notion of proletarian itself, the point of Rancière's distinction), worker narratives are a cultural and political horizon, a resource of hope in Raymond Williams's sense, in a world of more resolutely inevitable determinations.[3] Farmers and laborers will feature prominently in the case studies in the second half of this book, but the latter do not extend proletarian nights in Rancière's otherwise ardent provocation. Instead, I wish to "muddy the difference of natures" through a complementary and dialectical polemic. *Les Revoltes Logiques*, cofounded by Rancière, begins with a question: "How does one form, in its limits and contradictions, a class thought?"[4] It is a vital inquiry, not just for politics but for culture and one that must give us pause about the nature of inquiry itself (thus, although the question might be deemed inappropriate within a workers' inquiry, it is nevertheless the interrogative basis of its form). All kinds of conditions mediate what is appropriate to the question that simultaneously implies appropriation and misappropriation. A logical revolt for some can be revolting logic for others (a torsion that is at the heart of Rancière's project), and inquiry puts into play contradictions, of class, of workers, of working class, that bespeak the relations of their materialization and complex divisions. In this way, the problem of who makes the inquiry extends well beyond the subject who asks, and never more so when the subject *of* the question is the worker.

We take it as axiomatic that the key to working-class expression is the worker's experience; that the being of worker finds cultural articulation adequate to it. Much of my previous analysis of class and culture has cleaved to this principle, but only by questioning its meaning for knowledge. Interestingly, this position both confirms and contradicts Socrates' peremptory distinction. There is poetry, and then there is the worker's expression of her lot which is something else again. Or, the worker is aesthetically true to her experience which must mean there is gold in her soul or else that we have seriously underestimated iron. Mixing metals might seem to alleviate the tensions Socrates' divisions promote, but then the city in his judgment appears most secure when each is "in" their endeavor. Poets make poems, shoemakers make shoes, and philosophers make philosophy. Yet since it is obvious we are not solely defined by one attribute, and perhaps not by attributes in the conventional sense at all (which is one of the many lessons of intersectionality, if not of Spinozism), it seems there is more than ontological violence in making these distinctions in the first place. Two small points: first, the importance of Plato's *Republic* rests on how categories come to construct and negotiate the social—our souls may be of different mettle, but the logic of such distinction continues to overdetermine much of what we think of as social and aesthetic particularity; second, man's [sic] ideal state both undermines the position of the worker socially (for instance, on the question of social reproduction) while bracketing any aesthetic merit, especially if it might come to rest on mimesis. The social question can in part be explained by distinguishing the worker as an individual from labor in its relation to capital (in practice, of course, the distinction is necessarily problematized by different types of work and worker). Here, however, the mimetic faculty deserves special comment.[5]

Guardians of the city are not playing roles, they are not imitating anyone else; they simply are the position they inhabit and if they are to remain that way they must not be bewitched by mimetic art, by art's copying of an original rather than being it. The origins of the work of art and the distractions of mimesis are very much written into the quandary of the worker in her representation. The aesthetic representation of a life is paradoxically the ground of its authenticity: whether in poetry, fiction, drama, painting, etc., the worker's expression of worker life is its truth in correspondence, its *Erlebnis*, to borrow from Dilthey.[6] Yet it is just as much its misapprehension, a representation as misrepresentation, and for Plato undermines all claims to authenticity in its form. As is often the case, the philosophical distinction holds better than the actual processes of socialization in which mimesis is manifest (Bourdieu's entire project of *Distinction* is grounded by this tension[7]). If the carpenter makes a table, then later makes a poem about a table, we could argue both the latter is a copy of the copy that is the former, but that neither preclude the creativity in making. It is the instinct of creativity in mimesis that is missing from Plato's account even as we must acknowledge the situatedness of this elision for Plato in his own time. This is not to say he simply "mirrors" the concerns of history in which he is enmeshed. Far from it. Yet the logical consequences of his fear of mimesis, the lure of weakness and distraction through "copying," accentuate that worldviews, particularly those that aim to codify the social, are material through and through. Certainly the guardians today should have little trepidation about the mimetic per se since it has long been commodified and copying itself is the original condition of capital circulation. The question remains whether this development obtains for all forms of mimesis that occur within such a system of making. On this issue, mimesis must be further clarified and historicized.

Mimesis as an aesthetic mode challenges the pure gold guardian thesis of *The Republic* by mixing forms in its genealogy, by democratizing art without sacrificing the idea of some kind of artistic autonomy. It can be used as a foundation of human endeavor that Walter Benjamin in particular remarks upon (even in the age of "technical reproducibility"),[8] or as a specific historical aesthetics in the imposing mold Erich Auerbach presents. While Auerbach's philological tradition is unabashedly Eurocentric, the passage from high to low style in mimetic practices that is epitomized in the central example of Dante offers a trenchant answer to the purification procedures of Plato's divisions. The lessons of Auerbach's *Mimesis* for the representation of worker reality are many but here I will offer an initial assertion: representation in the present study is not simply a token of authenticity but a focus on the components of worker representation, however partial or flawed.[9] It is the belief worker representation is taking place even if the artist is not or does not claim to be a worker that riddles the wonder of the mimetic, a process that derives from a place where Auerbach's own commitment as an interpreter is at stake (although much of Auerbach's philology is unique, the practice of intimate identification, even if sometimes naïve and idealistic, is a reminder about what is and is not possible in cultural critique). For Auerbach, this approach often meant concern for the figural and for me this has always constituted a challenge for cultural representations of the worker. Why? Briefly, the figural proposes that a recent worker representation, for instance, may complete an earlier or otherwise disconnected figural realism but also that an instance of worker figuration may offer a representation of a worker yet to be and a future for workers not yet articulated or visible as such. One need not necessarily subscribe, like Auerbach, to Hegelian teleology to make sense of these connections (the figure disorders time), but the question of figura is resolutely historical in its inclinations and fosters dialectical thinking in cultural critique. Lurking in the background is a related discussion that links Auerbach and Goethe's thoughts on *Weltliteratur* to the knot of "world" where workers have not, in fact, united, a dialectic that is the very cultural and political ground of the current project.[10]

If this book's subtitle alludes to the final line of the *Communist Manifesto*, it also registers a Marxist dilemma. Should a cultural concern for the representation of workers be first and foremost empirically verifiable? Here we circle back to the problem of experience in contrast to the "as if" modes of identification in Auerbach. Discussion of worker representation necessarily entails a sociology of culture but what, if any, are the epistemological claims? This is not the place to suture the cuts between empiricism and rationalism, between sense and reason, which has a separate existence from that which the worker represents (for workers, knowledge is not an entirely philosophical problem of interpretation, especially where change is concerned). In a way, figura traverses and transforms such division, offering a spirit of relation that, like Raymond Williams' "structure of feeling," is its own kind of truth. For his part, Marx once pondered a survey, a workers' inquiry, to complement and complicate all thoughts of abstract labor. In 1880, *La Revue socialiste* asked Marx what questions for workers he could devise to elaborate the substance of their experience. Marx came up with 101 questions (in the "*Enquête ouvrière*," rounded off to a hundred in the *Workers' Inquiry*, the English translation[11]) and what they trace are the liminal spaces between workers' self-identity and the constituents of class for political economy, a space where the mimetic faculty lives to undo subject reason between the transcendental and the empirically sound. All this despite the aim, Marx argued, that was "an exact and positive knowledge of the conditions in which the working-class—the class to whom the future belongs—works and moves." This belief, and indeed the content of the inquiry, are fascinating on their own terms but are necessarily at some remove from the aesthetic and philosophical issues in which the worker subjects, and is subject. The idea one might check off these attributes of working-class existence against a contemporaneous cultural expression would seem ludicrous. Why should art, even art "about" workers, be verifiable and approximate to some arguably tendentious survey of "real" experience? The point is to hold these modes of representation in tension rather than to repeat endlessly they inhabit alien spaces of expressibility. Both might be said to objectify in the sense they assume a worker is being addressed in their elaboration, but then again it is the ambivalence of this knowing that drives the "inquiry" in the first place, even when the verisimilitude of the worker is at its most explicit. Marx's interest is clearly spurred by a desire for knowledge from below: the experience of exploitation is necessarily different from the formula for it. Like Auerbach's crafted argument for Dante's use of popular or "vulgar" language as enabling what we know as "literature" to exist (with the support that Dante's aim is "true reality"), so the revelation of the worker as integral to knowing the world has a cultural correlative that reaches beyond the basic questions of the inquiry. It acknowledges that representing the worker's reality is vital to the possibility of narrating per se, and especially when labor is vulgarized by value extraction or impossibly subjected. Marx's *Workers' Inquiry* has served more as a catalyst rather than as a model of investigation in its own right although some have been quite willing to limit it to a basic sociological framework. The story of the workers' inquiry is, whatever else it is, an allegory of the fraught imbrication of the working class and intellectual.

Perhaps one can mark its permutations by thinking of the questions in terms of their collective name. Clearly the questions are posed *to* workers, but the hope is the inquiry becomes the workers' by virtue of the knowledge provided in the answers. If the dice is loaded by the form of Marx's questions (certain information is being sought and Marx acknowledges that more questions could be asked), the worker emerges in the details of the reply. There is an expansive literature around the logic of such inquiry which is never far from the general problem of the representation of reality.[12] Even the grammatical question of possession (Does the inquiry belong to the workers? Is it ever their inquiry? Can it be an individual inquiry, a "worker's inquiry"? Why questions? Can't these be implied merely be narration itself?) points to key issues about knowledge, politics, and subjectivity. Marx knew his questions had a programmatic political bias and that those who answered were knowing in their own way—"We hope to meet in this work with the support of all workers in town and country who understand that they alone can describe with full knowledge the misfortunes from which they suffer and that only they, and not saviors sent by providence, can energetically apply the healing remedies for the social ills of which they are prey." "Full knowledge" is not in itself an epistemology and yet the inquiry, as a socio-political metric, is often read to do precisely this work. It is not a formula as such but a matrix of call and response produced in the rhetorical structures of industrial capitalism at that time. Indeed, from this perspective the worker inquiry necessarily pre-exists its distillation in Marx's 101 questions (just as the social pre-exists sociology) and is often registered in worker narratives (both about workers and by workers) throughout the period that forms the basis for Marx's understanding of political economy. Elsewhere I will connect this phenomenon to Rancière's extraordinary *Proletarian Nights*, but the point is to emphasize that worker inquiry "muddies" capital and labor as relations (synonymous, yet discontinuous) as its genealogy coalesces around the representation of (worker) reality. This does not make Flora Tristan's *Promenades in London* (1840) the same as the worker writing of *L'Atelier* (also first published in 1840), yet such examples often respond to an inquiry that has not been posed: how is the labor/capital nexus actually lived by those who are subject to it?[13]

The insurgency of the worker in representation is hardly the equivalent of the stylistic detail Auerbach brings to great works of Western civilization and there is no figura of the worker, metonymically or necessarily so, that might stand in for such deeply philological comparatism. I would say, however, there is more than one way to "discover the world anew" (183) and we are still learning how the forms of labor themselves are immanent to such revelation and that something as pervasive as worker experience has within it the lineaments of a properly global aesthetic. This is a challenge that mimesis implies but that Auerbach himself only hints at addressing:

> the meaning of events cannot be grasped in abstract and general forms of cognition and... the material needed to understand it must not be sought exclusively in the upper strata of society and in major political events but also in art, economy, material and intellectual culture, *in the depths of the workaday world and its men and women*, because it is only there that one can grasp what is unique, what is animated by inner forces, and what, in both a more concrete and a more profound sense, is universally valid: then it is to be expected that those insights will also be transferred to the present and that, in consequence, the present too will be seen as incomparable and unique, as animated by inner forces and in a constant state of development. (444—my emphasis)

A dialectics of figura would not necessarily entail such progression but the "workaday world" would always be coterminous with it, at least until that time in my schema when the worker as subject is superfluous to codes of subjection themselves.

Chapter 19 of *Mimesis* begins with a quote from Edmond and Jules de Goncourt's preface to their novel of 1864, *Germinie Lacerteux*,[14] the tragic tale of a servant (as Bruce Robbins points out, "signs of the unrepresented, servants haunt Auerbach's account of representation" [26]).[15] The Goncourts argue their novel must inevitably challenge readers used to smut, confessions, scandal and erotic trash for their project seeks to recast tragedy, and by doing so the novel, through narrating "the troubles of the little and the poor." One is struck not just by their sociological and humanistic verve (a later preface details the case which forms the basis for their narrative, an inquiry indeed) but by Auerbach's emphasis that will structure his subsequent critique. Indeed, he singles out the words "étude and especially enquête" (496) as if to underline how literary study and inquiry conjoin in the social realism and political economy of the nineteenth century (and indeed, in Marx's project for *La Revue socialiste*). Beyond that, however, is the Goncourt's enthusiasm for the scientificity of the novel, a literary positivism Auerbach finds indicative of "the extreme vanguard" (496). The Goncourts' view links empiricism with the kind of social verification found in Comte (and later Durkheim, who I have already invoked). Without deciding the philosophical and sociological debate, on one thing Auerbach is unequivocal: "The common people in all its ramifications had to be taken into the subject matter of serious realism: the Goncourts were right, and they were to be borne out in it. The development of realistic art has proved it" (497). As Auerbach writes this in the middle of the twentieth century his judgment is easy to gainsay. In the heat of proletarianization, socialism, and emerging communism, the representation of working people was all over the cultural map of Europe, but also in Asia, Africa, and the Americas. One could argue the proof of *Mimesis* lay in what it did not represent: the reality of the common people in Auerbach's cultural present. The twin paradoxes of his coruscating vision are first, the popularizing and populist styles Auerbach details in the Western (Christian) tradition form the basis for the largely elitist aesthetic predilections of European comparatism; and second, the representation of worker reality at the time is heavily overdetermined by the ideological needs of workerism and its opponents in which the very principles of "reality" and "realism" narrow the possibilities of stylistic combination (I would differentiate this general workerism as a kind of state presupposition from that of Italian "operaismo" of the 1960s and other examples below). What are the contraindications in "the subject matter of serious realism"?

The year after *Mimesis* was first published in Germany a pamphlet appeared in the USA called *The American Worker*, written by Paul Romano and Ria Stone (the pseudonyms of Phil Singer and Grace Lee [later Grace Lee Boggs] respectively).[16] It is a fascinating work that combines a worker's autobiography of life on a Ford car production line with a philosophical and Marxist account of theoretical activism, including the implications of a worker inquiry. Instead of a questionnaire the account emerges out of a single desire to render worker experience palpable as a narrative. Singer's contribution has been described as "a realistic representation of factory work and its repercussions on the psyche and political outlook of the worker,"[17] while Boggs' essay owes much of its insight to her collaboration with C.L.R. James (J.R. Johnson) and Raya Dunayevskaya (Freddie Forest) of the Johnson-Forest Tendency.[18] In their detailed genealogy of worker inquiries, Haider and Mohandesi go as far as to suggest Marx's *Workers' Inquiry* is "truly reincarnated" in the Romano/Stone pamphlet, but I would argue it is more significant in the ways in which it attempts to overcome the quandaries of representation indicated so far. Indeed, it pushes the question of mimesis back toward the problem of authenticating worker experience as cultural expression. Stephen Hastings-King will take Claude Lefort's phenomenological understanding of *The American Worker* as a refusal of its literary conventions and advance the somewhat practiced undecidability between its signifieds and referents. Such an elision or confusion in Lefort's "L'Expérience Prolétarienne" has serious implications for any putatively working-class cultural expression but cancels through one's understanding of Marx's *Workers' Inquiry* too.[19] It is not that one provides raw data of working-class experience in a way that the other cannot (personal reflections, somatic responses, etc.), but that the compositional contradictions of such narrative are the ground of the laboring subject. One is not more true or verifiable than the other but together they form the very substance of the limits in articulating the worker as a subject. On this level, labor in culture is a moving contradiction of cultural labor, irreducible to labor/capital as relations yet vital in expressing precisely this incommensurability. *The American Worker* emerged out of key debates within the radical Left of the USA over Bolshevism, "statification" (read by James as the state capitalism of the Soviet Union) and spontaneous worker praxis.[20] More specifically, it accentuates once more the creative tension between the worker and the radical intellectual as subjects, but also what constitutes appropriate forms of their expression. The question of representation in both concerns how to communicate "the life of the working class in the process of production" and thus stands in the lineage of the workers' inquiry, but by answering questions that have not been posed, as it were, from the outside. It is one of the great paradoxes of Marx's *Workers' Inquiry* that its legacy has come alive precisely when it abjures the form Marx gives it (there are notable exceptions, of which more below and one could add irony to paradox by underlining Marx never received a completed questionnaire; indeed, much of the difficulty of the worker for Marxism exists between questions posed but not answered and answers for questions not in fact asked). In *The American Worker,* the dangers of assumed authenticity remain, and this extends both to the reader and to Lee's interpretation. Singer's world is a copied reality, and Lee's analysis is caught in its mimetic relation. Yet surely this is a worker's understanding from within the texture of lived contradictions in the labor/capital relation—a manifest form of worker representation?

Singer's "diary" is intended, as he writes, to express the innermost thoughts of the worker to other workers, those who toil in the factories of the "most industrialized country in the world." The success of this dialogic of addressor and addressee is primarily sociological and political, the substance of the worker being measured in her relationship to capitalism. Yet to be a representation of that reality is to be active, aesthetically, otherwise the sociological itself becomes dry abstraction. This indeed is a danger Singer attributes to intellectual readers, who can only see "a repetition of an oft-written story," a confirmation of tenets rather than an expression of a worker in her lived relation. Singer's emphasis, therefore, is on "everyday reactions and expressions," in the belief that these are signs, to borrow from Auerbach once more, not only of the workaday world but the inner depths that make it so. Singer writes of a "subterranean frustration" distilled from the difference between the rewards of work and the urge to refuse this work. He details the effects of factory work on the worker's body, from skin and lung conditions to the physical and mental numbness produced by endless repetition. There is no sustaining character or individual in Singer's observations, just an accumulation of reflections and expressions of a worker as subject with all of the contradictions that implies. This may be read as problematic in its own way because it makes it harder to distinguish between subjective reflection and selective projection, between speaking as a worker and speaking for workers. At this level, the text demonstrates not just the ineluctable space between "worker" and "inquiry" but the antinomy of worker representation as such, a dialectic of the worker and her worlds. For the most part the prose is straightforward and unadorned, as if confirming the sentiment that ends Chapter 2: "The average worker has too much responsibility to be persuaded by words alone." Traditional elements and sentiments abound but Singer also registers specific changes in the experience of work like "speed up" that reflect the intensification of industry in the USA after the Second World War, including the effects of corresponding over production. The workers like efficiency, in their own performance and that of the factory, but this can also mean redundancy, just as much as poor work, absenteeism, and sabotage.

Within the composite picture of Romano's account (I use composite here to indicate "multiple," which is not a metonym of the universal in this worker's particularity), several representative yet specific features stand out. Romano, for instance, details the temporal conflicts of factory life where shift rotations and variations in hours are used by management to disrupt unity. The worker feels a strange attraction to the rhythms of the factory as if its decentering capacity in fact provides a stability the world beyond work is unable to secure. Romano offers sympathy for foremen who are squeezed between the largely irreconcilable differences of labor and management. There is, of course, no kindness for stooges and "company men." The image of the union that emerges is hardly rosy either, both because of a general worker hostility toward bureaucracy and because many see an all too cozy relationship between the union leadership and the company (the latter is perceived to have infiltrated the former). This is the point in the pamphlet that seems most directly connected to the work and outlook of those who would anchor the Correspondence group, those who were reacting not just to the dogmatism of Soviet workerism, but also to the ambivalence and sometimes outright resistance of major US unions to workers' direct action in the aftermath of the war. Chapter 6 reflects on the changing nature of the American work force and offers insight on racism and sexism in the work place, also in terms that reflect the discussions of Correspondence. "The Negro in the Shop" section still resounds with the realities of the factory but also underlines that the composite must risk speaking for "strata," as Romano calls them, already resistant to decades of American workers among whom their voices have been silenced or ventriloquized. One of the key splits in the American Left was over the primacy of race in working-class struggle, a struggle over the terms of struggle themselves; indeed, the rationale behind the Johnson-Forest tendency was that the radical Black politics of the time had to be seen in its autonomy, in its specific history and not simply as part of a necessary coalition.[21] The difference in authenticity compounds the dilemma in representing the reality of the worker and marks a constitutive aporia for politics and aesthetics. Whatever the mimetic pitfalls of the worker narrative, documenting from below provides an intervention on the meaning of worker experience for representation and, if the truth of testimonial must necessarily remain ambiguous, the challenge of the genre changes how the worker is read and indeed imaged culturally. I should say there is little ambiguity in Romano's conclusion, announced with a conviction that has shaped the account preceding it:

> The worker expresses his hatred of the incentive system by saying he should write the union contract. This is no less than saying that the existing production relations must be overthrown. It is also much more. It means that he wants to arrange his life in the factory in such a way that it satisfies his instincts for doing a good job, knowing that it is worthwhile, and living in harmony with his fellow men. It is deeply rooted in the worker that work is

the foundation of his life. To make his work a meaningful part of life, an expression of his overall individuality, is what he would attempt to put into reality.

It is because I feel all this and see it around me in the factory that I am a revolutionary socialist. Socialism is not merely an ideal to be wished for. It must grow out of the daily lives and strivings of the workers, and it must bring a new life to them in that which is closest to them and to society—their work.

Again, Romano's sense of self and situation is not only mediated by his experience of the factory but by the political debates of the Correspondence group, a context given substance by Ria Stone's commentary following Romano's narrative. The importance of the USA to how the worker is realized at the time cannot be overemphasized. The contours of *The American Worker* are girded by the transformations of the late thirties and the war: "The industrial reserve army of seventeen million unemployed merged with the millions already at the bench and created the largest and most powerful industrial working class that the world has ever known." Acknowledging such a place in history is vital to the problem of representation this project explores, particularly since it allows us to trace where that industrial reserve army might now lie, and in much greater numbers. Here, however, it is Stone's conceptual apparatus that galvanizes the worker's standpoint elucidated by Romano. Her reading of American political economy is substantial in its own right, but it is how she understands Romano's experience as evidence of ripening conditions that requires further comment. First, of course, she refers to Romano's emphasis on worker creativity, not just on the job but in all aspects of their life experience. Second, however, there is the stunting of such creativity, work for its own sake, by the needs of industrial capitalism which produces classic forms of alienation. To seek full employment under these conditions, Stone notes, is only to deepen the realm of alienation itself. Automation only intensifies the necessity of the worker harnessing his objective conditions over the machine, assimilating "the acuteness in perception which characterizes the operations of the objective world." Rather than pit the worker against the machine, the argument is for a dialectical process in which the creative and productive capacities of the worker are comparably unleashed. For the machine to become a truly social object in its productive capacities necessitates the production of a truly social "man," in the sense that the advent of the machine embodies or objectifies the totality of human activities that precede it. When Romano writes of the worker's desire to improve efficiency by modifying factory machinery, Stone interprets this through the prism of universality in which workers, to the horror of Socrates, would become authors of their own alchemy, the makers of their own metal/mettle. Whereas capitalism sees the machine as a means to undermine labor power through de-skilling and what is termed in the essay "tradelessness," full automation would in fact require "polytechnic literacy" in which ability as work would be fulfilled. As Stone notes, Marx saw this humanizing potential in the machine and the name for the unleashing of this productive capacity is communism. But where is the American worker in relation to this promise of human actuality?

In part, Stone believes the American working class is uniquely positioned because it is relatively new, large, and does not cleave to the same revolutionary tradition as its European counterparts. The key example, as in Romano's narrative, is the "Negro." Blacks in the factory find their racial marginalization compounded not just by the racism of bourgeois owners, but also by the racism of their fellow White workers, so that the contradictions between individual fulfillment and class conformity are most acute. The answer is not leveling in the crude sense, but a socialization of individuality in which the grounds of race are de-instrumentalized within codes of subjection. Partial socialization will only create new hierarchies and capitalism is intent on producing and reproducing these fragments (this is one of the meanings of racial capitalism). Only by making the worker whole will wholeness itself be recognized as a fully human actuality. The problem for Marxist politics and culture is whether the actuality of wholeness can be achieved without reproducing the false completeness of the subject (a question that will be taken up in other parts of the current project). Concomitantly, is radical theory's long pursuit of the death of the subject also active in the dissolution of the very humanizing potential revolution would otherwise desire? The difference between *Mimesis* and *The American Worker* is structured around a contradictory valence of the reality principle: in other words, the appeal to the "workaday" in Auerbach is only possible precisely because it does not confront the work of each day manifest in Romano's perception. This is not just an antinomy of realism, to borrow from Jameson, but the very dilemma that structures worker representation.[22] At the moment telling the story displaces the objectification of normative sociology, anthropology, and indeed philology, the disciplinary procedures of subject reason bleed the aesthetic from worker actuality. Stone's reading holds true to a belief that a radical politics freed from statist dogmatism can facilitate a sublation of such antinomies, but one could just as easily argue that pivoting the critique on Romano's revelations only reproduces the aporia of representation pressing against the possibility of transformation per se. Just as the contemporaneous *Dialectic of Enlightenment* of Adorno and Horkheimer (1944, revised 1947) tracked rationality's escape from yet subjection of nature, so creativity before the machine might also be said to suspend freedom within the actual productive logic in play.[23] Romano offers an antidote to abstract calculations, state, Party or theory inspired, of worker change but one is hard pressed to see how a record of worker experience in itself disrupts the material conditions of reason's need in production and reproduction.

Stone is clear that for intellectuals the universality at stake is overdetermined by the division of labor in which universality is thought. "Rescuing the individual from society," as she puts it, is only possible because of a prior misrecognition of what both represent (such is the tragedy of existentialism). Can the turn to worker experience overcome this méconnaissance when the worker herself is always already caught in individuation structured through the externalization and a concomitant abstraction of the productive process? Stone maintains that the intellectual sees the workplace as primarily one of degradation rather than the substance of human universality and thus is predisposed to look elsewhere in art, literature, science, and religion as if one cannot be sustenance for the other. This is one reason labor in culture is both everywhere and nowhere in terms of representationality. The converse danger is that by privileging worker experience as a political and aesthetic platform one risks substituting revolutionary desire for the deeper conflicts of worker actuality, something often detected in the more programmatic moments of proletarian culture. The idea of the project is salutary, but the discursive registers are often of a different order and are subject to theoretical nuance over practical complexity. Although Proletkult is little more than a historical curiosity, its relative absence is taken as proof positive proletarian cultures themselves are irrelevant to the matrix of labor and capital today. Of course, this remains a specific political shortfall but it is also, in true mimetic fashion, a challenge of social imaginaries.

That Stone accentuates Romano's understanding of the workplace in terms of gender and race rather than solely through class underlines how a transformation in productive forces also liberates the human from oppression in general. The emphasis is not to deny the concrete manifestations of sexism and racism in American society, including among its working class, but to link firmly the overcoming of oppression to the liberation of productive capacity in the worker. As long as that capacity is denatured through capital as a social and economic relation, there can be no freedom from necessity, including the necessity for deleterious social differentiation. Unions are seen to conspire in such differentiation not because they favor racism and sexism (although few need reminding there is plenty of evidence of this in labor history tout court) but because mimetically they reproduce the organizational structures of capitalist industry and copy their hierarchical logic. What is termed "labor bureaucracy" cannot undo the inhumanity of the workplace to the extent that its logic does not permit it to pose a "more productive mode of labor" than the system of labor relations in which it is embedded (a mode that would negate its own existence). Stone believes the workers are not bound to this realm of necessity and that yearning otherwise can be understood from Romano's account. As I hinted earlier, however, because the Johnson-Forest Tendency worked together on the pamphlet it is difficult to separate the creative spontaneity of Romano's narrative from elements that would merely confirm the group's already agreed position. This does not mean the analysis is wrong but that its basis may not be wholly attributable to the experience elaborated. Here we return to the representation of reality.

In a further distancing of Trotskyism, the Tendency would reform as Correspondence in 1951 with a still greater emphasis on the autonomy of specific political issues within the broader claims of the working class (especially on race and gender). That the worker for Correspondence corresponds to an objective reality of capitalism and its discontents is indisputable according to what is required of labor for social reproduction. This aspect of mid-twentieth-century American capitalism still offers a heuristic for today because of and despite the fact so much has changed in the social conditions and outlook of the American worker. The apparent paradox, contained within the idea of figura, cannot be understood by explaining away the historical distance of those "industrial" times but by negotiating the scales of representation themselves. Clearly, Correspondence faced immense barriers to the forms of collective praxis they imagined, but they placed their faith not in philosophical nuance but in what they sensed in worker self-representation. Given the vast literature and cultural expression available (the archive of the 1930s alone was formidable), what is surprising is their determination that direct action should be based on, as it were, direct narrative, as if mediation beyond intimate representation could only misrepresent the subject of social transformation.

While *The American Worker* might share strategic aims with Marx's *Workers' Inquiry*, its emphasis on relating raw experience of the workplace challenges the epistemological claims of inquiry. Both forms are overdetermined by political instincts (for Stone/Lee, for instance, Romano's reflections confirm the tenets elaborated in another pamphlet the same year, *The Invading Socialist Society*, penned by James, Dunayevskaya, and Lee[24]). True, the emphasis on direct experience inoculated their critique from the ideologies of state and party (by that time increasingly associated with the disasters of Stalinism), but why exclude all other forms of worker representation (e.g., social realism, documentary realism, modernist experimentation, and most pointedly, surrealism) that had nourished revolutionary desire, particularly in the pre-war period?

The story of "the representation of the reality" of workers should never escape the productive possibilities of this tension but it could be quite disabling in the immediate post-war era as all of those constituencies with an appeal to represent, putatively, the workers jockeyed for position. Just as the labor/capital nexus was changing under the economic dynamism of reconstruction and the geopolitics of American expansion, so the modes of identification with workers and workers' self-image entered a period of intense rearticulation. As the authenticity of a political movement began to fracture and falter and vanguardism became a point of departure rather than an explicit goal, the problem of mimesis and mediation seems to fade or is simply overcome in the distillation that is experience. The basic belief, shared by both Correspondence and by *Socialisme ou Barbarie* (that would translate "American Worker" within its pages), was that worker liberation was primarily articulated in the experience of work and that a proletarian could only be creatively understood by a radical intelligentsia keenly sensitive to the immediacy of such documentary. Again, what feels most like a historical curiosity (who now holds faith in the certitude of writing phenomenological experience?) holds lessons about the space for the worker in representational reality. The peculiarities of the crisis Stone elaborates form a chapter in American working-class history and is a subtext to any extension of Auerbach's "mimesis" for representing the worker today. It is also, for the current project, the theoretical knot in the dialectic of labor as relation and labor as representation which is hardly resolved by the truth in experience of worker culture, even as the latter remains the ground of its struggle.

Learning from labor would seem to be at once a suspect and forlorn exercise. If, from Marx's perspective, the inquiry was a necessary step in grounding socialist praxis in the material realities of the worker, Romano's auto-ethnography neither escapes the tendentiousness of the project nor indeed its very real practical limits. How much was the pamphlet read? To what extent did it achieve a measurable momentum for the Johnson-Forest Tendency, let alone worker movements at large? Should it be read alongside literature with broader appeal at the time, like Irving Stone's biographical novel of Eugene Debs, *Adversary in the House*, Mike Quin's *The Big Strike*, or the pulp predilections of Nelson Algren's *The Man with the Golden Arm*? Are workers "thinking and doing" in other cultural spaces? Of course, the point is the specific relation between narrating labor and political organization; one that, it seems to me, puts a heavy onus on the mimetic practice of worker representation. Such a focus not only draws attention to a genealogy, in Haider and Mohandesi's terms, of worker writing otherwise hidden from history, but to the pre-science of such mimesis on a world scale, where proletarianization everywhere must surely extend rather than limit the possibilities of inquiry.

Marx's *Workers' Inquiry* pivots on the nostrums of empiricism and positivism yet immediately faces the limits of a proletarian viewpoint mediated by a questionnaire (How random is the sample? How high is the response rate? Should open-ended questions be re-tested over time [e.g. question 100: general remarks!]?). A Workers' Inquiry in the present is, as Shukaitis, Figiel, and Walker put it, "part of the accepted social science repertoire: its techniques no longer seem dangerous, but familiar, at least at the methodological level."[25] I will return to the meaning of the Workers' Inquiry today below but here it should be emphasized that, compared to the questionnaire as genre and method, the work of the Johnson-Forest Tendency and then Correspondence is an interruption rather than continuation of the genealogy at issue. Stone's response to Romano's narrative obviously reproduces the false division between the worker and the intellectual and yet, by including both writers in the pamphlet, a unity of purpose is intimated.[26] For his part, Romano goes beyond descriptions of basic exploitation in the workplace by thinking through how these conditions raise consciousness and facilitate resistance. Stone reads this realization and activism as decisive: "[it is] an attempt on the part of the American workers to rise to their historic destiny and reconstruct society on new beginnings." The extent of this workplace derived consciousness becomes a worldview: the workers have "acquired an organic awareness of the inter-relatedness of production between one department and another, from coal mine to assembly line; between town and country, from continent to continent." This has always been the challenge and promise of the workers' inquiry: whether it could prove to be the catalyst of transformation not just in the workplace described, but in imagined workplaces across the globe.

In its immediate context Haider and Mohandesi argue *The American Worker* emerges "as a kind of paradigm" and it certainly inspires other projects within the Correspondence group. In 1952 Si Owens, using a pseudonym Matthew Ward, published *Indignant Heart: A Black Worker's Journal*.[27] The following year Correspondence released another pamphlet, *A Woman's Place*, by Marie Brant (Selma James) and Ellen Santori (Filomena D'Addario).[28] Both these works were in the mold of *The American Worker*, but more explicitly make race and gender the substance of labor. Like Romano/Singer's narrative, they both bear the burden of synecdoche, a knot of the social obligated by the subject. This transaction, an aesthetic exchange, necessarily questions all claims to authenticity, and on this level Haider and Mohandesi extend their point about Lee's interested "transcription" of Romano's text to the fact that *A Woman's Place* was the work of one woman, Selma James (D'Addario's name was added at C.L.R. James's suggestion to allow her talking points in public), and that Owens's *Indignant Heart* was actually written by Constance Webb, another member of Correspondence who, like Lee, actively "transcribed" a narrative by a worker who might otherwise have little experience writing in this way (in Hastings-King's study, which sometimes seems as cynical about workers as it is about Marxism, he states on two occasions, "workers simply did not write" [106, 109]). The inquiry is a space of desire that must seek an adequate response despite the troubling ambivalence between direct and directed narrative. Why must labor confess? Does the truth of social contradiction emerge in other ways than finding contradictions in its truth?

According to Owens' later explanation on the effects of McCarthyism, he sets his upbringing in *Indignant Heart* in Tennessee rather than Alabama, an admission that Haider and Mohandesi take to mean his journal is more like "historical fiction." Given Lowndes County's place in the civil rights movement and its history as a stark symbol of white supremacy and racist violence, Owens' relocation of his childhood is a stunning admission and inadvertently confirms the power of white intimidation even more than McCarthyism.[29] On the other side of fiction, however, the process of writing and the generic components of worker writing may not be as damning as the powers of verification make them seem. Obviously, it is important to Correspondence that the narratives are not made up, yet it is just as significant that worker stories must not be seen to adjudicate effortlessly the line between real experience and its expression. This is not to excuse embellishment or outright amanuensis, but is to take seriously the role of fictionality in presenting truth. As the Goncourts put it in their preface to Germinie Lacerteux "Le public aime les romans faux: ce roman est un roman vrai. Ill aime les livres qui font semblant d'aller dans Ie monde: ce livre vient de la rue. " ("The public likes false novels: this novel is a true novel. They like books that pretend to be worldly: this book comes from the street"). Auerbach argues that the way the Goncourts situate their text is a validation of what he terms the mixing of styles crucial to the democratization of culture. Their defense of the novel as a field of social inquiry (enquête) does not mean worker inquiry is necessarily better novelized, but that fiction has the capacity to be true to social inquiry, not as facts, but *as an inquiry*, as a questioning with social import. Again, such distinctions do not rationalize falsehoods and misapprehension. Instead, realism's push for the whole of reality might temper inquiry's insistence on the absolute real. Even if workers do not always write, or write accurately, they write enough to know writing is always already a creative act and can be mimetically sound without being consummately true.

Denby's journal is an important contribution to the representation of the Black worker in the USA in the twentieth century. If it gives life to Marx's *Workers' Inquiry* it is because it draws on experience without claiming to fulfill the metrics of political economy. Of course, Webb's writing skills might foreground certain themes over others, but one does not have to assume it is her voice that accentuates the persistence of slave ideology in the South, the movement from the land to the city and industry, urban racism as every bit insidious as its plantation forebears, and suspicions about unions, the Communist Party, and sympathetic whites. Overall, the success of the narrative is precisely in its uneven negotiation between what might be deemed typical and individual in a Black worker's experience at that time. What Marx refers to as "positive knowledge" is here based on how such unevenness is appreciated rather than elided; indeed, how a worker might not match the worlds in which she is situated. Like Romano's reflections, Denby's journal provides a vivid sense of the intricacies of factory work, but just as clearly how it is structured and overdetermined by race in American society. The offhandness of systemic racism still jars, as when Denby notes, "We have one or two segregated departments at this plant. Maintainers and tool and die, and crane operators are all white. The company has one hundred and one reasons for keeping Negroes out. The union, too, has one hundred and one reasons. There is one Negro in the carpentry shop and one Negro truck driver. The truck driver is a mulatto. When he was hired the company thought he was white" (160). Two other dimensions are also significant in this regard. First, a section of the narrative is devoted to Denby's wife: in particular, her experiences working at a Chevrolet plant in Detroit. The brevity of the piece is disappointing yet it adds another layer to the discourse of race and gender discernible in the rest of the narrative. Denby, for instance, remarks that Christine's experiences are "similar" but she makes a point of noting "how mad Negro men get when a white man goes with a Negro woman" (144) which has different race and gender implications for how the workplace is lived and divided. A second element that reaccentuates the piece is the addition of Part II, a quarter century after the initial observations. The stylistic contrasts are quite pronounced and reflect Denby's maturation as a writer (he would edit the Marxist-Humanist newspaper, *News and Letters* from 1955 to 1983[30]) over Webb's earlier influence. The mediation of history has also changed the angle of address. Part II, wrought by a deep consciousness of the civil rights movement (the first page alone references Emmet Till, Rosa Parks and the Reverend Martin Luther King Jr.), offers a maelstrom of Black worker politics across the USA. As the text moves from the journal to the journalistic much of the immediacy of Denby as a worker recedes and there are fewer occasions when the narrative privileges a "we-experience" consonant with shared practices in the shop or on the line. When it does touch on this, however, it is around the question of automation in the workplace that Dunayevskaya, for instance, reads as a catalyst for a new humanism in which "workers think their own thoughts" (274). Automation breeds crisis around alienation, speed up, even leisure, and suffuses the worker's experience of capital as a relation. It is in such crisis that new thinking emerges, which for Denby galvanizes his sense of race and class, and re-scales experience "to human freedom in this world" (294). The militancy in the text is part of its thesis, that the worker dialectizes the everyday and makes conscious global connections. The cynic may say that Denby's intimacy with intellectual activism predisposes scale jumping of this kind (tendentiousness from the Tendency, etc.) but not every lineament of an imaginary is simply an imaginary relation. *The Indignant Heart* does not end with resolution, even if its gesture to a totality of world might seem to affirm it.

If the division of labor is itself conceptually divided, the emphasis on the subjective claims of the worker opens up theoretical *and* practical questions about how labor is to be cognized and actualized as a material force. The more labor is elaborated (worked out) however, the greater the tension between subjective experience and the rationalization of a world-historical project. I have suggested this is constitutive of the effort, of the act of representing reality, but clearly much of this also comes down to historical possibility and political imperatives. In *A Woman's Place*, Selma James makes plain how labor at home is both made and marginalized, and also that women working beyond the home suffer hardships for their independence. Beyond its heteronormative assumptions and its projection of the "average woman," the pamphlet aims its critique at how patriarchy mediates relations of labor and how it can be challenged. As a place of labor, the home is a space of resistance: "The most universal organization of women is the action that women take in their own homes. Each woman in her own home is making a revolution" (71). The necessity to fight in this space is redoubled if a woman also works beyond it since it is assumed she will continue to perform all of the domestic labor as well. If this seems common knowledge within the literature on social production and reproduction it is in part because of pamphlets like James's, but its resonance is that the activism advocated is still necessary and ongoing. In the 1970s James's support for the "Wages for Housework" movement would inspire a complementary pamphlet, "Women and the Subversion of the Community" and *A Woman's Place* now appears with it. Silvia Federici would take up the charge of "Wages for Housework" groups internationally but notes "Of all the positions that developed in the women's movement, Wages for Housework was likely the most controversial and often the most antagonized."[31]

Despite the dynamic of politics and culture in which these texts participate we have already noted that their roots in "raw proletarian experience" are not unproblematic. While this might be explained as political exigency or, less charitably, as intellectual machination and hypocrisy, such worker narratives seem trapped by the relations they are seen to embody. Before concluding with some thoughts on mimesis and workers' inquiry today it is worth considering in more detail how the idea of inquiry at the time jumps scales between worker and world. In part this is the difference between a belief in creativity and spontaneity and one that finds interpretive frames relatively fixed and agreed upon; yet in practice worker experience might seem to support multiple modes of measure. Are there further studies that decide between the two? Claude Lefort's unsigned article,

"Proletarian Experience" published in *Socialisme and Barbarie* in 1952 is a reading of *American Worker* that takes up the challenge of its politics and aesthetics of representation for radical French thought.[32] The basic idea is that Romano's discourse of factory life was an inspiration for any socialism attempting to move beyond economic determinism around worker representation. As always for Lefort, the challenge of experience is about material forms of the political and how these can be articulated.[33] Crucially, Lefort's approach privileges class composition, which is not only a guiding thread in Marx's *Workers' Inquiry*, but is the strongest methodological link to interest in workers' inquiry today (my focus here is less on a "parallel sociology" but in its implications for cultural critique[34]). Romano derives socialism from his lived experience as an industrial worker but his account is already an interpretation of that experience, and Lefort's reading is a further phenomenological mediation of Romano's reality. There is a certain faith in documentary realism, a belief historically driven by resistance to the abstractions of Soviet workerism redolent in conjunctions of state and revolution (for some, therefore, a workerism without workers). What makes experience "proletarian" is not just descriptions of work as it is lived, but a conjoint intimacy in which a worker reveals a politics in her being, however at odds with the science of its appropriate constituents. To gauge this, Lefort argues, "the proletariat requires a specific approach that would enable access to its subjective development." Why? "The proletariat is subjective to the extent that its comportments are not the simple result of the conditions of its existence: its conditions of existence require of it a continuous struggle for transformation, thus a continuous distance from its immediate fate." Comportment is a mode of phenomenological relationality that both reflects and refracts its Heideggerian roots.[35] If for both Heidegger and Lefort it is an opening to the world as concept, a rather different genealogy of modernity is implied. In fact, the history of worker inquiry will shift comportment into a no less complex sociological rendering of elements, class composition. The representation of labor comes to rest on this necessary misalignment through which critical inquiry is itself composed. Critical worker inquiry at this level is not the shuffling in of the worker with the age of literary theory but is instead a means to think their entanglement as a key problem of the representation of reality itself. The story of the present is, whatever else it is, one of the maligned mimesis of the worker in which comportment and composition appear unhinged from the "subjective development of the proletariat."[36]

For his part, Lefort wants to emphasize subjective experience and its comportment at the point of production. This, of course, represents another way the worker may be delinked from the present since the production is industrial and fairly narrowly defined. Yet we should also acknowledge Lefort's approach to proletarian experience is sensitive to its unique coordinates at any one moment in capitalist history. In other words, if the spatial fixes of capital require more or less constant revolution, so labor's composition will either produce or approximate this challenge. If there are contingent inflexibilities these have often emerged within the analytical procedures otherwise primed to read the point of production. All kinds of factors weigh on the practicality and effectivity of worker inquiry from this perspective, from cultural logics to professionalization, from philosophy to technological means, from place to circulation, etc., but they all depend, to a significant extent, on an ability to read the worker as a composite of possibilities, as a source of lived and living experience. This is another way the worker inquiry asks questions in its own time and ours. Lefort returns to the key tension: how does subjective experience give us the proletarian and how does inquiry make this distinction beyond idealistic or ideological projection?

In Lefort's conception, the proletarian can indeed be produced in its projection but also by complex modes of ideological identification. Both have mimetic implications: the first, in a tendentious discovery of a subject that meets the category; the second, through an expressive affiliation whereby subjective consciousness folds into a political rationalization for it. This cancels through both the dry coordinates of Marx's inquiry, and those of post-war USA and France that seek proletarian documentary. Both philosophically and politically this constitutes the struggle within and between proletarian, worker, and working class (with further and deeper permutations around "poor" and "people" in the work of Rancière). These terms are more metonyms than synonyms, forms of mimetic méconnaissance redolent from the moment "Proletarier aller Linder vereinigt Euch!" of the *Communist Manifesto* becomes "Workers of the world, unite!" Each intervention, each inquiry, on "proletarian experience" necessarily reproduces this critical disjunction, even before one addresses a concomitant catachresis in capital's identification of its object and associated derivations. If Marx's questionnaire might desire a form of scientific certitude, at least in its objective claims, whatever the alienation of the worker the decentering has already begun in the designation which is also part of the organic composition of the worker in general. Lefort notes that since Marx there are only "literary" documents about the worker but more recently a sociology of the worker has developed, including a management-derived methodology, a "Taylorized form of humanism," bent on improving the soul of workers just enough to raise efficiency at the point of exploitation. Obviously, for Lefort, the worker inquiry has a different and agonistic foundation and his emphasis on experience is precisely to distance simultaneously overly deterministic economic scientism and the tendency to transform economic and class relations into a kind of personification.[37]

By focusing on the "progressive experience" of the workers within the process of work itself Lefort believes the "radical originality of the proletariat emerges again," in the sense that experience is the mark of preparation for assuming social control rather seeing this primarily in the moment of revolution itself. In its time this was a striking rejoinder to the efforts of Correspondence and sought some radical originality of its own. As another key member of *Socialisme ou Barbarie*, Cornelius Castoriadis, had pointed out, the tension between the scientific planning of a new society and the "creativity activity" of the people constituted the primary antinomy of anti-capitalist militancy.[38] Indeed, the inability to resolve this issue was a key factor in the break-up of the *Socialisme ou Barbarie* collective. Nevertheless, in "Proletarian Experience" Lefort is adamant that the "very nature of the proletariat requires that we collect and interpret testimonies written by workers" because this is the key to tapping their subjective experience, which is more than simply a description of existence or a tabulation of their productive capacities. More importantly, questions would be posed by reading the narratives themselves rather than waiting on a questionnaire to spur testimonies (the two Lefort has in mind are Romano's *American Worker* and Eric Albert's testimonial "La vie dans une usine" from *Temps Modernes* (Juillet 1952)).[39] The categories of concern that emerge are: (1) the relations of a worker to their work; (2) relations with other workers and social strata at the place of work, and the associated division of labor; (3) life beyond the factory and knowledge of the world at large; and (4) connections to proletarian history and traditions. Lefort acknowledges at once that differences in labor and location would sharply delimit the "universal import" of such narratives but he argues it would be just as reductive to deny all value to worker testimonials. The goal is evidence of "general signification," "worker attitudes," or a "proletarian standpoint." Statistical data will not help in this regard; like Marx, Lefort stresses individual responses permit a deeper engagement with living labor, "individual narratives are invaluable."

There are three sets of problems prompted by Lefort's argument that link both to the historical concerns of the worker inquiry sketched above and the representation of the worker that is the central focus of this cultural critique. The first is an entirely practical issue, and one that has been accentuated by Stephen Hastings-King's recent discussion of Lefort's project: if comportment is a phenomenological reduction (in the Merleau-Ponty sense) based on experience, one needs quite a large sampling of the latter to deduce something as declarative as a proletarian standpoint. Can a "proletarian optic" really be discerned in a sample taken only from the writings of Romano and Albert, however richly subjective their workplace experiences? As we have noted, Hastings-King points out that while *Socialisme ou Barbarie* actively solicited worker narratives, with examples published in the journal, the proletarian experience project never really got going because "workers simply did not write." I would qualify this overly brusque assessment with "enough": enough, that is, to justify Lefort's conclusions about the significance of worker documentary narrative itself. Workers write, but a proletarian standpoint requires more than the distillation Lefort discovers, and perhaps more than the genre of testimonial itself. The absence of writing is itself a challenge for materialist history and cultural critique; indeed, "to read what was not written" is precisely the imperative at stake in Benjaminian mimesis.[40] In Lefort's defense, however, the philosophical weight on proletarian experience is bound by contingency so that the limits on evidence are themselves a condition of compositionality. Indeed, this is a constitutive dilemma between the representational and the representative. A second and complementary group of concerns spring from the historical place of the proletarian in the political imagination. The situation that permitted radical identification (Hastings-King calls it "doubling") of intellectuals with proletarians had changed dramatically in the immediate post-war period. This in part answers an earlier query about why socialist and communist thinkers did not always draw directly from the political and cultural work of the 1930s. The plethora of pseudonymous writing alone is evidence that the Cold War and anti-communist state repression deracinated all kinds of political expression and identification (indeed, both Lefort and Castoriadis would break from Marxism over the theoretical and political implications of post-war exigencies in France and elsewhere). If the proletarian in the most dynamic centers of capitalist expansion was at once rearticulated, such a historical distinction had to be realized despite the concrete constraints placed on active engagement with that figure. The dialectical resonance of the worker inquiry of the 1940s and 1950s in particular has a compositional reality all its own and that historical complexity is still only beginning to be understood (the distance from now has encouraged amnesia as much as analysis). The third concern regarding Lefort's argument brings us back to the theoretical impasse in labor representation and the contribution of culture to its difficulty and denouement. Lefort is well aware that when the worker is writing, the worker is not directly in the moment of proletarian immediacy. It is not simply an issue of mediation accentuating the difference of signifier and signified, but of gauging the impact of narrativity on what is understood as labor. As Lefort puts it, "to tell a story is not to act within it," but he resists the notion form, or indeed any aesthetic resonance, might shape the elaboration of experience. His emphasis, instead, is resolutely upon the interpreter and the interpretation. The question of mimesis does not find a balance among the competing processes that meet in the worker inquiry; indeed, it is precisely because labor as relation and proletarian as subject(ive) are dynamic historical phenomena that we should not assume even the most basic proportionality (or "progress" in that movement). This is also why ideologies of the aesthetic are more pronounced around the cultural representation of labor, often to the point where the latter is deemed extraneous to the solemn categories of aesthetic value, judgment, and reason. Like postcolonialism, which also wears its politics on its sleeve, worker expression always already announces some element of struggle and interestedness and seeks an aesthetic adequate to it. What is vital in the complementary projects of *Correspondence* and *Socialisme ou Barbarie* is the sense of worker inquiry as a demystification of the hard data driving production line efficiency or, for instance, "time and motion" studies of the workplace. Worker documentary presents an alternative reality rather than a statistical regularity which is not averse to its own abstractions but nevertheless cleaves to an idea of experience as more than the alienation of work given it. The fulcrum rests on how work is comprehended for, as Marx put it, "only the comprehended world is reality" even as the realization of labor in the commodity is the loss of reality for the worker herself.

Lefort's work on proletarian experience attempted to bridge several conceptual difficulties simultaneously in trying to renew a socialist project that had, especially in its bureaucratic forms, seriously misrepresented working-class knowledge, both of its situation and of the means to overcome it. Part of the achievement of both *Correspondence* and *Socialisme ou Barbarie* was to take seriously the autonomy of the worker from normative and normalizing state forms, a difference through experience that would energize radical thought and practice in the years following these experiments as worker representation tried to escape its Cold War abstractions. To be sure, workers' inquiry holds most closely to a sociology of the workplace; indeed, its disciplinary traction is primarily in a sociological critique of the performance and management of labor, alongside a plethora of alternative strategies for solidarity within the intellectual and labor Left (with the proviso this division has much less practical resonance than it did in a world of vanguards and party nostrums). In *Socialisme ou Barbarie*, the litmus test for Lefort's theorization of inquiry as experience was the work of Jacques Gautrat, who published "Journal d'un ouvrier" within its pages in 1956–1957 under the name Daniel Mothé.[41] Yet, as several commentaries have pointed out, auto workers at the massive Renault-Billancourt plant near Paris provided their own response in 1954 by launching a weekly paper, *Tribune Ouvrière*, which encouraged worker expression at the place of work.[42] Indeed, the *Socialisme ou Barbarie* collective actively supported this project even as its autonomous and unofficial efforts seemed to question their own. Yet Mothé was also involved in the founding of *Tribune Ouvrière* and, as Hastings-King makes clear, his commitment to politics as a worker mediates every expression of his experience, including his embodiment or not of the bridge between intellectual and manual labor (Gautrat himself seems to favor splitting this subjective experience between his identification as Gautrat at the factory, and as the writer, Mothé, for *Socialisme ou Barbarie*). Lefort notes that for many (if not for himself) Mothé "represented" Renault (Hastings-King, 244) and this fashioning was symptomatic of the difficulties of workerism as a project.

Mothé's subjective bifurcation between the labor of inquiry at *Socialisme ou Barbarie* and metal-working at Renault is crucial to an understanding of labor mimesis in cultural representation. The worker inquiry is not supposed to be an articulation of labor as relation, that is, labor as a necessary process of valorization for capital, for this in itself (rather than in its effects) is necessarily unrepresentable. If the worker herself rarely appears in Marx's *Capital* this is precisely because labor's *relation* to capital is at stake, which certainly informs how the worker as subject is constituted but is not the essence of labor as such. Yet labor in culture is this relation, narrated, and the story of the worker in capitalism in all of its complex manifestations is a condition of labor mimesis, a kind of dialectical reversal. Whereas for Walter Benjamin, mimesis is part of the way words imitate nature as non-representational correspondence (*unsinnliche Ahnlichkeiten*), labor mimesis attempts to express the non-representational correspondence of labor as relation with the cultural conditions in which it is manifest. It is not that language, image, action, affect is simply the best we can do: it is that culture is the very scene of this expressability, the only way the Real of labor can be copied. In this regard, it is not a coincidence that "An American Worker" first appears in a journal and project called "Correspondence."

To some extent, the division in Mothé's self-identity is consistent with the incredulity before raw proletarian experience registered in readings of workers' inquiry above. However heartfelt the testimony, or evocative of the workplace, some mediating influence is seen to problematize its authenticity, some concept of culture, some intellectual category, some political prism, some aspect of language itself. To the idea of labor as relation as unrepresentable we should add the impossibility of labor representation itself, at least in terms of (false) conformity to what a worker should be. It is one of the antinomies of modernity that its most divisive subjectivity appears to pivot on Kantian a priori, and being true to form obfuscates its most discrepant figura. If, however, workers' inquiries are self-fulfilling and serve the ideological ends of those who conduct, encourage, or collect them, then they are questionably authentic in another key because they are a pure expression of intention: they are contaminated identities because they are ideologically pure. Even now, when almost all of the ideological sutures of party and state have been removed, to pose worker identity is to invite derisive responses about socialist recidivism, or shibboleths about communism, or sometimes accusations about just plain anachronism, out-of-jointness, some lost object of a lost cause. On the one hand, there is a historical and methodological necessity to understand the "sur-vivre" (the living-on) of the workers' inquiry; on another, the disconnection between the subjective claims and cultural substantiality have never been so stark. Workers are everywhere but labor in culture is obtuse, reified, and banal. Whatever the worker is, she is never and always the embodiment of proletarian experience.

Hastings-King tends to think of this contradiction as a definitive split in Mothé's work, which he extends to a crisis in what he calls "the Marxist imaginary" (It is never clear whether this is being used in Lacanian terms—which would make sense historically—an Althusserian reading of ideology, or simply as a worldview. Given the use of the definite article, a certain failure in imagination, if not in imaginary, is almost certain to follow[43]).

Mothé's "Journal d'un ouvrier" in *Socialisme ou Barbarie* (1956) is presented initially as an unsigned diary (a fiction, as Hastings-King points out, on a par with Denby's *Indignant Heart*, although for very different reasons) and outlines the political dilemmas of industrial action in the relationship of the AOC (Atelier Outillage Central, the tool workshop at Renault Billancourt where Mothé worked) to the rest of the factory, to *Socialisme ou Barbarie*, and to the French Left more generally. The workers, who Mothé represents in both the first and third person plural, do not necessarily think as one but do not take solidarity lightly, particularly over events that directly affect their daily lives, like the Algerian war (for which the majority of French combatants were conscripts). The text is riddled by the mediation of a class struggle as simultaneously an authorial struggle. When Mothé writes of the dangers of giving over a leadership role to a supervisor he also provides an allegory of the ambivalence in authorship of worker writing. From this view, a worker diary is highly appropriate in staging not the worker herself, but the conditions of her representability. It is the mutability of such substance, not its essence, Marx seeks in the *Workers' Inquiry*, so that its narrative challenge is to think both the specificities of the instance with the peculiarities of its changing composition. In Mothé's case, this is most easily registered, as Hastings-King points out, in the discrete antagonisms of proletarian politics overdetermined by structural changes in the workforce and the workplace, and the aggressive non-equivalence between putative worker states and the lives of workers in- and outside them. Ultimately, Mothé's narrative cannot bear the weight of the shifting scales in such identification, but this in part explains the continuing interest in the sociological import of a worker inquiry, especially since it is no longer assumed to correspond (that word, again) to the phenomenological certitude of a world historical project.[44] Of course, if the latter prospect remains, it must be tied not to a false singularity in the worker subject, but to the logic of worlding that would make the worker globally compound (a worker of the world[s]).

The immediate heirs to the challenge of the workers' inquiry in *Correspondence* and *Socialisme ou Barbarie* can be found in the autonomous worker movements in Italy.[45] As Haider and Mohandesi point out, the links are more or less direct and begin with Danilo Montaldi's translation of both "The American Worker" and Mothé's diary, and continue in Montaldi's own "inquiries" in *Milano, Corea* (with Franco Alasia), *Autobiografie della leggera*, and *Militanti politici di base*. Montaldi's reading of class composition was hardly formulaic and focused on the outsiders of the "lower orders."[46] The work with Alasia is particularly interesting since it highlights the south to north migration in Italy during the economic "miracle" of the 1950s that catalyzes autonomia (as we will see later, the connection between labor migration and capitalist expansion has not exactly dissipated). The question of worker autonomy at the theoretical level has had a profound impact on labor politics, indeed on every level of worker understanding about the workings of capital, even if its implications for the cultural representation of labor have been insufficiently elaborated.[47] *Operaismo* is a specific interpretation of workerism which itself can be read between Autonomia Operaia, the Workers Autonomy movement emerging in the 1960s out of the debates in the *Quaderni Rossi* (*Red Notebooks*) journal, and various discussions that led to the formation of Potere Operaio or the worker power movement by the decade's end. Operaismo deepened the critique of the worker state and bureaucratic forms of proletarian politics. If workers' inquiry sought creative knowledge of the everyday life of the worker, often if not always honed according to the criteria embedded in its central questions, work like Montaldi's placed greater emphasis on spontaneous responses and insurgency less codified or directed (particularly by the Italian Communist Party). It was not that such critique was beyond contradiction (Worker Power, for instance, was seen to overlook the specific power of women workers, and too much autonomy could be interpreted simply as independence from workers themselves—an autonomy from the social that could exclude the worker in her own name), but that workers' inquiry inevitably challenged class composition in the broad sense and how it might be narrated.

While there is much more to Autonomia than its genealogical extension of the workers' inquiry, it emphasizes both the continuities and limits in Marx's modest proposal. For instance, even if the political movement broke from the constraints of entrenched worker organizational models there was still relatively little autonomy from prescriptions about the experiences of Western industrial workers or indeed what C. Wright Mills calls elsewhere "the labor metaphysic."[48] An attention to class composition was placed front and center in Autonomist critique, yet this enthusiastic attempt to differentiate work and workers seemed to forestall any such corollary in inquiry itself (although Montaldi's work is a vital exception). Part of this can be explained by political exigency, and a specific attention to changing issues of self-management in the workplace wrought by technology (the problematic question of automation again). Within the movement, it was Raniero Panzieri who provided the most precise theoretical base for continuing the sociological work of the inquiry and, significantly, he returns the vagaries of personal narrative to the questionnaire, via "an autonomy based on consistent, scientific and logical rigor."[49] Here, experience is secondary to the political strategy or else experience does not articulate the politics as such:

> In this framework the method of inquiry is a permanent point of reference for our politics and underlies the illustration of this or that specific fact and investigation. This method demands the refusal to draw an analysis of the level of the working class from an inquiry into the level of capital. In other words, we wish to restate Lenin's proposition that the workers' movement is an encounter between socialism and the spontaneous movement of the working class. ("Socialist")

What Panzieri suggests is that inquiry should be pursued "in the heat of the moment and on the spot."

Panzieri's approach cuts across the philosophical framing of the inquiry in order to emphasize spontaneous creativity. He is not looking to norm the proletarian as a subject or as a political category but draw from the differences in class composition between the workers' everyday existence and moments of crisis (signaled for him in the contrast of conflict and antagonism). It is not clear whether this can be achieved by adding or subtracting questions or by changing the phrasing within questions according to whether conflict is at stake. Spontaneity can change the answers but much still depends on the nature of the questions. Whatever might be vague or diffuse in individual examples of worker narration, and whatever might be pinned to dialogic expectation, writing outside of the questionnaire permits a spontaneity all of its own, as if the very process of writing connects chance to personal experience. This is far from being an absolute difference, of course, and points instead to a basic tension in how a worker is discerned, predicated, performed; indeed, Mario Tronti's divergences with Panzieri within the autonomist movements of the time accentuate this contradiction. Like Panzieri, Tronti does not seek a typology of the worker based on the contents of inquiry, but he also pushes the reason for inquiry in an alternative direction, toward something like a science from a proletarian worldview. The difficulty in this move is that it focuses precisely on labor as relation while acknowledging that a capitalist science of labor had to be taken into account because it is premised on such relationality. For the most part, and especially in his *Operai e capital* (*Workers and Capital*), Tronti sees the workers' inquiry as a key to understanding the organizational nexus of capitalism and the workers' ability to out-organize it.[50] The inquiry is a bridge in knowledge, not to what capitalism knows as labor's productive capacities, but to the subjective contours of living labor, labor as living otherwise to the objective conditions of its meaning for capital. This is clearly a political challenge since it as posed as a revolutionary potential that is *within* capitalism but is not, in essence, part of it, and is also a profound demand on imagination since it asks that labor be seen beyond its abstract or objective form as social but is not represented as such (we should note that Tronti has to modify Marx on this point from the *Contribution to a Critique of Political Economy*, but the sense is there, as in *Grundrisse*, that the labor in question is "non-objectified" [nicht-vergegenständlichte Arbeit]). Indeed, we might say that as labor becomes more objectified for capital or, as Marx puts it, work loses its character as art (*Grundrisse*, 297), an inquiry of labor must seek its modes of non-objectification, and even the characteristics of art in its subjective forms. This, of course, is a leap of faith even greater than a workerist reaccentuation of *Grundrisse* in a refusal of work or a vaunting of general intellect, but it becomes more credible as a mimetic genealogy. How?

We began with Socrates' rationalization of social division through a critique of mimesis, as if the representation of reality could undo the certitude of such hierarchization. The story of workers' inquiry complicates this picture a great deal, not just because it expresses a concrete antinomy of labor and capital after the Second World War in my prime examples, but because labor mimesis itself strives to articulate the non-representational and the non-objective in its manifestations. It is as if the value of mimesis in an inquiry of labor comes to rest less on a measure of decision about authenticity, however pivotal that must be (who is represented and who is doing the representation?) and more on the extent to which it puts into play the very question of worker expressability, of a subject in semblance of the social (on and off the assembly line); indeed of a practical correspondence that would narrate the ways in which the worker might overcome the vagaries of correspondence itself. True, this can still be subsumed within suspect allegories of the intellectual, activist, and artist, even if the intention is to show how the worker cancels through those divisions. Sociologists committed to formulating the workers' inquiry today should maintain an incredulity about such mimesis somehow being the ward not just of workers, but of cultural critics and theorists, whatever the solidarity, consciousness, or roots. But it seems to me the furor created in the principles and practices of the workers' inquiry are actually creative in another way, both as historical moments and cultural coordinates. Marx believed the inquiry would offer "an exact and positive knowledge" of the worker to whom the future belonged. It is easy to say that, dialectically, it has become a barometer of political impossibility, a symptom of persistent idealism of labor in culture, or an almost hallucinogenic nostalgia for a workers' future that has not been. This cannot be wished away as ideological obfuscation since it is also part of the real foundations upon which Marx thought the workers' inquiry could be built. But it is not that the worker no longer corresponds, let us say, to the formulae given in the questions (such non correspondence is immanent to the inquiry itself); it remains a challenge, rather, in the ways worker knowledge is articulated, which has a cultural prescience both as genealogy *and* as mimetic practices now, in the worlds the worker makes.

Workers' inquiry today follows mostly in the traditions of Italian worker autonomy and this certainly invigorates what we understand as class composition. It also builds on specific interventions within the genealogy of workers' inquiry around the Campaign for Wages for Housework, for instance, and the research of Selma James, Mariarosa Dalla Costa, and Leopoldina Fortunati, among others.[51] James's "A Woman's Place" remains a classic in this history even if radical feminism has moved a long way from notions of the "average woman." Part of the reasoning behind the persistence of the inquiry is as a metric of the changed conditions of labor as relation and class as its lived formation. Nobody expects that either the questions or answers can simply mirror or would want to emulate the intent in Marx's appeals to science and, whatever seemed necessary in the intense post-war rearticulations of the inquiry, its present configurations are deeply affected by still more transformations in what the worker represents. If such moving contradictions are very much in the spirit of capitalism as a socio-economic dynamic entirely pinned to constant mutation, why would some sense of a mimetic faculty be relevant to reading the worker as active in those changes and in its changed self? Work, particularly the industrialized work that is the main focus of the workers' inquiry, rarely follows the mimetic desire for semblance and play; indeed, the assembly line takes semblance to mean reproduction without play (to borrow from Benjamin, this is the end of beautiful semblance[52]). To some extent, the inquiry seeks to measure this banalization of productive play in the disjunction between the demands of work and the workers' experiences of them (from this perspective sabotage is the return of play to the point of capitalist production, although such intervention is today more usually reserved for the poetics of consumption). As is clear now in the analysis of service industries, banalization through repetition, post-industrial line work, produces similar forms of disjuncture yet this would require reconceptualizing the cultural valence of assembly per se. Part of the point here is that both mimesis and worker inquiry share a capacity to address the outer and inner forms of labor but that dialectically, art preternaturally resists the inquiry's "positive knowledge" in the same way the inquiry tends to abjure the affective textures of worker experience. Both struggle mightily to do the work of the other. This in itself is a definition of labor in culture: it is constitutive of the labor of representation in representing labor as such.

Cultural analysis is always already an inquiry—"a voice for reasoned inquiry into significant creations of the human spirit" states the journal, *Critical Inquiry*, in its inaugural issue. Yet the obviousness of the declaration is belied by its objects and exclusions around "significant creations of the human spirit." Significance for the workers' inquiry has insistently been tied to political exigency and to an active and situated politics of knowledge. Auerbach elaborates mimesis to enable if not a politics of knowledge, then an aesthetic practice that still opens cultural expression to worker experience, to the subjects of "bronze and iron." What is fascinating is the present evokes a demonstrable need for the workers' inquiry as sociological method and political practice but the correspondence with mimetic critique is much diminished, as if this work is done or is done in by its impossible parameters (including those in the exhortation "workers of the world"). The historical context cannot be wished away, but no assembly of examples can ultimately stand in for the acute contradictions of a world system in which workers are everywhere, and everywhere out of sync with the cultural substance of representing labor. Modalities of inquiry are never conjoint, but the fact one can be pursued as if another did not exist might yet be remedied.

Notes

1. Plato, *The Republic*, Ed. and Trans. Allan Bloom, New York: Basic Books, 1991: vii (Plato 1991).
2. See Jacques Rancière, *Proletarian Nights*, Trans. John Drury. New York: Verso, 2012: x (Rancière 2012). The form of Rancière's critique is itself a countermyth since the worker stories elaborated insistently undo any and all claims to proletarian identity. If the current project cleaves to this sense of the worker as discrepant in the realization of proletarian being, it does not

root this in the joy of being artisanal but in the singularity of the worker before conflicting worlds of difference. The proletarian is not the sum of her stories but the divisions between them.
3. Raymond Williams, *Resources of Hope: Culture, Democracy, Socialism*. New York: Verso, 1989 (Williams 1989).
4. "Comment se forme, dans ses limites et ses contradictions, une pensée de classe ? " See *Les Revoltes Logiques No.1*. Hiver, 1975 (Revoltes 1975). This can be accessed online at: http://horlieu-editions.com/introuvables/les-revoltes-logiques/les-revoltes-logiques-n-1.pdf. The specific moment of this research and its accompanying theorization of the worker is a book in itself. While the current project often alludes to its provocation, it simultaneously critiques its "lesson." A half a century on from the attacks on Marxism, and particularly the Marxism of the French Communist Party (PCF) the importance of the initial question by "Logical Revolt" points to a different situation and material force, where the fading of state and party vis-à-vis worker identity has contributed to all kinds of corresponding dissolutions in the cultural representations of labor. For more on "logical revolts," see Jeanne-Phillip Deranty, Ed., *Jacques Rancière: Key Concepts*. Durham: Acumen, 2010. (Deranty 2010)
5. I am going to take this in the direction of Auerbach for reasons that will become evident but it is important to note that the problem of mimesis is integral to the function of the poor in Rancière's reading of Western philosophy, an emphasis highlighted in Andrew Parker's fine introduction, "Mimesis and the Division of Labor" to Jacques Rancière, *The Philosopher and His Poor*. Trans. Andrew Parker. Durham: Duke University Press, 2004: ix–xx (Rancière 2004). As Parker points out, for Rancière, the worker copying is a way to slip what the worker as subject is supposed to represent and what, culturally, is perceived as conditional or as constitutive limits.
6. Here I mark the difference between Erlebnis as individual life experience and what Gadamer will explore as Erfahrung (the experience of social interaction). Gadamer reads Erlebnis as a romanticization of experience and this is largely true in Dilthey's conceptualization. The difference in the idea of experience does not map easily onto that between, say, the personal life of testimonial and that of the communal thought as a sociology of life in general. Nevertheless, such difference asks questions about the mediation of representation and representability, both of which indicate how the worker "appears" in these pages. For more on Dilthey's conception, see Rudolph A. Makreel, *Dilthey, Philosopher of the Human Studies*. Princeton: Princeton University Press, 1975 (Makreel 1975). Much of Gadamer's position can be found in Hans-Georg Gadamer, *Truth and Method*. 2nd rev.ed. Trans. Joel Weinsheimer and Donald G. Marshall. New York: Continuum, 1993 (Gadamer 1993).

7. Pierre Bourdieu, *Distinction*, Trans. Richard Nice. Cambridge, MA: Harvard University Press, 1984 (Bourdieu 1984). Fields of cultural production, the sociological spacing of culture, appear to undo unmediated authenticity rather than confirm its cultural privilege. Plato's distinction is itself a cultural capital of its time.
8. Walter Benjamin, *The Work of Art in the Age of Its Technological Reproducibility*. Ed. Michael W. Jennings, Brigid Doherty, and Thomas Y. Levin, Trans. Edmundephcott, Rodney Livingstone, Howard Eiland et al. Cambridge, MA: Belknap Press, 2008 (Benjamin 2008).
9. The contention here is perhaps as old as that which mimesis represents for Plato and bears both aesthetic and political contradictions. On the one hand, it is not enough to settle for representation as the problem, as if allotted selves solve the question of the truth of identity, or as if non-representation can do all of the work of cultural transmission. On the other hand, if representation is not the vexed heart of labor in culture then the worker can be frozen in her metrics as a calculation outside the agon of subjectivity itself. Representation thus simultaneously throws light on what counts as an abstraction while revealing its limits for experience. This dynamic is not a version of the political, a representation of representationality, but is an indication of what is mutually compositional, the organic and technical composition of labor. See also Erich Auerbach, *Mimesis: The Representation of Reality in Western Literature*. Intro. Edward Said, Trans. Willard R. Trask. Princeton: Princeton University Press, 2003 (Auerbach 2003).
10. The basic premise is that Goethe's sense of world for world literature underestimates its internal differentiation and tends to project a world over and above its constitutive possibilities. It is no coincidence that such a worldview informs Marx and Engels' invocation of world literature in the Communist Manifesto, and is the same world in the final sentence of the English version of their pamphlet: "Workers of the world, unite!", although, as I have argued elsewhere, this world both muddies the German ("Proletarier aller Länder vereinigt Euch!") and undoes a specific articulation of proletarian being. Moving the "s" from worker to world does not solve the difficulty in apprehending the worker in her world, yet attempts to indicate an important cultural genealogy that grapples with the limits of proletarian unity in the idea of world. See Peter Hitchcock, "Defining the World" in *Literary Materialisms*, Mathias Nilges and Emilio Sauri (eds.) New York: Palgrave, 2013: 125–144 (Hitchcock 2013).
11. Karl Marx, "Enquête ouvrière" and "Workers' Questionnaire" in *Marx-Engels Collected Works vol. 24*. New York: International Publishers, 1880. The English version omits question 73 of the French version about a fall in wages in times of stagnation as if this might not contrast with question 74

on wage increases in more prosperous times. By rounding the number the English version appears to elide a significant source of crisis and resistance.
12. Asad Haider and Salar Mohandesi have provided an excellent background resource to the subject of the "workers" inquiry. See "Workers' Inquiry: A Genealogy." Available online at: https://viewpointmag.com/2013/09/27/workers-inquiry-a-genealogy/
13. To the charge that capital produces labor that is abstract, the inquiry seeks to render labor concrete in the form of worker responses. All kinds of assumptions are made in Marx's desire for "full knowledge" (not just about the pitfalls of sampling, location, even the time of day, but about the dialogic in play, the question of subjectivity, memory, self-consciousness and class codes—"who is this person asking questions, why should I answer, why should I care?"). Can a questionnaire possibly fulfill Marx's laudable aim to produce "an exact and positive knowledge of the conditions in which the working class—the class to whom the future belongs—works and moves"? At best the inquiry can only be a complement to the many forms of investigation already extant at the time, including of course Marx's own *Capital* and Engels's *Condition of the English Working Class*. For the trenchant intervention of Flora Tristan in this regard, see Flora Tristan, *The London Journal of Flora Tristan 1842: The Aristocracy and the Working Class of England*, Trans. Jean Hawkes. London: Virago, 1989 (Tristan 1989). Tristan's understanding, mediated through a provocative and contradictory logic of "promenades," accentuates that labor in culture is inexorably tied to conditions of expressibility themselves, to beliefs in the veridicality of recorded experience, mimetic practice. Such belief is itself historical and has repositioned the truth of Tristan's identifications. See, for instance, Susan Grogan, *Flora Tristan: Life Stories*. London: Routledge, 1998 (Grogan 1998). For a polemical discussion of the worker journal *L'Atelier*, see the third section of Rancière's *Proletarian Nights*.
14. Edmond and Jules de Goncourt, *Germenie Lacerteux*. New York: Book Jungle, 2010 (Edmond and Goncourt 2010).
15. Bruce Robbins, *The Servant's Hand: English Fiction From Below*. Durham: Duke University Press, 1993: 26 (Robbins 1993). Robbins's book traces the haunting of labor in a number of critical ways that inspire the present work. In discussing Auerbach Robbins notes: "The presence of servants signifies the absence of the people. Signposts left at random in the no-man's-land between what can and cannot be represented, they indicate only that the other side of the border is inhabited" (27). The signifying absence of the worker is deeply contradictory, not just in *Mimesis* but in the Workers' Inquiry where presence would seem most obviously present. It is not that the worker is unseen, necessarily, since global cultures are saturated with a

worker symbolic; the problem is always the apparent randomness of association as if the worker can *only* appear in her singularity.
16. Paul Romano and Ria Stone, *The American Worker*, 1947 (Romano and Stone 1947). Available online at: https://libcom.org/history/american-worker-paul-romano-ria-stone. Also available online at http://www.prole.info/pamphlets.html. Both sites emphasize how new media preserve and disseminate representations of labor in culture while linking them to specific political projects in the present.
17. Nicola Pizzolato, "The American Worker and the Forze Nuove: Turin and Detroit at the Twilight of Fordism," *Viewpoint* 3 (2013) (Pizzolato 2013). Available online at: https://viewpointmag.com/2013/09/25/the-american-worker-and-the-forze-nuove-turin-and-detroit-at-the-twilight-of-fordism/. See also, Nicola Pizzolato, *Challenging Global Capitalism: Labor Migration, Radical Struggle, and Urban Change in Detroit and Turin*. London: Palgrave, 2013 (Pizzolato 2013).
18. The Johnson-Forest Tendency occupies an important place in American Marxism. Its formation marks keys rifts within American Trotskyism and the travails of the Socialist Workers Party in the 1930s and 1940s (indeed, James and Dunayevskaya would be instrumental in the split to form the Workers Party in 1940 but would rejoin the SWP later the same decade). Eventually Johnson-Forest would coalesce around Correspondence, another splinter group and later a publishing venture. An early pamphlet of 1947, *The Invading Socialist Society* would strongly inflect Lee's contribution to *The American Worker*.
19. See Stephen Hastings-King, *Looking for the Proletariat: Socialisme ou Barbarie and the Problem of Worker Writing*. Chicago: Haymarket Books, 2015 (Hastings-King 2015). Hastings-King's book is important on a number of levels. It works just as well as a history of *Socialisme ou Barbarie*, of which Claude Lefort was a fulcrum, as it does as a theory of revolutionary writing. The phenomenological emphasis of the analysis is key, although I have a very different reading of social imaginaries and the futures to which they bend, one which must differentiate looking for the proletariat (the title) from looking for the working class (the chapter), just as it separates the worker from labor.
20. These exchanges intensified after the Second World War as more doubts were cast about actual worker power within the Soviet system and the specter of "state capitalism." For more on the historical currents, see Paul Buhle, *Marxism in the United States* (3rd ed.). New York: Verso, 2013 (Buhle 2013).
21. Such a polemic has its own vital history, epitomized for me in the Black Radical Tradition detailed by Cedric Robinson but also evident in many movements of decolonization and anti-capitalism of the global South. It is

the difference in these worlds that complicate the assumed solidarities of the worker, multiplied. See Cedric J. Robinson, *Black Marxism: The Making of the Black Radical Tradition*. London: Zed Press, 1983 (Robinson 1983).
22. Fredric Jameson, *The Antinomies of Realism*. New York: Verso, 2013 (Jameson 2013). Interestingly, Jameson begins the book by acknowledging that "mimesis" will not be a fulcrum in the argument and that his own reading of realism will be very different from Auerbach's. Yet Auerbach's study hovers quite close to Jameson's even when the latter resists the former's idiosyncratic rendering of realism as mimesis. Thus, while Jameson correctly identifies realism's role in modernity as a kind of globalizing democracy in Auerbach's reading that is focused on European texts, it is sometimes difficult not to see Jameson's critique following the same trajectory, albeit with a stronger sense of its dialectical contradictions. When Auerbach invokes the everyday as a "realism to come" (Jameson), Jameson also hints at the nuance in his own sense of futurity.
23. Adorno, T. W., and Max Horkheimer, *Dialectic of Enlightenment*. Trans. Edmund Jephcott. Stanford: Stanford University Press, 2002 (Adorno and Horkheimer 2002). Adorno and Horkheimer attempt to correlate the moments of fascism, Stalinism, the advent of mass culture and the absence of revolution in advanced capitalist societies with a withering critique of "Enlightenment." A central text of Critical Theory and the Frankfurt School it is also in conversation, real or imagined, with the problems of labor and mimesis of its time. How, for instance, can Romano's account of worker experience disrupt or subtend the aura of a pervasive counter-revolutionary symbolic, what Adorno and Horkheimer call "the mimesis of mimesis" (152)? Reification and occultation roll back revolutionary desire at every turn as creative mimesis is met by the magic of the market and the pleasures of social inertia.
24. See C.L.R. James, Freddie Forest and Ria Stone. *The Invading Socialist Society*, 2nd Ed., Detroit: Bedwick Editions, 1972 (James et al. 1972). Note in this second edition Dunayevskaya and Lee retain their pseudonyms. Available online at: https://www.marxists.org/archive/james-clr/works/1947/invading/.
25. See Stevphen Shukaitis, Joanna Figiel, Abe Walker, *A Workers' Inquiry Reader*. Available Online at: http://www.ephemerajournal.org/events/politics-workers-inquiry. See also, the special issue of Ephemera edited by Shukaitis, Figiel, and Walker, Available online at: http://www.ephemerajournal.org/issue/politics-workers-inquiry.
26. There is some debate about the process of the pamphlet's production. C.L.R. James is credited with suggesting the idea of a diary but Romano's narrative is something else again and indicates a more creative transcription on Lee's part. See, for instance, Paul Buhle, *C.L.R. James: The Artist as Revolutionary*. New York: Verso, 1989: 90 (Buhle 1989).

27. Charles Denby, *Indignant Heart: A Black Worker's Journal*. Boston: South End Press, 1978 (Denby 1978). This edition uses Owens' preferred pseudonym, Denby, rather than Ward. As Haider and Mohandesi note, Owens continued to use pseudonyms long after the pall of McCarthyism that nurtured them.
28. See Selma James, "A Woman's Place" in *The Power of Women and the Subversion of the Community*. London: Falling Wall Press, 1972: 57–79 (James 1972). The original publication was in February 1953 in *Correspondence* under the names Marie Brant and Ellen Santori.
29. For more on Lowndes County's key role in combatting racism and advancing civil rights, see Hasan Kwame Jeffries, *Bloody Lowndes: Civil Rights and Black Power in Alabama's Black Belt*. New York: University Press, 2009 (Jeffries 2009).
30. Central to the work of the journal and its associated organization is the writings of Raya Dunayevskaya; indeed, Denby recommends her key text, *Marxism and Freedom*, in this section of his book. Dunayevskaya's importance to the Johnson-Forest Tendency, Correspondence, and *News and Letters* cannot be overemphasized. *Marxism and Freedom*, for instance, not only laid the groundwork for a defense of Marxist-Humanism but the first edition (1958, introduced by Herbert Marcuse) included English translations of Marx's Economic and Philosophical Manuscripts of 1844, and Lenin's notebooks on Hegel's *Science of Logic* (Dunayevskaya had worked with Lee on a translation of the former in the 1940s). Dunayevskaya's works on philosophy and revolution, Rosa Luxemburg, and women's liberation extend the significance of her legacy and provide a materialist understanding of the moment of inquiry foregrounded in this chapter. See Raya Dunayevskaya, *Marxism and Freedom: From 1776 to Today*. New York: Humanity Books, 2000 (Dunayevskaya 2000).
31. Silvia Federici, *Revolution at Point Zero*. New York: PM Press, 2012: 54 (Federici 2012). The consciousness that invigorated the Wages for Housework campaign emerged in several places and spaces in the women's movement but connects to the kind of communal voice James explores in *A Woman's Place*.
32. See Claude Lefort, "Proletarian Experience" Trans. Stephen Hastings-King. Available online at: http://viewpointmag.com/2013/09/26/proletarian-experience/. The original critique appeared as "L'experience prolétarienne," *Socialisme ou Barbarie*, 11 (Novembre/Decembre 1952): 1–19. See also, Claude Lefort, "L'experience prolétarienne," in his, *Éléments d'une critique de la bureaucratie*. Paris: Gallimard, 1971 (Lefort 1971). *Socialisme ou Barbarie* published a translation of Romano and Stone's text in issues 1–8, March 1949–April 1951. Available online at: http://soubscan.org/.

33. For more on Lefort's intervention, see Eric Herrán, *What Is (The) Political? Notes on the Work of Claude Lefort*. Shelbyville, KY: Wasteland Press, 2013 (Herrán 2013). On Lefort's work with Castoriadis on *Socialisme ou Barbarie*, see again Hasting-King's *Looking* (2015).
34. Joanna Figiel, Stevphen Shukaitis and Abe Walker, "Editorial," *Ephemera: Theory & Politics in Organization* 14(3): 308. The idea here is not to make the compositional elements of class and culture synonymous but different *because* of their relation.
35. Not surprisingly, comportment for Heidegger slips any ruse of consciousness and is a direction towards, but it fits Lefort's emphasis on the possibility of spontaneity. The opening for *Dasein* here may not lie in proletarian subjectivity, but in the world that attends being as such. See Martin Heidegger, *Being and Time*, Trans. John Macquarrie and Edward Robinson. New York: Harper Perennial, 1962 (Heidegger 1962).
36. In other words, labor in culture might imply the "subjective development of the proletariat" but can also mark a prescient absence: that labor "appears" where the proletariat is not subjectively composed. This puts an onus both on organizational claims and on the procedures of critical elaboration.
37. Clearly the difficulty here is rendering experience as class inflected without reproducing the conflation of the individual with class coordinates. This is a living contradiction in the dialectics of proletarian representation itself and is only overcome in the sublation of class as a socio-economic category.
38. See Cornelius Castoriadis, "Proletarian Leadership" in *Political and Social Writings (Volume One, 1946–1955: "From the Critique of Bureaucracy to the Positive Content of Socialism")*, Trans. and Ed. David Ames Curtis. Minneapolis: University of Minnesota Press, 1988: 198–206 (Castoriadis 1988).
39. Eric Albert, "La vie dans une usine," *Les Temps Modernes* 81 (Juillet 1952): 95–130 (Albert 1952).
40. Benjamin argues that language is the highest form of mimesis but that there is reading before writing and thus the necessity for magic. I am not suggesting that labor representation depends on such magic but that the unwritten must be figured into proletarian inscription. See Walter Benjamin, "On the Mimetic Faculty" in *Reflections: Essays, Aphorisms, Autobiographical Writings*. Ed. Peter Demetz, Trans. Edmund Jephcott. New York: Schocken, 1978: 333–336 (Benjamin 1978).
41. His diary was also published as a book: *Journal d'un ouvrier*. Paris: Minuit, 1959. Hastings-King's chapter on Mothé explores his shifting identities, and those indeed of *Socialisme ou Barbarie*. These are read here less as caprice or opportunism, and more about the subjective ambivalence of worker identification.

42. See, for instance, Henri Simon, "Workers' Inquiry in *Socialisme ou Barbarie*" posted as part of the special issue of *Viewpoint Magazine* on the workers' inquiry. Available online at: https://libcom.org/library/workers'-inquiry-socialisme-ou-barbarie.
43. Hastings-King suggests the Marxist Imaginary "refers to the entire range of socio-cognitive creations instituted in ways shaped by the sedimented history of [the Marxist] tradition." (*Looking*: 5) There is a tension in this formulation between the ability to imagine as itself a political force and a notion that the sediments in play are themselves "imaginary."
44. As Haidar and Mohandesi point out, part of the problem is that only Mothé himself fits the parameters of his worker inquiry. Thus: "The worker must not only be the most politically conscious of his class, but must also be capable of expressing his experiences in such a way that they could be theorized. This required not only a high degree of general literacy, as well as a fair share of confidence, but also some fluency in a more challenging political lexicon. 'In this sense', Mothé clarified, 'those workers most suitable for writing will be those who are at the same time the most conscious, the most educated but also those who will be the most rid of bourgeois or Stalinist ideological influence.' So Mothé wanted a worker who could not only reflect on his situation and transcribe it into a narrative that mimicked the natural oral culture of the average worker, but who would also be free of all non-revolutionary ideology."
45. The literature on operaismo is extensive. A good introduction related to the current discussion is Steve Wright, *Storming Heaven: Class Composition and Struggle in Italian Autonomist Marxism*. London: Pluto, 2002 (Wright 2002).
46. This is particularly true of the *Autobiografie*. For *Viewpoint's* special issue on the worker inquiry, Mohandesi translated Montaldi's introduction of the American Worker in *Battaglia Comunista*, XV: 2 (febbraio-marzo 1954). See https://libcom.org/library/introduction-l%E2%80%99operaio-americano-1954.
47. A key tome in this regard is Sylvere Lotringer and Christian Marazzi, Eds., *Autonomia: Post-Political Politics*, originally published as a special issue of the journal Semiotext(e) in 1980. A second edition, in book form, appeared in 2007. The collection captures the heat of political turmoil in Italy in the Seventies while also providing political principles and terminology for worker struggle, if not workerism, today.
48. See C. Wright Mills, "Letter to the New Left," *New Left Review* 5 (September–October), 1960 (Mills 1960). For Mills, the labor metaphysic was a belief in the working class in late capitalism that defied the specificity of its agency within early industrialization. He termed this a "Victorian Marxism" out of touch with the realities of contemporary social and political

upheaval, much preferring the activism of a youthful intelligentsia. Viewed historically, this might now be read as a misreading of both the working class and the intelligentsia.
49. Panzieri's belief in Marx's *Capital* as a primer for sociology was not a consistent line among the *Quaderni Rossi* cohorts, but reveals a pertinent dialectical flux despite a general resistance to dialectics in theories of Autonomia. Panzieri's argument for the workers' inquiry, for instance, ostensibly pits socialist science against capitalist principles of organization, while actually deconstructing the scientific proclivities of the Communist Party. The second moment of Autonomia, heralded in the second edition of Lotringer and Marazzi's tome, finds that disassembly complete, especially after the collapse of "actually existing socialism," and this permits a new science of anti-capitalism, in theory. The question here is about the possibilities of workers' inquiry in that endeavor. See Raniero Panzieri, "Socialist Uses of Workers' Inquiry." Trans. Arianna Bove. Available online at: http://eipcp.net/transversal/0406/panzieri/en. See also, Raniero Panzieri, "The Capitalist Use of Machinery." Trans. Quintin Hoare. Available at libcom.org.
50. Mario Tronti, *Operai e capital*. Turin: Einaudi, 1966. Although this text has been translated, a full version in English is not yet available. Haidar and Mohandesi's critique of Tronti is useful, as is Tronti's "Strategy of Refusal" from *Workers and Capital*, translated in Lotringer and Marazzi: 28–35. For Tronti's reflections on operaismo, see Mario Tronti, "Our Operaismo" *New Left Review* 73, January–February 2012 (Tronti 2012).
51. See, for instance, the aforementioned book by Mariarossa Dalla Costa with Selma James, *The Power of Women and the Subversion of the Community*. Bristol: Falling Wall Press, 1972 (James 1972). Also, Mariarossa Dalla Costa and Giovanna F. Dalla Costa, Eds., *Women, Development, and Labor of Reproduction: Struggles and Movements*. London: Africa World Press, 1999 (Dalla Costa and Giovanna F 1999); Leopoldina Fortunati, *The Arcane of Reproduction: Housework, Prostitution, Labor and Capital*. New York: Autonomedia, 1996 (Fortunati 1996); and, of course, Federici's *Revolution at Point Zero* (see note 31 above).
52. See "On Semblance" in Walter Benjamin, *Selected Writings: 1913–1926, Volume 1*. Ed. Marcus Bullock and Michael W. Jennings. Cambridge, MA: Harvard University Press, 2004 (Benjamin 2004). Mimetic labor is structured by seeming, a cultural space in which the assembler, and the worker per se, is assembled.

CHAPTER 2

The Worker Subjects

One of the more slippery signifiers in cultural and political theory is the "worker." Entire histories, epistemologies, political platforms, economies, and indeed states have been formed around the worker, and it is no exaggeration to say that the long worker century (longer than all those others that trespass beyond a hundred years) has been epochal in how we understand the human subject. Of course, that the concept of subject is so easily associated with the edifice of bourgeois thought (and white, male, European too) has presented itself as a catechresistic nightmare for thinking the worker. Is she a mere epiphenomenon of bourgeois categories, a kind of anarchistic edge to cultural Cartesianism? Is the worker the great orphan of socialization, the passionate progeny of modernity disavowed by those who yet draw on her labor? Is the worker just an alibi of the male subject, something its logic requires but is actually positioned elsewhere, beyond its primary protocols, in some ontological wasteland that permits a contrasting fecundity to appear? But then we have killed the subject have we not? We are always "after" it, beyond its "death," so sure of our demystification of its substance that it exists only as a ghost, a spirit, or, for the more materialist, an exquisite corpse. Could this be the trick of theorizing the worker: that she is so tied to the life of the subject that she has expired with the concept and, while work must be done to sustain species being, there is no subject form for the worker to inhabit? Humans still need food, water, clothing, and shelter; they might need smartphones, fiber optic cable, and all kinds of energy, but these do not guarantee the worker as subject even if the worker facilitates all of it. If she is alive in her materiality and immateriality, the worker exists in modalities other than the subject, or at least in a subject other than what is given in theorization. To the extent the subject prescribes and/or underwrites the category of subjection, the worker is always a subject; to the degree the waywardness of the designation threatens all manner of elements deemed constitutive of what makes a human, the worker subjects the ways we ground the relation of work to the human to uneven but incessant interrogation. Is attention to worker subjects primarily a cultural practice, expressive discourses that undo the facts and fictions of worker existence? Is it a political lever, one that prizes apart the platitudes attending "representation" and the praxis of our collective endeavors? Is it first an economic category, one that comports with the labor relation as such and in that capacity is a key to the logic of capital and its dominance over the social order? Together, these questions constitute something of a dialectical weave, and one to be undone within Minerva's flight of history. Here I will concern myself with the cultural and philosophical elements not to revivify a subject made impossible in the discourse of science (a rescue akin to bringing back the manual typewriter), but to clarify as much as possible why the worker subjects all "metaphysical subtleties and theological niceties" to category confusion in its own name (when did the worker become as much a fetish as the commodity?). And this is an impasse we are not so much "after," but in.[1]

The worker pre-exists its designation within modernity and, whether as serfs, slaves, servants, or staff, its genealogy traces who comes *before* the subject. My interest is primarily in what the worker signifies in the nexus of capital, labor, and revolution, for three reasons that seem to me to represent a major theoretical, cultural, and political challenge. First, the shift in the meaning of worker when figured into labor as relation has thoroughly changed the possibility of the human, a revolution that "subject" can at best only refract. True, the question of labor as relation is itself historical, but how we understand the worker derives from the substance of this relation which is not a type of worker or of labor but is, to borrow from the poet Philip Levine, "what work is."[2] Second, and following from this observation, ontology does not belong to the worker: being, as such, is distilled in work and, while we may have cause to define work so that philosophy is work, identity is work (the work of performance), the state is work (a work of art, perhaps), and death is work (where at least we work as one), being exceeds such assignation and the worker is its complementary void. The worker, of course, has being but this belongs to a different order of self than that of work. Work is life, work is existence, but it is not all of the worker's life and existence and she belongs to it only in work (a being that stands even in the absence of work). But third, because work has ontology in a way the worker cannot, we fill the void of the latter with equivalents, just as the money form attempts to solve the riddle of price and value. This is the time of now in which all talk of temporal progress, including modernization itself, is suspect, and the signifier is secured by speculative ambivalence. Time, indeed, is not a sequence of "befores" and "afters" but complex constellations of otherwise arbitrary measures without hierarchy, except perhaps for those of philosophical decision. We might say this is the market of equivalents, one in which the fading of the subject, its inexorable aphanisis, allows the worker as sign to float even more.[3] An ontology of work remains but the worker herself is composed in ether and assumes any form that eludes rather than exudes orthodoxy, dogma, doxa, or state prerogatives. Even while I question these categories, the hard line of politics, the straight line of history, one can still cleave to worker praxis, that the worker is active in her remaking, although not alone or under conditions of her own choosing (again, just like the philosopher). We may be much more sensitive now to the geo-location of proletarianization (even more than Wal-Mart or Apple, although they are two of its prime producers) but we have so unlearned the worker assignations of state and party it has become increasingly difficult to read the worker in her cultural and political possibility, one that is not only post-Soviet but post-presence. The worker is still an excuse for state authoritarianism, most obviously in China, but in general she evokes statistical dissimulation or is a citational social force rather than a concrete one. The point is not to redefine the worker as concept to account for its allusive register but to come to terms with whether its subjective divergence is actually a break from the ossified political components known mostly as "workerism."[4]

To address the tension in the "worker subjects" (its doubling, its seemingly inappropriate otherness) the following will link the comments above to an agonistic schema, an argument between methodology and system. In part, the doubling of "subjects" in my title contests how the worker "appears" for cultural theory (as in Jacques Rancière's "The Proletarian and His Double"[5]). This structure of feeling, "which is not one," underlies attention in other parts of this work to bodies of workers, a trust in problematic visibility that is yet concomitant with a specific genealogy of the sensate, the forming of the five senses through work.[6]

Such formation, overdetermined in modernity by capital, articulates the worker if not the subject as such. After the actual existence of the worker state the worker only seems to assume subjecthood as a phantasm, a specter, or as a dream. I do not view these as excluding the active presence of the worker in politics or culture, but they are too readily read as a displacement rather than as an engagement with the force of capital in contemporary species being. As the worker state recedes in memory the antinomy of work and workers becomes more pronounced. Its function as alibi and ideology are transcoded, but this only serves to accentuate a historical reckoning with capital that remains relatively unaccounted for in the present. I often trace this moment of non-encounter historically as worker eventness (the complex process through which the worker "appears") in the cultural and the literary in particular,[7] but it necessarily presses attention on theoretical correlatives, most pointedly in the work of Rancière. The "lesson of Rancière" troubles the cultural conditions, the very problem of work in labor as relation.[8]

There may be some dialectical valence in addressing Rancière's conspicuous post-structuralism, the aleatory post-Althusserian radicalism of dissemblance. Rancière is at once the victim of his own (non)method—here the furious deconstructor of working-class essence who yet finds his *Proletarian Nights* dubbed "essential reading." It may be the fate of radical theory that it has so ironized the present, the present can only make a gift of irony. I will have more to say about this "present" of work in Rancière's labor but here would affirm his historical importance as a philosopher whose work has spanned the great upheavals of the 1960s in French thought and in particular its implications for thinking the worker since. In his preface to the new English edition of *La Nuit des prolétaires: archives du rêve ouvrier* (a newness that marks both the difference from its French original of 1981 and from the translation, *Nights of Labor* of 1989, coincidentally published on the eve of the death of the worker state[9]), Rancière notes the out-of-timeness of the project, a kind of temporal schism he accentuates with illeism, a third-person Rancière sensibly distributed across time rather than in it. This splitting of Rancière in his re-representation is not disingenuous but is symptomatic of his politics, a logical revolt in which he and his work are themselves the part of no part, in the sense he cannot simultaneously be active in the agonistic politics he describes while he is writing it (if the act of writing itself is the revolt then Rancière has performed the very substitution he bemoans in others). This is one of the great lessons of work, but specifically in Rancière's philosophy, the paradox of the "poor," who have no place in the community because they have no time to take it.[10] This quality of out-of-timeness in the present is crucial not just to reading Rancière in general, but to understanding his intervention on work and workers as a chronotopic critique. I will augment the division Rancière elaborates not to suture it but because what is so suggestive in his worker aesthetics—work as dream work, for instance—exceeds the grammar he accords it. In the same way, the Rancièrean register of "proletarian," "poor," and "people" is sufficiently volatile or dissimulated to catalyze the difference in work and worker, ontology and epistemology, redolent in labor as relation. "The worker subjects" marks the charged space between the worker's praxis, an active struggle from within the contradictions of work, what Rancière calls subjectification, from the phenomenological content of that existence.[11] The collapse of these two elements is what founds a subject; their division is what renders it impossible.

The difference in understanding labor as relation is that between equilibrium and equality. Rancière's theorization of the latter is based on a democratic appeal to the people. Although *demos* is not an economic category (still less an aesthetic one), Rancière continually invokes equality to do the work of the economic. Over and over again, Rancière states the problem for workers is "inegalitarian symbolic violence" as if capitalism is first and foremost an intellectual exploitation and prejudice (*Philosopher*, 221). Few would doubt the condescension heaped upon workers by those who believe workers are thoughtless enough to be suited to their labor, to the world of production for instance. But the translation of economic logic into an arena of moral superiority necessitating opprobrium might be deemed poor from another perspective. Quite simply, while there are constant moments of equilibrium in the conditions of labor and capital as relation, there can never be one of equality, even if equality is presupposed in general. The idea of economic justice between labor and capital historically appears as a bourgeois rationalization for inequality dressed as its opposite. It is for this reason Rancière's understanding of the economic must insistently bracket basic conditions in the formation of labor (the selling of labor, its circulation, surplus and relative surplus value, debt, rent and ownership, forms of political opposition, revolt, etc.) in favor of obtuse appeals to a kind of new abstract labor (the "part" as an aestheticized *objet à*, dissensus, the sensible, fabula, "ethics," disagreement). The question is not one of the powers of invention (when has the aesthetic not been revolutionary?), especially against the myriad gods that have failed Rancière (the Soviet Union, the PCF, Maoism, Althusser), but one that addresses the material contradictions constituting labor under actually existing capitalism. The appeal is not for a resort to the economic determinism and corresponding reductionism propelling Rancière's principled retreat from Marxism (that history has been decided), but whether there is a continuing role for worker discourse in the dissolution of capitalism and how, if at all, this is being manifested. All kinds of critical elements are reconstituting the worker (unemployment, migration, urbanization, environment, technology) and to this extent Rancière's analyses are enmeshed in vibrant and provocative epistemologies. But if we start from work in its ontology, to what extent does the worker subject her logical aphanisis to cultural and political scrutiny? It is this sense of labor as relation, one of both worker subjects and force where the worker subjects that might now be usefully theorized.

It is important to stress what is an antinomy between work and worker is, like that between capital and labor, not simply binaristic. Each term betrays its logical exception which is not its truth but the contour of its relation, its dialectical impress. To say the dialectic is itself subject to dialectics is not license to a charmed circle but to the possibility of constitutive supplementarity. Thus, a logical impasse in the concepts of dialectic and dialogic, for instance, particularly over their status as science, can be enabling of theory in ways pure oppositions foreclose. Even subject/object, long the most baleful of these examples, is readily deferred/deconstructed in relation, as if the shorthand in the designation cannot possibly meet the actual processes the categories imply. In addition, work and workers do not dissemble according to better policing that indicates Leftist astuteness over and against Right Wing muddle-headedness. Marx often takes a position on workers that problematizes his theorization of labor. In the *Communist Manifesto* he and Engels interpellate workers of all countries to unite in their opposition to capitalism, but *Capital* can hardly be said to extend the politics of such subjectification, especially since the worker as subject is largely absent from its elaboration. Indeed, a key to political economy in the conjuncture of work and workers is precisely *not* to proceed on the grounds of subjecthood for the latter. Just as *Capital* is about capital more than capitalism so its theorization of labor is not simply the basis of worker politics given in its name. Put another way, when the worker is taken as subject, labor as relation is banalized, for the latter exists in social production and reproduction not in subjectivity per se. For capital, the worker is a false subject in the sense that it wants her labor not her subjecthood. For their part, workers are not duped by forged subjecthood. Historically, worker struggles against capitalists have constantly revealed the real foundations of value extraction rather than waiting on the social capital of subjecthood, the "fiction of *animal laborans*," as Rancière terms it. Jean-Luc Nancy suggests the subject exhausts all possibility of "being in the world" and to the extent a specific genealogy of self-presencing and metaphysics have historically deracinated an ontology of collective reciprocity there is much to recommend his intervention (which forms the core of the essay collection, *Who Comes After the Subject?*[12]). Yet capital places a peculiar bar on subjecthood, so that the worker pivots on a specific value form, one that not only prohibits being in the world but being itself, whose ontological coordinates remain in work. When Nancy asks, "Who comes after the subject?" the end of metaphysics seems largely a philosophical disposition (and insistently French at that) but for the worker such a question is already the scene of deferral, for it is an answer to a regime of truth whose kernel lies in the materiality of a specific value form. To some extent, this is the classic reversal Marx ponders in *Capital* (Volume Three) when noting the difference between the form of appearance (*Erscheinungsform*) and essence.[13] If the commodity is considered as the finished article, this risks an understanding based on surfaces (although not always on visibility), one that misreads the role of labor in value and a concept (*Begriff*) adequate to it. If the subject, like the commodity, is viewed as completed the same elision can occur not because they are identical, but because they are co-extensive, the only ways in which they can appear under capital. The question of labor lies before the question of the subject, which is its very effect. Co-extension does not mean at the same time but reminds us that "befores" and "afters" may function within the logic of an identical, or identitarian, apparatus.

True, Nancy understands the potential of this paradox in posing the question, and the philosophers who answer his call (which becomes *Who Comes After the Subject?*) do not spend a great deal of time on premises and assumptions because of it. Of those who respond, Balibar's answer with "Citizen Subject" is more interesting to me than Rancière's "rewriting indefinitely" since the question of "after" is, as above, suspended in favor of a richly symptomatic reading of the Cartesian ego as its own "afterlife." The subject appears for Balibar, "after," not "in" the *Meditations*, a reverse engineering provocative for understanding the *Erscheinungsform* of the proletarian (in contradistinction not only to the worker, but also, as we shall see, in relation to the poor and the people). For some, the founding contradiction of the subject in its non-appearance in Descartes would be enough, but Balibar is at pains to distinguish what becomes the subject for the substance of citizen, a substance of the subject *as* citizen. This notion of an inessential subject, an appearance of substance, not its essence, will feature again in *We, the People of Europe?*[14] Here the problem speaks to the doubled nature of subject as identity and constraint, as a sovereign ground and the very suppression of that freedom. The freedom to subject can never produce a subject of freedom and it is because so much of Western metaphysics is grounded by this paradox that it is the scene of its philosophical agon. It is not that the history of worker struggles simply reproduces this dilemma but it has proved politically and philosophically expedient, particularly when it comes to issues of realism and representation. For his part, Balibar recognizes the short answer to Nancy's question is the non-subject, but this is largely a philosophical conceit (a "sophistic" question) and a means to think the citizen as its sublation. The only contributor to *Who Comes After the Subject?* who answers the question by reference to workers is Gerard Granel, for whom the idea of the worker is hamstrung in the French context by a vague adherence to the "Firm," an apparently communist or socialist belief that prevents the worker from understanding when labor is dead. Granel does not pursue whether the emergence of dead labor is itself an allegory of the subject (the afterlife once more) but at least the worker is conceived as more than an occupation, or indeed an occupational hazard.

In his elaboration of the citizen, Balibar argues the transcendentalism of the subject is a projection by Kant onto Cartesian categories of the "I" while simultaneously bracketing its substantiality. The question of substance is an important one and finds no home as cause between Descartes and Balibar's own preference, Spinoza. The category of the subject renders "citizen" insubstantial and the non-subject citizen can only come "after" the subject. We might offer that subject is the substance of the citizen to the extent the latter must break with the former's causal influence in order to "be." This is a revolutionary rupture and for Balibar the key date is 1789. Whatever the epistemological break Balibar discerns, this does not quite work the same way for ontology. If substance is a ground, a primary support, the edifice of the Ancien Régime is certainly overcome by the French Revolution, but the antinomy Balibar describes is contained *within* bourgeois thinking (as are many of its solutions according to Balibar, including socialism and communism), as if the tension of subject and citizen is philosophically substantial to ruling class ideas in the modern period (yes, there is a "subject prince" as Balibar offers yet this can hardly be said to represent the subject in Descartes, Locke, Kant, Hegel, etc.). The politics Balibar accords the citizen are appreciable but it is not easy to expunge the citizen from barbarous documents of the subject that, as Walter Benjamin reminds us, are offered in the name of civilization. However blind Marx may have been to the bourgeois premises of his social divisions (he always extolled the revolutionary virtues of the bourgeoisie, as he did those of capital), the political economy of subjection is not a bourgeois monopoly. In this sense, "citizen subject" works the category of the subject to the citizen's advantage even as it is the sign of the subject's exhaustion, for which revolution is an entirely necessary response. Balibar's invocation of the citizen is a way of unthinking the subject in the service of an alternative genealogy of the human, in its scientificity or materiality. Yet it remains primarily a philosophical response to the antinomy of the subject, one caught between power and the subjection to it. The wonder of Balibar's concept of the citizen subject as a conceit is that the citizen cannot be if anyone is excluded/subjected by its designation. Short of universality, the citizen cannot be, and this is why the citizen comes "after" the subject.[15]

There is more nuance to Balibar's argument than this, framed as it is as a meta-discourse on philosophy's subject. Yet, if he reminds us, for instance, of the distinction between subjection as compulsion and subjection as obedience, Balibar resists reading the subject ideologically, which might make the subject something other than a philosophical dispute, the substance, as it were, of Nancy's question and corresponding book. An ideological critique opens up the chiasmatic overtures of citizen subject to an interested, material history not altogether dependent upon nominating one's exception. This, indeed, is part of the logical impasse of the subject that chooses its attributes and subordinates irrespective of self-consciousness. Power may not admit ideological contradiction but it is always "handling" it in some way until that capacity is overcome. The symptom of such ideological work is precisely the oscillation within the subject as adjective and substantive, between its necessary interpellation and implication, a contradiction citizen may reveal but not solve in its constitutional deployments. Balibar's original thoughts about the citizen subject appeared in a special issue of *Les Temps Modernes* on "L'immigration maghrébine en France."[16] This is important for a number of reasons. First of all, the initial theorization is "citoyens ou sujets" which immediately conjures the dialectical tension over and above a new conjunction. Second, this research should be read in light of Balibar's deep criticisms of the PCF and his subsequent expulsion from the party in 1981. Third, the project is indicative of a long-term commitment to fighting racism, but one in particular that develops out of Balibar's understanding of Beur political movements in France at the time. Finally, Balibar's intervention is contemporaneous with his new thinking on ideology, and on the significance of the proletariat as concept. The Beur activism concerned both immigrant rights (the burning question of state subjectivity and citizenship that pervades the essay) and their specific meaning for employment. State-sponsored marginalization of immigrant workers was compounded on the left by the PCF's support for anti-immigrant workerism (new forms of the latter, of course, pervade the present). President Mitterand may have stabilized the legal status of long-term migrants but new legislation split migrant communities along lines of "regulars" and "illegals." It cannot be overemphasized the change in thinking these events produce in Balibar's theorization of, for instance, race, nation, and class (to borrow from the title of his subsequent book with Wallerstein[17]). But here some significant clarifications are in order. On the one hand, the break from the PCF enables Balibar to rethink productively key categories of political philosophy, especially as they leaned on and learned from Althusserianism; on the other hand, the nexus of subject and citizen (in particular, how the French colonized could be French subjects but not French citizens) could easily be misread as an elision of the problems of ideology and the proletariat even as they constitute the discursive horizon of the intervention. But this is the difference between Balibar's formal response to Nancy and the articulation of subjects and citizens born of social crisis in the essay for *Temps Modernes*. Here the worker subjects the philosophical *dispositif* of the later iteration to the initial conditions of its problematic. The struggle over citizenship and its idea takes many forms in the immigrant movement in France but includes basic rights of work. In the auto industry, unskilled immigrant workers from North Africa staged well-organized strikes against redundancy at Citroen-Aulnay and Talbot-Poissy in 1982 and 1983. The occupation of the Talbot factory in 1983–1984 by immigrant workers sparked a violent and generally racist response from non-striking French national workers. Not to be outdone, the prime minister at the time, Mauroy, described the strikers as "Islamic Fundamentalists," presumably to underline their labor was eminently disposable (this term, including its relation to labor, continues to inform the non-said of Western racism). When Balibar is thinking of what the subject excludes he is simultaneously pondering what citizenship has meant in the materialization of the French state. It is for this reason the polemic must be reconnected to questions of class, race and nation, but above all to the fate of the worker in that schema. And ideology?

As Balibar is thinking through worker struggle in light of the prohibitions introduced on behalf of the citizen subject (the Sans Papiers movement is of course, the culmination of that struggle in France, about which Balibar has written[18]) he was also elaborating why ideology was aporetic for Marxist theory. The "vacillation of ideology," as he describes it, goes to the heart of the antinomy between worker and subject.[19] The essay begins by remarking on the political and ideological uses of Marxism, including "conservative recuperation," which continues his more general critique of the PCF. The basic point, however, regards the position of ideology in political struggle. If workers are subject to ruling ideology does their struggle against a ruling class include a corresponding dominated ideology, one which both unites opposition and makes strange the ideological structures of domination itself? But if ideology subsists on representations, illusions, and imaginary projections, can a class be revolutionary if it also embodies these same capacities? How can there be a proletarian ideology if the proletariat itself is radically exterior to the perquisites and imperatives of bourgeois class formation? Marxist theory, Balibar argues, vacillates on this question, and the proof he finds is in the twenty-year hiatus of ideology in Marxist thinking between the *German Ideology* and the *Anti-Dühring*. I have argued elsewhere how such vacillation is constitutive in materialist thinking and is distilled not by nomination but by the actual logic of crisis it confronts.[20] The purification of Marxism, as Balibar terms it, leads precisely to the ossification of revolution in state mandate, or a pastiche of freedom by decree and not by praxis. Proletarian ideology is not to be found in *Capital*: indeed, both the proletariat and ideology are conspicuous by their absence from Marx's critique of political economy. As we have stressed, if *Capital* is written on behalf of proletarian subjecthood, that subjectivity remains unformulated and largely missing from its analysis. *Capital* is about one class, the capitalists, and the relation through which they subsist. Just as the commodity inverts the value form through an appearance that can be exchanged, the process and form of fetishism, so *Capital* itself elucidates capital as relation only by turning upside down the substance of the subject that is its politics, or by using the commodity itself as its ghostly surrogate (the proletariat therefore haunts *Capital* as communism is the ghostly goblin of the *Communist Manifesto*).

Balibar points out these conceptual difficulties as part of a thoroughgoing critique of the theoretical dead-ends in PCF orthodoxy. A reduction, and reductionism, on behalf of the International obfuscates the material contradictions of key concepts and the role these notions *and* their contradictions play in the manner in which capitalism can be overcome. Fair enough, but as I have also indicated, in answering Nancy's question Balibar's theorization of "citizen" comes to work metonymically for the migrant labor struggles in which it was initially precipitate. If the proletariat and ideology drop out so that Marx can better critique the components of capital as relation, so in Balibar's otherwise trenchant thoughts on the citizen subject, the worker largely disappears. It is as if Balibar's polemic is itself an effect of the deconstruction of subjectivity that provokes Nancy's question. Who comes after the worker? The citizen. It is more complicated than this of course, but I would like to think the worker exits Balibar's critique of the citizen according to the same logic the proletariat drops out of Marx's discourse throughout the project of *Capital*. The elisions are materially determinate and are not simply acts of volition or tautological conveniences. Yet oscillations always imply some form of return (all theoretical models seek a homeostatic moment without which they decompose). Is the illegibility of the worker in Balibar symptomatic of the divide opened up within theory's relationship to actually existing worker states that, by the time of its English publication, had been settled more or less in favor of dissolution? The vacillation between subject *or* citizen and citizen subject is also a poignant remark upon the antinomy of worker subjects. Does the worker go the way of the subject and if so what becomes of labor's relation to capital?

Rancière's dilemma in thinking the worker is not outside the materiality of this moment, and not simply because Rancière, like Balibar, begins his theorization by "reading *Capital*" (both Balibar and Rancière were part of Althusser's original "Reading Capital" undertaking[21]). The proletarians of *Proletarian Nights* are not the proletarians Balibar elaborates in relation to political struggle. As Rancière reflects on the project, "They were old-style artisans, dreamers who versified or invented philosophies, who met together in the evenings to set up short-lived magazines, enthused about socialist and communist utopias, but generally did not get involved in putting these into practice" (vii). Just as Balibar rethinks his position to the French Communist Party because of its inability to articulate politics beyond race (and racism) and nation (and nationalism) when it came to immigrant workers, so Rancière offers an extraordinary history of nineteenth-century

French workers in sharp contrast to what he believed to be the pseudo-science of Althusserian philosophy and the concomitant forms of socialist and communist politics in France of the 1970s. Both thinkers write of equality but reject on principle the rationalization of the present to achieve it (in the spirit of '68, they continue to "demand the impossible"). What lessons, if any, do the dialectical limits we have explored so far have for Rancière's extensive engagement with the problem of work and workers, and furthermore to the knot of worker subjects around which this cultural and political project congeals?

First, and emphatically, Rancière's repudiation of Marxist dogma means any Marxist terminology that remains is discontinuous with and sometimes simply contradicts genealogies of Marxism themselves. This is not simply a case of favoring the aesthetic over the terms of political economy (one could argue that emphasis is precisely Marxist, especially in *Capital*) but of finding an alternative register to "the dissenting invention that this difference offers" (STP 18). While Rancière is not beyond caricaturing "real relations," his understanding of labor in terms of precariousness, ambivalence, and ambiguity are hardly outside the radical traditions of worker culture and politics (even if their valence in Balibar, for instance, offers a very different philosophical and political apparatus). It has to be said the break from Althusser and the critique of the servant's hand in philosophical discourse was a much greater intervention in its own time than now, which is more about their relevance to understanding the *longue durée* of Rancière's thought than the precise battles of post-1968 French theory (Warren Montag has pertinently discussed the role of Althusser's shadow for Rancière in this regard[22]). If the worker has a double, as Rancière puts it, it is also in the non-contemporaneity of Rancière's own theorization in a context where the act of de-dogmatizing Marxism seems about as crucial as the embargo of Cuba. Still, as David Harvey reminds us, the Left has struggled mightily to understand the play of "co-evolution" in the development of and critique of capitalism (the multiplicity of contradiction rather than the singularity of labor) and to that extent Rancière's reading of difference across its political discourses serves a vital heuristic function and more.[23]

Rancière's dissertation, "La Formation de la pensée ouvrière en France," presented as, according to Rancière's transcript, "Le Prolétaire et son double" would develop into *La nuit des prolétaires: archives du rêve ouvrier* (*The Nights of Labor*, then *Proletarian Nights* in English), signs not just of a philosopher's career, but of a colloquy of concepts. Just as the proletarian is doubled, according to the difference between an empirical existence and a discursive formation, so the elaboration of the worker dream in Rancière's argument oscillates between a philosophical condition and a historiographic trace. Where Balibar will fathom such conceptual sway as a dialectical impasse in Marxism, as a materialization of its limits, Rancière argues the complexities of the shift are signs of a fundamental incompatibility: Marxism is caught in a classic bind because it cannot read simultaneously how to live the working-class condition philosophically alongside the perquisites of its political program. Further, while I might mark this as a Lacanian disjunction within subject formation (in other words, such *méconnaissance* is not the monopoly of malevolent Marxizing) Rancière distances this possibility, seeing the constitutive gap as proof positive worker subjectivity and Marxist discourse are doubles without consanguinity. In his presentation of the dissertation Rancière responds to the divided loyalties of '68 by asserting the radicalism of the working-class subject is covered up, or overlaid, by Marxist discourse. An analysis of "origins" (a loaded word in the argument of an avid deconstructor) underlines the fecklessness of a Marxist discourse "graphed" onto "the voices of working-class protest" (STP 22). Class consciousness, "conceived in the Marxist fashion," is similarly met with robust incredulity as is the "supposedly natural road from exploitation to emancipation" (STP 22). Balibar responds to the crisis of the French Left, and Marxism in particular, through a deep engagement with the conceptual sway or founding contradictions of its discourse. Rancière, on the other hand, always seems to read an antinomy as bad faith and that "an encounter with the impossible" (STP 30) means adherence to the impossible as such, a kind of negative dialectics without the dialectics, or an anti-Marxism without the Marxism (redolent in the "chronology" appended to *Proletarian Nights*, although to be fair, given the temporal coordinates Rancière elaborates, the very notion of a "chronology" must be taken as ironic). No amount of "revisiting" or "revising" Rancière's dissertation can escape the rejection it proposes (a lecture available online of Rancière in Delhi celebrating the Hindi translation [from English] of *Proletarian Nights* cannot decide if he is revisiting or revising the book). Yet this nonconformism from Althusserian non-conformism also helps to unravel how worker subjects, like Balibar's proletariat, act on the present. We need not leave Rancière to adjudicate the prescience of this intervention; indeed, he would be the first to admit it is overdetermined. Instead, I would argue the imbrication of worker with proletarian, people, and poor in Rancière's critique offers an answer to a question that could not be posed (for the conceit is Althusser's): "What is the value of labor?" (a question that will also form the focus of the next chapter).

This trope of answering a question that has not been asked, drawn from Althusser reading Marx reading Smith and Ricardo, is not some revenge of history on Rancière's critique but is a means to grapple with the subject division which is my chief concern. How so? Superficially, Rancière's modest proposal is that the formation of working-class thought must include, precisely, the kind of thinking, writing, painting, dreaming necessarily undermining the "supposed" (STP 10) truths of its historical mission. All that talk of propaganda, proletarian ideology, worker states, and worker parties, is "an alibi for a certain politics" (STP 24). More than that, as Rancière has recently explained, it has become an excuse for right-wing politics. In the preface to the new English edition of *Proletarian Nights* Rancière suggests the experience of work today may be closer to "the artisans of the past" (xi—i.e., the subject of the book) than the images of "non-material work" constantly posed as present reality (he makes the same point in his essay on "Communists without Communism"[24]). While that argument is not supported and perhaps would not hold within capitalism's proletarianized globality, it has the distinct advantage of provoking further reflection on subjective remains in worker identity, experience and speech for instance, in contradistinction to its objective correlatives in class and the labor theory of value. Part of the lure of Rancière's discourse is exactly this appeal to subjective remains as indeed the real of relation over and above the truths of radical scientificity (Althusser's claims for philosophy, Marx's understanding of political economy, etc.). Yet this aspect of Rancière's reading of labor, the emphases on experience, art, thinking, etc., is anti-Marxist (if Marxism's historical fulcrum has been class, party, state) but hardly anti-Marx. When Rancière ponders the Gauny collection and "how to live the working-class condition philosophically" (STP 26) he is using a mode of synthesis and elaboration Marx himself would have appreciated. There is nothing in Part One of *Proletarian Nights* that could not be read alongside rather than opposite Marx's understanding of Balzac on the aesthetics of lived conditions. Gauny, "Le philosophe plébéien," is more of a philosopher than Marx (especially the Marx of Rancière's *The Philosopher and His Poor*) but both are joiners in their own way, expounding on the *philia* of filiation. Indeed, reading Rancière's reassessment of Saint Simonianism or the fortunes of associations of the time one feels more the nuance of solidarity rather than its absolute difference. Where such comparisons begin to break down is around what elements of synthesis affect a transformation of their overall composition, be this cultural, social, economic, political, and so on. From the radical dissensus of his work for *Les Révoltes Logiques* to his critique of consensus through chronicles, Rancière has seized the leisure to think as much as Gauny, but the path of worker subjectification to this end remains tantalizingly obtuse. In part this is due to a hypostatization of the worker as artisan (there is an untranslatability in the experience of Gauny through which all things artisan have been recoded; indeed, "artisanal," like "natural," is as much a niche market today as a way of life). Rancière sometimes writes as if the banalization of skill sets of the last 150 years is merely an exception rather than a central fact of the commodification of everyday life crucial to capital accumulation and circulation. This does not mean the artisan is dead or that the figure cannot be aspirational or inspirational, but it is so far from the concrete forms of the transnational division of labor it constitutes an end not a means. Why then is the artisan the emblematic worker for Rancière?

Radical equality, as it was for another of Rancière's key thinkers, Jacotot (Cabet's teacher—Cabet features in another chapter of *Proletarian Nights*), is demonstrably individual, not collective. This, for Rancière, is the primary way an identity becomes a subject. If one of Rancière's realizations is that working classes do not need Althusserian science, he goes on to stress a working-class subject needs her individuality as a practice of identity, but because this is individual the principle forms a bar on solidarity to the extent self-emancipation is not a collective will. The discourses of the artisan exude professionalism and skill, but also something of free association, sometimes ethical, sometimes religious, or sometimes poetic. The extraordinary detail archives like Gauny's provide do not add up to a collective identity even though every element of working-class consciousness, resistance, and revolt in their tropes, figures, and rhetorical flair finds expression in Rancière's reading.[25] Strategically and theoretically, this is the reason why Rancière terms these dreamy artisanal associations "proletarian," because if it cannot contain such "spirals of impossibility" then the basis of changing the workers' fundamental conditions must be rethought. One could respond sociological content is not simply incompatible with individual reverie, as if revolutionary possibility ever needs brute facts and aesthetic perquisites to cohere. Yet part of Rancière's polemic is undoing the worker as subject to accentuate prescriptions and prescribing as eliding the power of partial links in the political configuration in favor of formulaic or positivist positions. What if the problem of proletarian is actually, as the *Les Révolte Logiques* texts aver, what does it mean to think? While it is hardly surprising a philosopher is emancipated enough to offer this speculation it nevertheless provides insight on the question of value coextensive with the concept of proletarian. Whether or not this is an imaginary resolution to a real contradiction, a further ideology of the proletarian rather than its disambiguation goes to the heart of how the worker subjects.

Obviously, for a philosopher value is first and foremost of a moral and ethical suasion, a kind of axiology of goodness (or lack thereof). Rancière is rarely declarative about social value but always demonstrative about aesthetic value. If, as he argues in *Dissensus*, Rancière's creed is declassification (demystification without a theory of ideology) then the proletarian is the most challenging subject for such a modus operandi.[26] Balibar will seek the proletariat in the interstices of Marx's texts, not in the assumptions drawn from them. Rancière, by contrast, will recast the proletariat without a labor theory of value (he alludes to it of course, but is not interested in its axiom for the economic or a politics necessarily derived from it). Marx does not begin with a value concept but determines one through his analysis of the commodity, which expresses a concrete social relation of value under capitalism. Exchange value is a form of appearance of the commodity from which its value as a product of labor has largely been erased. Value for a proletarian can be many things, a collocation of all sorts of evaluative criteria, but for capital as relation value extraction from the worker is relatively specific and represents a surplus over and above the price set for the work done: value, as it were, is the objectification of abstract labor. Marx's understanding of the worker is laden with value theory (use, exchange, surplus, relative surplus, etc.) but is not determined in advance but through commodities in exchange. The value of labor power is hardly uncontroversial, as is Marx's exposition of the value form in *Capital*, but Rancière steers well clear of political economy and the social conditions of the proletarian under actually existing capitalism.[27] If Rancière is correct to question the prospect of "communists without communism" we might usefully press the notion that a concept of proletarian shorn of any sense of its economic coordinates is a little less than a sensible distribution of the subject. One can easily accept Rancière's aestheticization of the political and the equality of intelligences as radical philosophical interventions, but if the double of the proletarian is dissociated from the value form we come close to reducing the worker to assertion more than a social force, a historical curiosity more than an active presence in the economic fabric of human existence. It is not, of course, a question of truth versus falsity and certainly not one of science versus aesthetics, but an issue of whether "declassification" is but another "soft liquidation of proletarian vigor" (STP 8) that Rancière otherwise ascribes to the "new philosophers."

Yet the insight of the critique lies precisely along the trajectory of both distancing and recomposing. The aesthetic claims of proletarian realization must hold the grand aims of labor power and class abolition with suspicion when they seek legitimacy in advance of a more complex matrix of logic.[28] Rancière's target here is not actually a recalibration of the proletarian (bearer of value minus the economic) but how the fate of the proletarian affects the constituent claims of the intellectual. In many of his texts of the Seventies and Eighties, Rancière is interested in those elements of worker analysis that reflect upon intellectual method as, paradoxically, non-method. The slippages between proletarian, poor, and people are in the end not about hasty metonymy so much as concrete effects of changed relations in the composite of the intellectual and power. In stark relief, however, this is a poor answer to the question of labor value (i.e., that whatever the economic interest, the kernel of the issue is the logical contradictions of the intellectual), but it reflects a basic point the value of labor is also realized in its intellectual elaboration, the ways in which the subject is "staged." Does this resistance to the usual policing of the proletarian reinvigorate the worker as subject after '68 or does such doubling participate in the very displacement it is otherwise at pains to delineate? For many the difference implied is hollow, hollowed out by history, since most invocations of the proletarian now are instantly allied with relics of productivism, shibboleths of the Soviet era, or gestural politics. By contrast, I would read this in parallax with Badiou and Zizek's more recent predilections for communism, not because proletarians and communism are ripe for nostalgia or resurrection, but because the contradictions their thinking engage are unresolved in the history of capital.[29]

Rancière is far from wanting to "fix" the instability of the worker as sign or as possibility but he has tried to show how specific divisions of labor inform what is sensible or not, visible or not, aesthetic or not, without returning the politics of discourse to the realm of sacred truths, laws or, of course, science. Indeed, Rancière's *Disagreement* is precisely about the problems of divisibility in economics and politics that do not seem to offer the viability of synthesis.[30] I read this, however, as a question of social dynamism and the challenge of a dialectical impasse rather than as the simple reproduction of a false distinction. Thus, the point of thinking through worker dreams of the nineteenth century, for instance, is to challenge the divisibility of worker time. This is more of a provocative supplement rather than a dismissal of Marx's analysis of the "working day" in *Capital*, yet what is its significance for worker subjects in either sense of my focus? Clearly, what is deemed experience in the nature of work is less than what the worker represents in history, in politics, and in culture (this is also a lesson of the previous chapter). Precision in the definition of the proletarian is, for Rancière, a block on the expressive forms of radical opposition—she can be as much "poor" in her economic condition as "people" in her democratic impulses (there is no space here to detail the genuflections of the genealogy Rancière brings to this belief but in a crude way all roads lead to ancient Greece and the *demos*). The instability in terms reflects the changing conditions of the worker in what the community represents. In my schema, this inclusion/exclusion, Rancière's part of no part, means that in any analysis of the cultural representation of labor the substance of labor is not decided by critical fiat, by terminological nuance, but is instead mediated by community possibility, its participatory logic. The difference between labor as work and labor as worker subject is not, however, in itself an aesthetic division. As I have implied earlier, this is where Rancière fails to measure the impact of commodification on the aesthetic, a moment of capital that permits the aestheticization of politics in modernity, the exchange between the universal and the particular. The first contradiction of capitalism is that of capital to labor in which work produces a specific being that is supposed to ensure the survival of capitalism as a mode of socio-economic existence. The worker as subject is overdetermined by the forms of this antinomy not just as cause and effect, but as an organic composition of the relation. This neither negates the role of the intellectual in such composing, nor that of the worker in self-subjectification. Indeed, when the worker in particular subjects the forms of the capital/labor relation to scrutiny the organic nature of this active presence is emphasized. The present effect of the worker is the tissue of subjecthood, something that finds expressive content in everyday life. The necessity for worker subjects exists in this space which is by all means one of articulation, description, measurement (a subject produced by data) or categorization (a division of labor in perhaps the more literal sense). When subject is a verb, worker subjects denotes both struggle within labor as relation and pressure on the forms of knowledge this is assumed to provide. It is not simply "living the working-class condition, philosophically" (STP 26) but seeking sublation of the living contradiction capital constructs and that its subjective forms help to secure. Paradoxically, it is capitalism that is most interested in constructing proletarian futures and it hedges in any number of ways on the struggles this can produce, including the once-feared dictatorship of the proletariat that was often used to justify novel accumulation strategies via embargoes, protectionism, union busting, and the odd war. It would be hyperbolic to suggest the worker subjects the proletarian as subject to futurelessness, but to the extent states and parties were points of transition *from* proletarian subjecthood, thinking and writing about the worker can be hinged to that process.[31]

Balibar deconstructs the proletarian of Marxist thought by showing its ambiguous identities are unexplored signs of changed forms in the relation of capital to labor. The critique of racism is pivotal in this regard since it recomposes the whole field of French and European thought on labor in its migration. Rancière's unraveling of the post-political brackets the economic in subjectification in order to reveal a worker less dependent on the iron law of value extraction and whose popular democracy cannot distill in contemporary structures of the state. As we have seen, they both subject the subject to a kind of radical dissimulation in which the worker as subject becomes the instance of political bad faith: the subject as a "policing" of insurgent identity. In the "worker subjects" I am suggesting an alternative (and not always complementary) trajectory of inquiry, one that tempers any philosophical position "after" the subject, with a cultural understanding of the worker sufficient to measure the subject's persistence. Rather than separate off with suspicion the ontic elements of the worker's economic position I would read such symptoms as antinomies in the concrete forms of work themselves. The ontic nature of work can be measured and a worker's ontology belongs to it. The being of work is mediated by specific socio-economic forms which, while hardly static, inform work's reason to be. If we begin with the worker as subject as an ontology we inevitably diminish the economic substance of labor as relation because it is read as the subject's trap, the limit on being in its fulfillment. I would say this problem remains even if, like Hardt and Negri, we recode the arena of ontological construction as the "common."[32] Several possibilities emerge from shifting the problem of ontology from the worker to work (from the "who" to the "what" of the subject).

First of all, the proletarian's dialectical limits for capitalism remain in play. We can identify myriad forms of labor relations (migrant, immaterial, virtual, contingent, industrial, service, etc.) without trivializing certain necessary inclinations in capital to produce and reproduce itself, temporal and spatial "fixes" that cannot be wished away if capital is to continue to survive. We can describe short-form versions of these limits but the point is to resist dismissing the economic as some ontological or "scientific" fib. Second, however, while the economic is invested in the production of the worker as subject, this does not diminish the force of culture in its configuration. The visibility or not of the worker in contemporary culture is a field of political possibility even if it is not simply an overlay of Rancière's category of the aesthetic. If one "finds" the proletarian in cultural representation this is less a proof of existence or experience than it is an arena of contestation, a space of articulation where labor as relation may not be obviously at stake (labor, like capital, is not a representation and is therefore always represented). Indeed, it is precisely when labor as relation is questioned that proletarian representation becomes a significant cultural event, that the worker subjects. Third, the instance of the cultural event is doggedly discontinuous with transformations in the economic substance of the human. The worker dreamers, poets, philosophers of *La Nuit des prolétaires* are hardly conjoint with the revolutionary fervor of the period, although their outsideness is also a reason for the movement's failure. This point leads to a fourth one on the temporal coordinates of intervention, both that of the worker herself and that of the other intellectual, the philosopher or cultural critic, who finds substance in the act. When the worker subjects, time is both particularized and "misplaced." It is not just that a temporal disjunction messes with capital's will to regulate the working day, to commodify leisure, and to medicate sleep, but that it facilitates a consciousness of time as such. A protest may be of "now" but not of its present: does it repeat, recall, or perhaps invoke a future whose own temporal logic may be barely articulate? The mixed messages of Occupy Wall Street, for instance, are also signs of multiple times, a longue durée perhaps insufficiently articulated in its moment. Fifth, it is not only the worker as subject that is ideological. If the "worker subjects" is for me, a cultural problematic I would also claim it partakes in class warfare as, whatever else it is, ideological. It would be glib to suggest Rancière lets go of ideology as concept as he had to let go of his teacher and theorist of ideology, Althusser, but it is the exiting of ideological critique that permits the "poor" and the "people" to appear in Rancière's work, and even perhaps the "citizen" in Balibar's post-Althusserian theorization. In the immediate aftermath of his break with Althusser, Rancière attempts to reconfigure ideology in its disparate and not simply scientific distinctions.[33] The proletarian ideology of *L'Atelier*, for instance, the organ of Christian Socialist ethicists, is seen as elitist, and as no less illusionary than both contemporaneous bourgeois pronouncements and subsequent labor organizations of the twentieth century. In his initial critique of Althusser's theory of ideology, however, Rancière is at pains to distinguish the positive impress of proletarian ideology while acknowledging "it is a system of power relations that is always fragmentary because it defines a certain number of conquests always provisional because it is not produced by apparatuses but by the development of struggle" (10). At this level, the distillations of aesthetic ideology in representations of labor are not all bourgeois fantasies of working-class subjects. In ideology the worker subjects again.

Finally, however, I must conclude with a warning about the scattered speculations above on the meaning and persistence of "the subject" for cultural readings of the worker. I have alluded to the conditions rather than the content of worker experience here not to reproduce the assertive mode of Balibar and Rancière but to tarry with the negative of proletarian "presence" in the present. In keeping with Harvey's thoughts on the necessity for renewed unmasking of the "enigma of capital," the "worker subjects" seeks to address theoretical coordinates in this critical juncture around and through the *enigma of labor*.[34] Obviously, such articulation is a project not a statement, and one cast against an aura of cultural critique in which "all that is solid has been 'posted,' thank you very much." For some, recent invocations of the 99 percent are proof again that the class politics and cultures of the worker are unrecognizable and irreconcilable with its main currents in Marxist thought. Such difference is instructive but the crux is whether further analysis of labor as relation has been rendered superfluous before capital. The confluence of worker and subject suggests otherwise, not because they are there to be resuscitated but because the forms of their relation have been transmogrified. If globalization, for instance, has interpellated the woman worker of "developing" economies as central, new and multiple modes of de-subjectification are at stake. Perhaps forms of labor relation are markedly absent from contemporary cultural theory because, paradoxically, it is the only way they can appear, for theory. This has a deeper significance for labor in the present that often has to the live the consequences of its smaller share of the fruits of work. The imminence of such crisis does not offer the truth of "worker subjects" but the substance of its dialectical challenge as more than a philosophical conundrum. From this perspective, the value of labor is also about the ways in which it is lived and whether it can continue to live under the sign of capital.

Notes

1. The reference here to the "metaphysical" and "theological" is to Marx's reading of the commodity in the opening chapter of *Capital*. See Karl Marx, *Capital*, Volume One. Ed. Ernest Mandel. Trans. Ben Fowkes. London: Penguin, 1992. Needless to say, *Capital* seethes with an allegory of labor, and labor representation, but the commodity itself is no mere metonym of such narration. The invocation of "after" is a familiar knot in the politics of "post." What temporal logic permits the proletarian to be posted while capitalism persists? This question of the subject and subjectification pervades the current chapter.
2. Philip Levine, *What Work Is*. New York: Knopf, 1991 (Levine 1991). One of the themes of the title poem is the degree to which work, or the lack of it, shapes all relations including, in this case, one of brother to brother. It is a poem about alienation but also about the being of work itself, an ontology that the worker inhabits but does not own, in several senses.
3. This is not the place to revisit in depth the question of equivalent form and its peculiarities in Marx, but in the relation of abstract human labor to the commodity, equivalence suspends the real of labor, the work that is not the commodity itself or its universal equivalent, money. See Marx, *Capital* (Vol. One), chapter 1. For a discussion of how relative and equivalent forms of value emerge in Marx's text, see David Harvey, *A Companion to Marx's Capital*. London: Verso, 2010 (Harvey 2010), especially chapter 1.
4. Given the argument of the previous chapter, including about the distinct workerism of Autonomia, the point here is a warning about a fetishization of the worker that stands in for the specificity of work and misrecognizes the cut between labor as relation and labor as work, the worker and the proletarian, and class struggle and the end of class.
5. See Jacques Rancière, "The Proletarian and His Double" in *Staging the People: The Proletarian and His Double*, Trans. David Fernbach. New York: Verso, 2011: 21–33. This presentation for Rancière's doctoral thesis (that would become *La Nuit des prolétaires*) is provocative on a number of levels, both in the way it reads the proletariat overreaching its categorization (a doubling, and more) and in the emerging sense Marxist theory was

discontinuous with its subject. Here, instead of an inquiry that pulls discourse closer to worker experience via a chronicle of work, Rancière's reading of Gauny stresses "a genuinely philosophical experience: how to live the working class condition philosophically" (26). These approaches are not necessarily incompatible, and certainly not within Marxism, but increasingly lead Rancière to reject the formal representation of the proletarian for a doubled (at least), mimetic practice of ambivalence and "failed encounters" (27). This is an instance where the worker as subject demonstrably frays. Further references to *Staging the People* in the text will be abbreviated as STP followed by page number.

6. I am running two ideas together here, both Raymond Williams's notion of structure of feeling as a cultural problematic and Irigaray's deconstruction of "le sexe" as a sliding signification of the Real, the symbolic, and the imaginary. The lesson of the former is about what might constitute class consciousness (affect, for instance, rather than dogma); the lesson of the latter is that feminism's troubling of the subject opens up all instantiations of the subject (as in, this worker who is not one). See Raymond Williams, *Marxism and Literature*. Oxford: Oxford University Press, 1978 (Williams 1978); and Luce Irigaray, *This Sex Which Is Not One*. Trans. Catherine Porter and Carolyn Burke. Ithaca: Cornell University Press, 1985 (Irigaray 1985).

7. See, for instance, Peter Hitchcock, *Working-Class Fiction in Theory and Practice*. Ann Arbor: UMI Research Press, 1989 (Hitchcock 1989). The notion of eventness is adapted from Bakhtin. See, in particular, M.M. Bakhtin, *Art and Answerability*. Intro. Michael Holquist. Trans. Vadim Liapunov and Kenneth Brostrom. Austin: University of Texas Press, 1990 (Bakhtin 1990); and *Toward a Philosophy of the Act*. Ed. Vadim Liapunov and Michael Holquist. Trans. Vadim Liapunov. Austin: University of Texas Press, 1993 (Bakhtin 1993).

8. Clearly, this refers not just to the shape of an intellectual life but to a way of reading, which is partly the polemic of Rancière's first book, on and around Louis Althusser, See *Althusser's Lesson*. Trans. Emiliano Battista. London: Continuum, 2011 (Rancière 2011). For a contrasting methodology in reading Rancière himself, see Samuel A. Chambers, *The Lessons of Rancière*. Oxford: Oxford University Press, 2013. Alain Badiou has also taken up this challenge: see Alain Badiou, "The Lessons of Jacques Rancière: Knowledge and Power after the Storm" in *Jacques Rancière: History, Politics, Aesthetics,* Gabriel Rockhill and Philip Watts, (eds.) Durham: Duke University Press, 2009: 30–54 (Badiou 2009). And Slavoj Zizek uses the title "The Lesson of Rancière" for his postface to Jacques Rancière, *The Politics of Aesthetics*. Trans. Gabriel Rockhill. London: Continuum, 2004 (Rancière 2004).

9. Jacques Rancière, *La Nuit des prolétaires: archives du rêve ouvrier.* Paris: Fayard, 1981 (Rancière 1981). *The Nights of Labor: The Workers' Dream in Nineteenth-Century France*, Trans. John Drury, introduced by Donald Reid. Philadelphia: Temple University Press, 1989 (Rancière 1989). Edition with new preface by Rancière translated by David Fernbach: *Proletarian Nights: The Workers' Dream in Nineteenth-Century France.* New York: Verso, 2012 (Rancière 2012). The basic point here is that the difference of worker and proletarian is continually being recontextualized. Rancière locates this shift in the writings of artisans outside of the kinds of interpellation used to hail revolutionary subjects (think here of the *Communist Manifesto*), but this is very much connected to specific crises in the French Left in the sixties and, of course, Rancière's break with the scientificity of Althusserian discourse. The use of "labor" in the title of the 1989 translation is of a different moment and perhaps a deeper crisis, with the very idea of the proletarian increasingly buried under the contradictions of the worker state. The new edition reveals yet another time and out of timeness that I will discuss, related both to the abstraction of the proletarian once more in terms of political realities, and the impact of Rancière's other writing.
10. Rancière's critique of such subject categories is not only aimed at ancient philosophy but an entire genealogy of Western thought. See Jacques Rancière, *The Philosopher and His Poor.* Trans. Andrew Parker. Durham: Duke University Press, 2004 (Rancière 2004). Two questions immediately come to mind: first, can philosophy only produce the "poor" as a conceptual crutch or alibi?; and second, can the use of "poor" possibly mediate differences in the social and economic as a category of the subject?
11. For more on subjectification, see Jean-Phillippe Deranty, Ed. *Jacques Rancière: Key Concepts.* Durham, UK: Acumen, 2010 (Deranty 2010). As with other aspects of Rancière's theorization, subjectification is a way to conceptualize the subject of politics beyond its obfuscation for the social and the political. For an essay that reads this in terms of the figure of the worker, see Jason Read, "Politics as Subjectification: Rethinking the Figure of the Worker in the thought of Badiou and Rancière," *Philosophy Today*, SPEP Supplement, 2007: 125–132 (Read 2007). I thank Christian Haines for bringing this piece to my attention.
12. See Eduardo Cadava, Peter Connor, and Jean-Luc Nancy, Eds. *Who Comes after the Subject?* London: Routledge, 1991 (Cadava et al. 1991). The reference to "animal laborans" by Rancière to decenter the subjectification of "proletariat," "working class," or "labor movement" appears on page 250.
13. See Karl Marx, *Capital*, Volume 3. Trans. David Fernbach. New York: Penguin Books, 1993: 956. This misalignment between appearance and essence is also crucial to labor mimesis explored in Chapter 1.

14. See Etienne Balibar, *Nous, citoyens d'Europe?: Les Frontières, l'Etat, le peuple*. Paris: Editions la D´ecouverte, 2001 (Balibar 2001); subsequently translated with additions and subtractions as *We the People of Europe?: Reflections on Transnational Citizenship*. Trans. James Swenson. Princeton: Princeton University Press, 2004.
15. I would suggest this is also the dilemma of the worker vis-à-vis the ontology of work: she can only appear as its expression. One of the problems at stake in this project is the extent to which representations of labor in culture disrupt this inevitability.
16. Etienne Balibar, "Sujets ou citoyens? (Pour l'égalité)," *Les Temps Modernes* 40 (March–April–May 1984): 1726–1753 (Balibar 1984).
17. Etienne Balibar and Immanuel Wallerstein, *Race, Nation, Class*. Second Ed. New York: Verso, 2011 (Balibar and Wallerstein 2011).
18. See, in particular, the collection, Etienne Balibar et al., *Sans-papiers: l'archaïsme fatal*. Paris: La Découverte, 1999 (Balibar et al. 1999).
19. In Etienne Balibar, *Masses, Classes, Ideas*. Trans. James Swenson. New York: Routledge, 1994: 87–124 (Balibar 1994).
20. See Peter Hitchcock, *Oscillate Wildly: Space, Body, and Spirit of Millennial Materialism*. Minneapolis: University of Minnesota Press, 1999 (Hitchcock 1999).
21. See Louis Althusser and Etienne Balibar, Eds. *Reading Capital: The Complete Edition*. New York: Verso, 2016 (Althusser and Balibar 2016). This fiftieth anniversary edition restores essays by Roger Establet, Pierre Macherey and Jacques Rancière that were not available in previous abridged versions.
22. See Warren Montag, "Rancière's Lost Object," *Cultural Critique* 83 (Winter 2013): 139–155 (Montag 2013).
23. Harvey has remarked on this on more than one occasion but see, for instance, David Harvey, *Ways of the World*. Oxford: Oxford University Press, 2016.
24. Jacques Rancière, "Communists without Communism?" in *The Idea of Communism*, Costas Douzinas and Slavoj Zizek, (eds.) New York: Verso, 2010: 167–177 (Rancière 2010).
25. Rancière has edited some of Gauny's work for publication. See Gabriel Gauny. *Le philosophe plébéien*. Ed. Jacques Rancière. Paris: La découverte-Maspéro, 1983 (Gauny 1983).
26. See Jacques Rancière, *Dissensus: On Politics and Aesthetics*, Ed. and Trans. Steven Corcoran. London: Continuum, 2009 (Rancière 2009). Dissent, as such, is always a symptom of reconfigured sense, and therefore aesthetic. Although this can be read as an aestheticization of the political, the politics of sense perception remains a vital thread in Marxist critique, from Marx's early philosophical manuscripts onward. Yet this does not simply exclude

ideological critique. See, for instance, Terry Eagleton, *The Ideology of the Aesthetic*. Oxford: Blackwell, 1990 (Eagleton 1990).
27. The question of value cannot be settled here, although I will return to it in a subsequent chapter. Part of the point is that at the moment one eschews or elides the problem of value in the proletarian as subject, aesthetics becomes a metonym rather than a complement or integral dimension that may render obtuse the labor/capital relation.
28. Aspects of this polemic can be discerned in Jacques Rancière, *The Intellectual and His People: Staging the People, Volume Two*. Trans. David Fernbach. London: Verso, 2012 (Rancière 2012).
29. While radical theory is forever rethinking communism, specific crises or political conjunctures intensify such concern, and this is obviously true in the aftermath of the 2007–2008 financial crisis. I have already referred to *The Idea of Communism* volume(s) but there are many other texts and events associated with this moment (including components of the project here). See, for instance, Bruno Bosteels, *The Actuality of Communism*. London: Verso 2011 (Bosteels 2011); Jodi Dean, *The Communist Horizon*. London: Verso, 2012 (Dean 2012); Tariq Ali, *The Idea of Communism*. London: Seagull, 2009 (Ali 2009); and Alain Badiou, *The Communist Hypothesis*. Trans. David Macey and Steve Corcoran. London: Verso, 2010 (Badiou 2010).
30. See Jacques Rancière, *Disagreement*. Trans. Julie Rose. Minneapolis: University of Minnesota Press, 1999 (Rancière 1999). Rancière notes, "We should take disagreement to mean a determined kind of speech situation: one in which one of the interlocutors at once understands and does not understand what the other is saying" (x). This becomes the field of politics. The Duranty volume above provides a useful gloss on Rancière's specific elaboration of the term.
31. Put another, there may be a future for workers but there is no future for proletarians if indeed capitalism is a historical mode of production. Obviously, the end of an economic logic is simultaneously the attenuation of its realms of subjecthood.
32. This is a substantial component of what Hardt and Negri term, "commonwealth." See Michael Hardt and Antonio Negri, *Commonwealth*. Cambridge, MA: Harvard University Press, 2009 (Hardt and Negri 2009). For my own reading of the Spinozist dimensions of the commons, see Peter Hitchcock, "Commonism," *Mediations* 25(2011): 1.
33. See Jacques Rancière, "On the Theory of Ideology." Trans. Martin Jordin, *Radical Philosophy* 7 (Spring 1974): 1–14 (Rancière 1974). One can sense the heavy imprint of the present in the tone and terms of Rancière's polemic here that are symptomatic of the ways in which the French Left attempts to theorize its way out of the impasse legible in the events of 1968. The necessity for theory always has its historical moment.

34. See David Harvey, *The Enigma of Capital*. London: Profile, 2010 (Harvey 2010). Part of Harvey's argument is that capital is not as enigmatic as it is often portrayed. The stakes are different for labor but I maintain this wariness of inexorable abstraction.

CHAPTER 3

On the Cultural Representation of Labor (Value)

What is the value of labor? If labor is as contestable as we have already indicated, then value is no less disputed. Within Marxist critiques of capitalism, the labor theory of value attempts to show how the socially necessary time of the worker is embedded by workers in the commodity. The value of the workers' labor power is the market rate of that power as a commodity. This division of value between time and power is central to how labor's value for capital is understood. Labor power is a specific capacity for producing use value that is commodified at the moment it is sold. The labor theory of value, however, which pre-exists Marx in the thinking of Adam Smith and David Ricardo for instance (from whom he rearticulates the concept) concerns the degree to which social production and reproduction constitutes the value of labor time in the commodity. In contrast to classical political economy, Marx argues that labor *is* value, a measure over time of how a socio-economic formation organizes the conditions of socialization in general. The market, of course, can change labor value, and it has been argued therefore that the labor theory of value is simply false, but such judgment tends to misinterpret the abstraction of Marx's claim and fixates instead on the data set of short-term fluctuations in a market economy.[1] Still, even within Marxism, there is much disagreement over what is called the transformation problem of labor value between prices of production and value for labor, leading some to suggest that it should at least be bracketed or at worse pilloried as incoherent when it comes to understanding actual social relations.[2] My interest is less in the transformation problem per se but more in the translatability of labor value for cultural representation. One might expect a correlation between whether labor value is figured in reading capital and problems in the cultural representation of labor (i.e., whether the latter has a value that modifies along with the fate of the former). As independent variables, the ideas of value in both mediate one another without being reducible to some kind of universal principle (including that notion sometimes attributed to money as a universal equivalent); their specific explanatory power (for each other) is prompted by the question with which I began although, as I will detail, answers can arise in the absence of the question. Indeed, the relationship between absence and representability is vital to understanding how labor is constituted culturally around the question of value. When the value of labor is in play the conditions of culture assume a specific valence, one which complicates any attempt to jump metrics between the instance of cultural value and the worker as its expression on a global scale or within capitalist globalization.

Clearly, how concepts of value and labor are defined will affect the struggle in their combination. To then think of this in terms of cultural representation would seem to offer the prospect of "a riddle, wrapped in a mystery, inside an enigma," but the aim at least is to take seriously the dialectics of their non-equivalence as productively agonistic in contemporary critique. Indeed, within worlds of the worker, a labor theory of (cultural) value on a global scale remains more necessary even in its prospective impossibility (impossible at the level of thinking economic and cultural value as purely commensurate). The question of the value of labor seems so omnipresent that it actually does not need to be asked since life or subjectivity is its substance as both question and answer. The existential here, of course, could be an alibi for not posing a question that can just as easily take one to abstractions of exchange, surplus, and use, or the foundations of labor as relation rather than as a material being. One could argue that Marx does not always ask the question precisely to enable the abstraction of value in constituting labor by way of a materialist elaboration as a reply. When labor is a subject, value is more obviously objectified within a grammar of object relations in general. From this perspective, something as mighty as Marxian value, even as a law, has a more modest position among value practices as a whole. While it may indicate a specific crisis in principles of value and of labor, the knot in their relation that produces different constellations and contradictions, one can now write an entire book on capital, as Thomas Piketty has done, without addressing a labor theory of value, even as something to be dismissed.[3] This, for instance, permits one to make tax propositions without recourse to class critique. Once the labor theory of value is subtracted from an analysis of capital, socio-economic division tout court becomes a gestural metric. The 1 percent is no more a class than the 99 percent—it is a statistical reference not one of unreformable socio-economic contradiction, and well suited to elongating, via trickle up (accumulation) or trickle down (redistribution) logic, the value of capital, rather than encouraging its nemesis—even the invocation of a "middle class" partakes of this vagary vis-à-vis the actual processes of capital as relation. In this light, if labor has value it appears paradoxically today to have insufficient measure to make a question of it. In value critique according to Robert Kurz,[4] labor itself, banalized by exchange, is the problem in value formation, and thus any adherence to a concept in which labor and value are conjoint is only to reproduce the fetish in which the valorization of value for commodity capitalism proceeds. This is a significant problem that I can only intimate in this chapter—I would say that battling on the ground of an opponent is not the same thing as fighting for that opponent. It is no small irony of history that Piketty's statistical understanding of accumulation might meet value critique's passionate ultra-left evisceration of labor and class from anti-capitalism on the plane of post-revolution and post-subjectivity. In one, class struggle is arithmetically obtuse; in the other, class struggle is moribund (at least in part because it is highly evocative of things like the old Germany and pre-Fall of the Berlin Wall thinking—seen in films like *Goodbye Lenin*, etc.). As some liberals and anarchists divest themselves of the labor/class nexus, conservatives inevitably seize on any symptom of state egalitarianism as quintessential class war. Capital can make labor precarious; theory can make labor expendable. Yet proletarianization can increase within this cruel antinomy, within the void of the quotidian question. Proletarianization is not just statistical but is intrinsic to the logic of capital; interestingly, in pure numbers more proletarians were produced in China alone in the last quarter century than in Europe's entire Industrial Revolution. A major concern is the cultural and political correlatives for this transformation. As urbanization claims the majority of the world's population, the proportion of those who subsist on the sale of their labor power has also increased. How do we account for this phenomenon? Is it only an ideology of capitalism? Is it the last remainder of modernity? What is the value of labor? The absence of the question, because so immanent to the eminence of capital, resounds itself in silence or radical esotericism. Is it because every breath is assumed to be expended in its name, no breath need actually be spent? Or is it because, as Hardt and Negri somewhat laconically put it: "The world is labor."[5] Within an aura of omnipresence, the value of labor need not be expounded: the question is, by definition, the subject of superfluity. It is against the superfluousness of the question that we should further examine its logic; again, not to speak simply the question or to assume some abject universality, but here to come to terms with the role it plays in accounting, in the narratives we tell ourselves, to make the question palpable if not always representational as such. I have two possible and interdependent claims that link value to the worker discussed so far. First, that accounting for value is a theoretical impasse in making accounts (accounting) per se; and second, that representing labor undoes the cultural desires of capital at the very moment the value of representation itself is problematized, accounted for. The former contention will necessitate consideration of value's hold for labor; the latter, an excursus on cultural theory around representation and realism. What happens to cultural accounts of labor if they begin from value rather than descriptions of work itself?

The conceit of my opening, the question posed but not expended, comes from Althusser's reading of Marx.[6] The notion here is not to resuscitate Althusser's structural Marxism but is to acknowledge the salience of symptomatic critique when labor has become the non-said of both capitalist boosterism *and* anti-capitalism in the same moment. Althusser notes how Marx's confrontation with Ricardo and Smith pivots on an answer to a question they have not asked, about the value of labor. Capital may interpellate labor as instrumental for surplus but this does not mean their relationship is obviously antagonistic. A key question for Smith, for instance, is what is the value of markets (significantly, the invisible hand he invokes is less about the freedom of markets but the consonance of rational self-interest with the state's desire to distribute public good, a calculus that places the domestic market before the international one). Marx has an answer for that question too but, on the whole, for him the invisible hand is a laboring one and value comes to rest on the market for labor power. Althusser reads Marx on labor as a philosopher; that is to say, with protocols that may not begin with labor's economic substance over its conceptual valence. It is important to note that prior to Althusser's posing of the symptomatic question, "What is the value of labor?" he has offered, "What is it to read?" as its polemical parerga. To our initial paradox, that the absence of labor is a function of its omnipresence, we can add another, that even if labor does not disappear in a flourish of philosophical ardor (recall, that for Rancière it is just this critical lever) its legibility as value is hinged on the practice of reading (of invisibility—indeed, labor's value is a signature of the invisible[7]). Marx has to provide visual clues so that we might glimpse congealed labor as value in the commodity. Here we cleave closely to the notion that labor can never be read in its objectifiable form as value and that this only appears in the apparent formlessness of its abstraction. If we expend form, "This is the worker," then value itself paradoxically disappears in its realization. The problem of abstract labor remains but is specifically linked to the possibility of reading.

We should recall that Althusser ascribes Marx's earlier more Hegelian thinking to a naïve reading of "abstract essence in the transparency of its concrete existence" (*Reading*, 16). *Capital*, however, examines "a distant and internal dislocation" in such reality in which immediate reading is the very mark of displacement and illusion, of fetishism. It is this sense of reading, Althusser argues, that permits Marx to read the oversight in what Smith sees, lacunae produced by a kind of scopophilic desire to visualize the object of reading. This is less about the value of an individual visual pleasure but more about visual pleasure *as* value, as a logical representation of the form of value (something that will return in my final example). That Smith should proffer the invisible hand is a confirmation not a contradiction of formations of desire since what is invisible depends on visibility as such. Similarly, Marx shows that classical economics speaks in silences or, as Althusser puts it, in the blanks that permit its formulations to appear. The absence concerns the gap between the value of labor and labor power, the non-said that riddles the calculation of average cost. Thus, and this is Marx's epistemological break with some Hegelian Absolute, the question not asked becomes "What is the value of labor power?" This is not a simple affirmation of Marxian economics which necessarily differs on this calculation—my point is merely to accentuate how the supplement is the foundation, the potential is greater than the visual form, and that the possibility of surplus is co-extensive with a specific logic of reading. But how can one read a surplus that is not narrated or at least is not extant in the visual surfaces of narration?

We see labor more or less all of the time. It is our constructed reality, all those things we note, think or feel that constitute a pulsion or trace of human presence (the work of other species is discerned, for better or worse in relation to the labor of our own). We see labor power as commodified embodiment or something as translucent as an old Nike Airmax sole. But the form of labor is not necessarily the objects of its activity. Labor power is a living thing, an attribute of the living that, once expended, cannot be returned (as that power). This is something of the pathos of extraction under capital. Labor is expending but is only seen in what is spent. It is a condition of necessary expenditure. Althusser's argument is that Marx demystifies such doxa by inserting a narrative of production where pre-given realities are described; indeed, within Althusserian critique this becomes a way to understand ideological structure. At least three imbricated levels of reading are implied. First, Smith necessarily produces labor as the object of his reading; that is, his reading produces labor as a function for the economic logic he analyzes. Second, Marx does not dispute what Smith sees, but articulates the constitutive aporia of his procedures. Marxism thus emerges out of the voids in capitalist logic. But third, these are all moving contradictions, which is to say that labor and capital never stand still and neither does any other condition of economic interaction, including those which doubt the very relevance of labor power to species being. If the second reading links labor power to production, the third reading can dismiss productivism per se or at least reassign its capacity. These too are signs of what Althusser calls "immanent necessity" (*Reading*, 25).

For instance, while capital still seeks surplus from labor this is in no way a constant of capitalist desire. Indeed, there are conditions where capital actively seeks less labor value and the worker herself becomes increasingly surplus to her own capacities within regimes of production and consumption. Now we could say this is but a reflex of ideological class struggle and an argument can be made given my comments so far on how ways of seeing, to borrow from John Berger, are constructed. Yet the kind of thinking that produces *Farewell to the Working Class, Goodbye Mr. Socialism, The Jobless Future*, and *The End of Work* shares no particular ideological agenda but constitutes reflections on a world where class consciousness is low, the actual existence of socialism is minimal, and technology continues to achieve cost efficiencies highly detrimental to full employment and the average price of labor.[8] In the 1970s workers were powerful enough to refuse work; today, work itself appears to exclude the worker at rates that permit the worker's value to diminish. The problem with such readings is not the tendencies they identify (which are demonstrable) but the implications drawn for the future of capital and labor.

The refusal of work is just, but just dependent on other refusals to sustain it (class struggle as a matrix of refusals and resistance). Again, I find it useful to ponder these "eventualities" in terms of reading logic.

If one reads for the content of subjection one will find labor, not as a relation but as a subject to be seen—the must-be-seen of labor, the figure of the worker. It is quite possible to write about proletarian culture only on the basis of such sociological content and gather a politics of reading around documented toil. This is not false: it is as verifiable today as it was in Zola's *Germinal*. Yet there is another dimension to the fictiveness of work that can be elaborated from the same material which we can term labor's abjection. Abjection here is not the alienation, the sense of self that can be described in the realization of dispossession; rather, it is that part of the relation of labor and capital that is unresolvable by representing value. Part of the problem in deriving labor value from Marx's writing is that he often holds these elements in tension: there is content in the commodity that is labor's abstraction as abjection that can be represented (metrics that gauge the difference in use and exchange value, but also as a representational imaginary, "congealed substances," etc., as Marx puts it in the first chapter of *Capital*) Just as various exchange values manifest themselves in a commodity (market rates, price gouging, obsolescence, etc.) without being identical with it, so labor's manifestation in the commodity does not correspond at the level of identity. I have argued elsewhere in this book that the exchangeability of labor as relation with worker as subject constitutes an ontological fallacy bent on a certain subjectification of worker being. The more interesting agenda is how work produces being, not how the proletarian "has" being (proletarian being is only produced in the instant of its *Aufhebung*). Why is this important either for understanding value or for the cultural representation of labor?

The conundrum in value is key to the hypostatization and reification of labor in its representation. Rather than measure the impasse or absence in presence of accounting for labor as an exhaustion of labor's meaning for capital, I am concerned with the difficulty of value and labor as code shifting in the order of representation which, if not a material structure in the Althusserian sense, is a constitutive ground with cultural implications and beyond. First, exchange value for Marx is a "form of appearance" that cannot be seen in a commodity in isolation, but only in the context of exchange in general with other commodity values. Second, and following on from this, the form of appearance is an abstraction to the extent it does not depend on utility, or use value, the individual nature of the commodity, or how it is consumed. But third, this abstraction resolves itself into one property of a commodity for capital, the "being products of labor."[9] The difficulty of the latter is that its abstraction opens out onto a fecund hermeneutical field. Put *Sein* close to labor and suddenly, despite Marx's warnings, the worker as well as the infamous table in *Capital* is dancing in the commodity form. The "being products of labor" is not the being of labor, much less that of a worker herself, even in the alienation that Marx describes. One reason value is so hotly debated is because once labor as *Sein*, if not sign, is bracketed the contradictions of value appear only as functions of capitalist cycles and short-term imbalances, a more or less direct confrontation between use and exchange (which is another way of reading Piketty), rather than something systemic and imbricated with labor in its mode of production that is historical and potentially transformative.

Piketty believes the Marxian apocalypse has been rendered moot by virtue of growth in productivity and there is more than a little evidence to support this view (globalization, technological and spatial fixes, and the shifting tectonics of proletarianization have all facilitated the notion growth can cheat communist redistribution at every turn[10]). But what has growth meant for labor in this regard? Even a cursory glance at Piketty's analysis affirms the matter is complex and vexing. Several elements are worth mentioning beyond the fact Piketty has no problem bracketing *Sein* from labor (Marx's *Capital* is not a work of philosophy, but at least he read some[11]). By analyzing data on national income in France and England from the eighteenth century to the present day Piketty estimates capital's share of income at around 40 percent, and labor's at 60 percent. Many caveats are introduced, especially around mixed income anomalies and non-wage occupations, as well as the amorphous but no less significant impact of informal economies. Obviously, if you begin with informal labor or domestic labor, indeed the panoply of labor in social reproduction for instance, all kinds of measure seem out of joint, which is to say Piketty cleaves to the most comprehensive (and normative) data. The arbitrary and the imaginary are much more difficult to graph, but by crunching the numbers Piketty comes up with a "pure return on capital" of about 4–5 percent per year for the last three hundred years, if trending lower in more recent decades. This does not mean the system is absolutely stable but it does help to explain capitalist longevity amidst specific variables and even what George Henderson pithily calls "the persistence of value in a more than capitalist world."[12]

Marx used the literary to de-nature the substance of data in his analysis; Piketty, on the other hand, deploys it chiefly to confirm the veracity of the metrics by what the literary lacks. In a section on the return of capital in historical perspective we are offered the following perceptions: "In classic novels of the early nineteenth century, such as those of Balzac and Jane Austen, the equivalence between capital and rent at a rate of 5 percent (or more rarely 4 percent) is taken for granted. Novelists frequently failed to mention the nature of the capital and generally treated land and public debt as almost perfect substitutes, mentioning only the yield in rent" (207). Elsewhere, "Similarly, neither Austen nor Balzac felt it necessary to specify the rate of return needed to transform a specific amount of capital into an annual rent: every reader knew full well that it took a capital on the order of 1 million francs to produce an annual rent of 50,000 francs" (53). This is not quite what Pierre Macherey (or Althusser) means by explicating what the text is compelled not to say.[13] The determined silences of the literary are certainly part of its ideological tissue and it is important to gauge the regulative assumptions therein, but it is a strange kind of materialism, and even stranger Marxism, that would assume direct correspondence between capital/rent equivalence and "classic novels." The truth of social realism does not reside in statistical correspondence. On the one hand, Piketty is right to connect the economic to literary possibility (words alone are not food, shelter, or clothing but do not exist outside matrices of exchange) but is one account simply the repressed truth of the other? And why is this "historical perspective"? Here we can begin to dis- and re-ambiguate the value of labor in the current conjuncture. It remains a cost, a capital expenditure, yet the literary may fathom the logic of its relation to capital, its expense ratio and *ratio*. How?

The worker in the novel is often a metonym, standing in for the great realm of unrepresentability in labor power itself. We can argue over the role of consciousness in such representations and the ways in which imagination interrogates Piketty's reading on every page. To be sure, however, Piketty well understands the internal polemic of the imaginary. He notes: "Nothing prevents us from imagining a society in which the capital/income ratio β is quite high but the return on capital r is strictly zero. In that case, the share of capital in national income, $\alpha = r \times \beta$, would also be zero. In such a society, all of national income and output would go to labor" (213). This is not the formula of communism but is at least a calculable precondition. The problem of substitutional salience remains, though, because even without any mention of labor as subject or as relation, economic activity has taken place and is taking place. The mode of production argument is well known in studies of the novel (one thinks of Lukacs, or Macherey, or Feltes[14]) but accounting for value is no easy corollary. The entire history of literary criticism has been devoted to separating aesthetic value from economic equivalence whether or not it sits on labor and capital as much as any other activity. To force the value of labor into this reckoning may be deemed creative accounting but it is closer to a non-standard deviation in representational aesthetics rather than falsehood for short-term gain. Again, borrowing from Piketty, labor's non-appearance presses "the elasticity of substitution" in labor as relation so that its cost is always present as such, but can never be reasonably fixed. If expense is a responsibility, or answerability in my schema, then this is also to the variegations of value in its expression. At this level of abstraction, all of the stories are about workers; we just create them as if they aren't.

Such debt is an obligation but it would not be capitalism if all debts were paid (debts are certainly productive in the maintenance of capitalist longevity). This does not mean when capital claims a greater share of surplus one can track a corresponding diminution of labor in cultural representation. Conversely, when the worker appears this does not connote righteous anti-capitalism is always in play and the demands of answerability have been met. The capital/labor split, even when putatively stable, is about contradiction, mediation, and ambivalence, elements that no representational certitude can correctly handle. If there is an increase in labor capital in relation to its other forms (land, plant, finance) there is no equivalence in cultural representation; indeed, there are contraindications even with capitalism where the substitution of capital *for* labor is increasingly greater than one. In Marxist terms, rather than the falling rate of profit I understand the cultural condition as a falling rate of labor. Yet this virtual disappearance (which I will explain further below) should not be confused with capitalist triumphalism. The question of profit over labor persists and deepens around the problem of growth. Place all of your bets on automation, for instance, and you risk stagnating worker income to the point of consumption crisis. Lower prices, and profits are pinched and growth is stifled. Finance capital may be awash in notional value but the value of notional labor is a contractual nightmare. Dystopians believe capitalism will run out of what David Harvey calls "spatial fixes" around about the time it has killed the planet (a convenient if rather drastic form of debt settlement). Again, Piketty suggests that national economies have largely avoided the social cataclysms implied by Marx because of growth (and, it should be emphasized, what makes up the very notion of work). Yet while this means he does not have to address labor value, its concept remains restless even in his more rigorous account (he seems to view Marx's obstinately narrow data set as phenomenologically quaint). This may require we return from substitution to exchange.

Labor's contribution to capital is to facilitate exchange value. There are certainly economies on which exchange need not be based on labor (potlatch systems, etc.) but capitalism is not one of them. Apple's market capitalization may make it (depending on the day) the world's largest company but it did not become it by eschewing the labor theory of value (in 2010, its subcontractor, Foxconn, employed up to 450,000 workers in one factory complex alone, the "Longhua Science and Technology Park"—that, we can say, is a lot of abstraction as extraction). But until unpaid workers started leaping off dormitory roofs at the factory the techno consumer thought the iPhone was a marvel of autogenesis. This is not to say the iPhone is not epochal in its moment (it has sometimes seemed a micro version of the obelisk as fetish in *2001 A Space Odyssey*) but must a worker fall to her death in order for labor to be visible? Being the product of labor, rather than labor products as being, is a hard sell to those who think their services are simply non-productive labor. For many years, so-called white-collar workers fervently believed days of factory drudgery were over as they populated endless lines of drab cubicles. True, many companies are tearing down those walls (especially those based on the exploitation of workers elsewhere) but the division of labor among wage earners is more about the difference of proletarian and working class than it is what makes labor power and the logic of value extraction.[15] Exchange value remains an externalization of what work is; yet if capital reifies labor representation, theory can produce similar effects by rejecting value and work as precisely blocks on radical transformation. Is the matter of materialism now that the value of labor does not matter?

Recall that Marx at the beginning of *Capital* wants us to see labor's part in value extraction using subtraction: the being product of labor can be glimpsed by abstracting this congealed quality from all other elements of the commodity. Today there is a robust tradition in Marxism of applying abstraction by subtraction to Marxism itself. Althusser used an epistemological break to crack Hegelianism; Negri deployed *Grundrisse*, principally one section (the fragment on machines), to push Marx beyond Marx by subtracting the value/labor nexus from his critique; Zizekian dialectics of the negative requires that Marx equals Lacan plus Lenin; Caffentzis filters out any abstraction that is not, in essence, thermodynamic, etc.[16] Perhaps, after all, capitalism is Hannibal Lecter and Marxism, like Krendler, sits quietly eating its own brain. We can say that any value theory of note is always the play across its additions and subtractions, but the value of labor power has something akin to ultimate tensile strength, beyond which it lies only in its historical fragments. If it is broken, maybe in the transition from formal to real subsumption, we have pursued subtraction to a point beyond remainder (the material remainder of value production). The question then is not to prove the law of value, which is a formidable if generally thankless task, but to wonder if labor power persists in another key. This does not mean abandoning value in our understanding of labor, nor does it necessitate transcoding labor value so that it is aesthetic value in disguise (it is the dialectic of this relationship that in part inspires Marx's *Capital*). Accounting, as Piketty well knows, is measurable, yet when we consider the cultural representation of labor, such accounting has also to figure immeasurability.[17] Value here is not homologous: it is a mediatory plane between immeasurability and unrepresentability. Such terms indicate the difficulties of measure and representation in labor value, not a lack or negation. It is to this dimension of expendability that I now turn.

You do not really need a theory of value to measure labor exploitation, just ask a worker. Clearly, however, the royal road to science, as Marx called it, is littered with such subjective claims. Marx did not seek to dismiss the subjective experience of exploitation (hence the workers' inquiry) but to understand the specific form it could take in the relation of capital and labor. Yet in terms of cultural representation we revisit the conditions of value and price; that is to say, a transformation problem. On the face of it, because value is a function of production and price is an integer of circulation, the former can be assessed independently of the latter and socially necessary labor time, perhaps paradoxically, can be argued either as a conceptual pivot or as necessarily redundant. Is it the case the cultural representation of labor *qua* labor as relation comports with the commodity as the form of appearance of labor as abstract? Does representation somehow combine abstract and concrete labor even though or especially when representation itself is commodified? To be clear, this means more than seeing abstraction in representational aesthetics; it means tracing labor as relation in representation regardless of whether a worker is actually represented.[18] The form of appearance refers to the abstraction of labor under capital not worker representation per se. Just like value and price, labor and labor representation can be pursued independently but I would like to think they share the same problematic, reading capital.

The methodology at issue here has in part already been suggested by Althusser and his associates in the "reading capital" project and is the non-said of capitalist modernity. Yet the theorist who is most provocative in this regard rarely engages with the labor theory of value or representing labor at all: Fredric Jameson. I want to deduce several lessons from Jameson's *Representing Capital*[19] (whose cover features Yuri Pimenov's socialist realist painting, "Increase the Productivity of Labor" [1927]). This, indeed, is a transformation problem for a value-informed theory of labor's cultural representation. Of course, Jameson begins with labor to remark upon its comparative absence from *Capital*, a dialectic figured between the unrepresented (the unemployed) and the unrepresentable (capital). One could argue that, even with his opening caveat, Jameson repeats at least part of the absence he notes in his book title "Representing Capital" (as Jameson says of Marx's tome, "the book apparently imitates its object of study" [19]). From the troubled accounting for value I have explored so far the impasse emerges around representing *labor* in the twenty-first century. Jameson works with the labor of dialectics rather than offer a dialectics of labor as such but, as I have noted elsewhere, the advantage is that it tends to foreground the spatial components of time in capital and this may have purchase on the limit of labor for cultural representation.[20] How?

Jameson's text abounds with insights on the "play of categories" in *Capital*, where the qualities of work, skill, the organic existential components of labor, must be deracinated for abstraction to occur, and permits Marx to subsequently reveal the well-known "crystals of social substance" in his understanding of the commodity.[21] The abstraction to simple labor allows for the measurement of time; in other words, it is a precondition for Piketty's analysis. But Jameson also notes how labor time is displaced onto transactions of buyer and seller (basically, how most of us see economic activity from day to day, with the pall of price hanging over value), thereby producing a representation of the worker devoid of class struggle (42). At this level, the dialectic of cultural representation oscillates between Jameson's representation of *Capital* as a reading, and the logic of Marx's own critique of capital as political economy. As soon as one attempts to "show" the valorization of labor power in exchange something other than the labor power in use value is brought to account and temporal coordinates (co-ordination, a relation of number) come tumbling out as rates, ratios, proportions, etc. (51). Time divides labor by number, the "working day" chapter of *Capital* is the way labor "appears," it is the *Erscheinungsform*, a formal representation of labor. The counter-valence, for this is dialectical thinking after all, is to be found, as both Harvey and Jameson affirm, in the chapter on "Cooperation" (in the disjunction of coordination and cooperation one glimpses a history of capitalism to the present).[22] Industries that want to work the magic of relative surplus value invite cooperation by gathering workers (the factory dorm system in China, for instance), an efficiency that can often breed its opposite. True, the expansion and intensification of technology can tame labor, liberating both its ardor and its capacity to fight the capture of its surplus. Indeed Jameson is "tempted" to propose the machine is the form of appearance. The labor power of living labor may make the machine (even the machine that makes machines cannot gather and produce [or produce and gather] its own components: it is a creature of relative not absolute autonomy in automation), but obviously technology can rapidly replace labor and labor time. Yet machinery as constant capital, according to Marx, produces no value: what it permits is a concentration of value derived from labor use. As we know, this is both a controversial and slippery formulation. Why build machines of "no value"? Let's just say efficiency in itself is not surplus but its potential. The point is to mark a difference between the role of labor time and the force of its abolition. The cost of technological efficiency is always and everywhere the narrowing of the rate of profit unless, of course, you can make labor exceedingly cheap via subcontracting, which is the most brilliant aspect of Apple's design.

Jameson claims Marx represents capital as a law, one of immiseration, in which capitalist expansion and domination over labor produces an ever larger reserve army of labor who live their surplus as pauperism. Marx grants the situation is "modified in its working by many circumstances" (for which we have various names: bare life, precarity, subsistence, etc. [*Capital*, 798]), but in all of Marx's writings this is the only "absolute general law of capitalist accumulation." The lesson here is that labor appears almost literally by its suspension (that is to say, it is not in use). What this means for the cultural representation of labor, rather than capital, is once more paradoxical: the value of labor power is defined by its absence; the worker's substance for accumulation is represented by not working (hence, one could argue, Jameson's focus on unemployment).[23] It is not the case that by representing capital one simply slips the representation of labor, but to demonstrate how capitalism works such an elision can become a methodological principle. Yet, this tends to accentuate the benefit of Jameson's key trope in representing capital, that of figuration. Clearly this does not mean figures, like those of workers on the cover, but it does not necessarily exclude them (it is closer, once again, to Auerbach's principle of figura). Representation as figuration opens up all kinds of interesting possibilities for culture (Jameson's favorite iteration remains allegory) because it permits an attention to process over identification or subjectification. It has the advantage of allowing utterance but also internal polemic, extant speech as well as the non-said, reality without an untroubled mimesis, etc. Allegories of labor are everywhere even if the laborer may not be found. Is allegorical figuration the form of appearance in which value and labor are enmeshed, articulated, concrete? On the one hand, this would allow for an understanding of labor "stripped of its sensuous characteristics" as Marx puts it when considering labor value in the commodity; on the other hand, it is hard to gauge culturally what is to be gained by figuring labor in this way. Does it merely confirm the machinations of capital logic? And why should representation be limited to the figural? What of realism, for instance—is this the enemy of labor's liberation from capital; is it just a sign of capitalist realism in general?

In the history of class struggle produced in the labor/capital nexus, realism stands supreme as the aesthetic of worker representation. In the Twenties and Thirties for instance, socialism was ecstatic about the ekphratic, as the worker was subject to detailed and verifiable description. Marxism was not taciturn about such enthusiasm not least because realism appeared to resolve the antinomies of bourgeois thought by assuming its freedom from ideological taint. As Lukacs was at pains to show, reification was not beyond aesthetic mediation but realism might yet succeed in its depiction of social totality, a complex issue especially in the later Lukacs where it is negotiated between Hegelianism, Leninism, and Stalinism.[24] In general, "Proletkult" was a traitor both to bourgeois *and* socialist aesthetics, deploying labor as a cultural symbolic over and above realism as lived experience and contradiction. There is no space here to recount this history, but clearly modernism offered an alternative matrix of reality effects even as its propositional faith could be no less problematic vis-à-vis the cultural representation of labor. But if realism has provided a positive resource of hope in the cut between value and representing or reading capital, is it because labor always appears despite the travails of reification, mystification, hypostatization, and ideological obfuscation?

Jameson's *Antinomies of Realism* provides a historical and dialectical sense of the mediations between narrating (here, accounting) and showing (here, the form of appearance).[25] The discussion of affect, of course, is immediately notable but does not provoke a sustained engagement over the role of affective thinking between, say, Marx and Spinoza, or Spinoza and Tomkins.[26] The codification of affect, as he calls it, continues apace which might be deemed problematic since realism itself is subject to dissolution according to Jameson's schema (a contradiction accentuated by Jameson's previous association of postmodernism with the waning of affect, a phrase he develops from *Do Androids Dream of Electric Sheep?*[27]). Jameson here returns to the philological materialism of *The Political Unconscious* (particularly in the commentaries on Balzac) in order to rethink realism's charge, including but not limited to, the emergence of a bourgeois body and consciousness.[28] When critics like Klaus, Zandy, Foley, Rabinowitz, Haywood, Kirk, etc., think through labor and working-class culture, disjunctive or otherwise, realism in general remains relatively under-theorized or historically amenable.[29] Symptomatically, *The Antinomies of Realism* reveals why this might be so, not because it refuses to engage with the literature of labor, but because culture appears to extend the elision discerned in representing capital: that labor as relation is featured as embodied workers or not at all. One cover of *The Antinomies of Realism* features a painting by Gustave Caillebotte from 1875, "Les Raboteurs" ("The Floor Scrapers"—most probably they are depicted working on the artist's own floor—the home as a site of work and art, and the work of art), but you will have to scrape very hard to find this kind of labor depicted in the book itself. It is an outstanding work in many ways because it demonstrates how impressionism trumps realism while seeming to do the opposite. But there is an alternative cover for Jameson's tome, this time revealing Vilhelm Hammershoi's typically mute painting of "Interior with Ida Playing the Piano" (1910—in this picture the floors are already finished). On the one hand, the difference between these paintings is a classic antinomy of bourgeois thought, one which acknowledges the making of interiors, the other which celebrates the interior for its generative interiority; on the other hand, both stage the limits of representation for any account of labor: how to mark what has been expended beyond the work of the artist herself.

Jameson's *Antinomies* includes a chapter on the resurgent historical novel and this is apposite when the world is labor but not bound to represent capital as such, a world where "revolutions are always confiscated, when not already defeated" (261). The generic distinction, the historical novel as a subgenre of the novel, only works if the historical claims of the former have an impress not to be found in the latter. This is less a stylistic option, a kind of thick description that can be verified beyond novelistic discourse itself, but is rather a comment on the meaning of history for fiction that questions the reality of generic differentiation.[30] It is not that the nineteenth-century realist novel was blissfully devoid of commodity values in exchange (whatever else it is, it is also its very effect), but that, just as the dialectic is dialectical, so history as concept is historical and the novel in its difference mediates its own non-coincidence. In stark relief this may reveal the historical novel as a market niche although not one without import since a nostalgia for richly evocative detail offers its own symptom about a certain depthlessness and presentism in other parts of contemporary culture. One of the more melancholy aspects of Alain Badiou's philosophy is that he theorizes the Event in a manner more or less precluded by the present (1789, the Paris Commune, or '68 are integral to the Event's present impossibility; they can, therefore, make historical novels).[31] But this is not Jameson's argument, which reads in Hilary Mantel a new engagement with history for the historical novel, such that Robespierre, for instance, becomes a believable character.[32] This is an enviable achievement for a grand historical figure whose personal intervention ended with the privilege to see the guillotine blade as it descended to his neck. The question here is not one of corresponding believability in a working-class subject, but *that* portrayal's relationship to labor as relation in the present. Jameson allots Mantel a relevancy test, seeing in her analysis of corruption an allegory of late-capitalist predicaments. One could argue, however, this ability to round, or humanize historical figures sutures individualization to a particular genealogy of self-presence that extends rather than ruptures incredulity. Clearly, this is not the lot of realism or of the historical novel, but let us return to the fate of the "raboteurs."

Caillebotte's painting was dismissed by the jurors at the 1875 salon in Paris for its "vulgar subject matter"; indeed, some have suggested this is one of the first representations of proletarians (part of the idea here is to separate what is proletarian in value from the subject in representation). The hallmark of Caillebotte's realism is its compositional precision. "Les raboteurs de parquet" is laid out in squares with the floorboards and wall panels permitting a very academic distribution of spatial relations. The scrapers themselves are shirtless which corresponds less to reality than it does to Greek or Roman heroification. This is a scene of labor yet one in which the laborers are rigorously contained. When Caillebotte displayed the painting in 1876 at the Second Impressionist Exhibition, Zola commented it was a rendering "so accurate that it makes it bourgeois." Its mathematical aspects are supposed to verify its content without political or ethical embellishment but Zola understands there can be no innocence in such depiction.

In the "E-verk" or worker series of Attila Richard Lukacs from the early 1990s, the Canadian painter invokes a similar classical discourse of the body, banalized less by bourgeois discernment but more by the lineaments of fascism and socialism in the twentieth century (the paintings themselves are set in Berlin after the fall of the wall). Lukacs celebrates virility and homoeroticism through the male worker's body while the skinhead symbolic unpicks any easy political recuperation (this is also an allegory of the new Germany). The antinomy Jameson foregrounds in the historical novel between "world historical figures" and collectivity is resolved narratologically by representing, synecdochally, the mob, the "skirmish for the battle" (as in Eisenstein's *October*), but this may work better for literary value than it does for social change; that is to say, the difference in form between literary value and the value of labor power is both determinate yet essentially undecidable. This might be thought in terms of Gödel's "Incompleteness Theorems": there is something axiomatic in the consistency of Marx's theory of value but it cannot be proved on that basis (this often centers on the transformation problem alluded to earlier); synecdoche may offer the value of collective cultural representation but it is demonstrably incomplete vis-à-vis labor as relation. This is one reason, for instance, Piketty can explicate inequality without solving it; he points to reforms that adjust the ratio of inequality depicted while preserving the structural contradiction that produces it. Incompleteness, however, does not mean without answer, and can be thought between labor representation and undoing.

Jameson concludes *Antinomies* by proposing the historical novel of the future as science-fictional. Borrowing from the complex visuality of Christopher Nolan's film, *Inception*, Jameson suggests the historical novel must be seen as an immense elevator moving up and down time (given Jameson's key theorization of postmodernism this might productively be read into his analysis of the Bonaventure Hotel with the inside/outside nature of its elevators). Such a "temporelevator" provides a cognitive map in which David Mitchell's six (at least) layered novel *Cloud Atlas* proceeds (if somewhat more awkwardly in the film version—despite Jameson's approving comments, the film is obtuse rather than complexly cinematic).[33] To those who think *Cloud Atlas* is told by Sheherezade as a latter day Christine (Chris Costner Sizemore), a dissociative identity disorder well-suited to detached referentiality, Jameson responds that style here "constitutes the superstructure of a mode of production" (308). *Cloud Atlas* finds a syntax of memory and history through technological transitions which is a rather brilliant way to indicate history without in fact writing it. Jameson's argument is that "valuable works are those that make their points by way of form rather than content" (311) but let us take this literally as *Erscheinungsform* where labor is structured in relation rather than only subjectivated. The world of work in *Cloud Atlas* is suitably multi-various and often forced. From the Moriori slaves of the Maori to the no-rest utopia of the fabricants, work in the novel is primarily figured as oppressive but not beyond creative sublation. The "Orison of Sonmi" sections offer a future of still more factories and corporations that prefer to engineer docile workers than risk their human counterparts (the robot/cyborg's cultural history has always leaned heavily on ideological schisms and at that level is an imaginary resolution of a real contradiction). As with all futures, this one is ripe with present indications: "Medicorp opens a weekly clinic for dying untermensch to xchange any healthy body parts they may have for a sac of euthanaze. OrganiCorp has a lucrative contract with the city to send in a daily platoon of immune-genomed fabricants, similar to disastermen, to mop up the dead before the flies hatch" (316). Forty years after Dick's portrayal of the Tyrell Corporation the future remains ominously familiar. Here, Unionmen are still fighting the stranglehold of corporate Unanimity, and the collective is radically particularized, even Souls are commodified and implantable ("the souling of a fabricant" brings Frankenstein's vitalism into the twenty-first century). As the character Hae-Joo comments, "Travel far enough, you meet yourself" (320). There is a story of labor in *Cloud Atlas* but does it speak back to the moving contradictions where we began?

The sliding temporalities of the narrative are indeed an interruption of normative ontology (one, for instance, "capital is") but the formal innovations strain under the crude social divisions the content reveals. Yet even as each section is a sketch (of a novel whose series is itself a history of the genre), the chronotopic profusion picks away at what would otherwise be a figural impasse: labor becomes. When the fabricant, Sonmi 451 quotes the Xecs on Catechism Seven, "A Soul's value is the dollars therein" (325) the *ratio* of the remainder, the abstraction of labor elaborated by Marx, is measured by an altogether impossible calculation: such value cannot be secured. The Union in the story pursue their own version of extraction, "revolution," which is no less conceptually incomplete as the contradictions in the value form they wish to overcome, but the point would be to read for capital as the condition of its own subsumption, as an unreality of realism. As soon as the word "labor" is mentioned the perils of representation are at once deeply prescient, irrespective of whether its invocation is structured or overdetermined by economic or social naïveté. In the play of Jameson's *Representing Capital* and *The Antinomies of Realism* the possibility of reading capital seems abrogated by the waning of realism, as if the postmodern passion for unreferentiality has concretized abstraction as just one more symptom of the triumph of commodification in general. Must the value of labor power always recede in representation?

Let us say representation is an immense elevator moving up and down labor time, but also elliptically. Its revelation of value often stops at the figuration of workers ("they cannot represent themselves, they must be represented"), but labor itself seethes in its own abstract excess, as Marx underlines in the *Grundrisse*, "Labor is the living, form-giving fire: it is the transitoriness of things, their temporality, as their formation by living time" (361). In this we register not superfluity but fluidity per se. True, this kind of indeterminacy can easily precipitate knowing disavowal (pre-capitalist, capitalist, post-capitalist in some version of exception), but this hardly renders the value of labor redundant. What it means is that at any one moment, determinate and determining, culture's non-representation of labor may align with the problem of unrepresentability itself, as a confirmation of the quotidian "thereness" in the concept rather than as a challenge to figure the new forms of its constellation. The dangers of what Diane Elson calls "misplaced concreteness" remain (130), but so too does the promise of the disambiguation of the "value representation of labor" in cultural formations. If we follow a cultural account of labor *from* value the emphasis will be on formal characteristics rather than characterization, the abstraction of labor rather than the figure of the worker. I would argue, however, that the differences of such accounts are coextensive and do not resolve themselves in the essence of narrative modes, realism, etc.

The "raboteurs" are among us still. Not long ago an image went viral on the Chinese microblog network, Sina Weibo. The *People's Daily* had reported on the ardor of a sanitation worker at Shandong Airport, where a waiting passenger observed her for fifteen minutes scraping the floor with a razor blade to remove a single piece of gum. The responses to the photo range from pro-government sloganeering to quintessential bourgeois self-management (throwing gum on the floor reveals a disciplinary deficit, etc.). The worker does not speak in this account but it is another example of the question posed but not uttered, "What is the value of labor power?" The answer must always leave the instance, the value of a particular labor; or as Marx puts it, the phantom-like objectivity, the being product of labor, only appears when one considers "human labor power expended without regard to the form of its expenditure" (*Capital One*, 128). Rather than maintain this makes the worker disappear once more (a position where Leftist defeatism meets capitalist desire) it is, dialectically, a critical process in which labor can emerge in the knots of representationality themselves. The stories are everywhere but mostly untold, which is the heuristic and not just the hubris, in taking account of them.

Notes

1. The literature on these matters is immense and I will not attempt to summarize it here. The labor theory of value, for instance, can be discerned all the way back to Aristotle. In the modern period, the differences between Adam Smith, David Ricardo, and Karl Marx on the question have become a genre of political economy in itself. In addition to the work of these three on the subject, the following have been pertinent to my reading: David Harvey, *Limits to Capital*. New York: Verso, 2006 (Harvey 2006); George Henderson, *Value in Marx*. Minneapolis: University of Minnesota Press, 2013 (Henderson 2013); and Diane Elson, Ed., *Value: The Representation of Labor in Capitalism*. New York: Verso, 1998 (Elson 1998). For more on labor as always already an abstraction in value critique, see the extraordinary work of the Wertkritik project, Neil Larsen, Mathias Nilges, Josh Robinson, and Nicholas Brown, Eds., *Marxism and the Critique of Value*. Chicago: MCM', 2014 (Larsen et al. 2014). While not focused on the labor theory of value per se, Gayatri Spivak's intervention in such debates remains for me a provocative rejoinder. See Gayatri Chakravorty Spivak, "Scattered Speculations on the Question of Value," *Diacritics* 15(4) (Winter 1984): 73–93 (Spivak 1984).

2. See, for instance, Richard D. Wolff, Bruce B. Roberts and Antonio Callari, "Marx's (not Ricardo's) 'Transformation Problem': A Radical Reconceptualization," *History of Political Economy* 14(4) (1982): 564–582 (Wolff et al. 1982).
3. See Thomas Piketty, *Capital in the Twenty-First Century*. Trans. Arthur Goldhammer. Cambridge, MA: Harvard University Press, 2014 (Piketty 2014). It is hard to exaggerate the event horizon of this book, much of it driven by a perception it provides statistical proof about how inequality is produced and therefore provides fiscal remedies in that regard. Like many brilliant books, it is more referenced than read. Here I am interested in its challenge for understanding value between the economic and the aesthetic.
4. See, for instance, Robert Kurz's contributions to Larsen et al., above.
5. Michael Hardt and Antonio Negri, *Labor of Dionysus*. Minneapolis: University of Minnesota Press, 1994: 10 (Hardt and Negri 1994).
6. See Louis Althusser and Etienne Balibar, *Reading Capital*. Trans. Ben Brewster. New York: Verso, 2009 (Althusser and Balibar [1970] 1998). I address this reading practice in Peter Hitchcock, "Defining the World" in *Literary Materialisms*, Mathias Nilges and Emilio Sauri (eds.) New York: Palgrave, 2013: 125–144 (Hitchcock 2013). A new edition, *Reading Capital: The Complete Edition*. New York: Verso, 2016, restores essays by Roger Establet, Pierre Macherey and Jacques Rancière from the original French version, a non-said in translation of fifty years.
7. The reference here is to Fredric Jameson's ardent polemic, *Signatures of the Visible*. New York: Verso, 2007. Jameson's essays are on the subject of an ontology of the visible, on the saturated visuality of the present. In part, the visual mediates both reification (rendering social relations as things) and the division of labor, where we began in "inquiry." With all the "elaborated codes" Jameson addresses in the book, the "elabore" of labor remains generally under-theorized in terms of the visual, except around the commodification of labor in general. This signature of labor's invisibility will return later in the current volume.
8. See Andre Gorz, *Farewell to the Working Class*. London: Pluto, 2001 (Gorz 2001); Antonio Negri, *Goodbye, Mr. Socialism*. New York: Seven Stories Press, 2008 (Negri 2008); Stanley Aronowitz and William DiFazio, *The Jobless Future*. Minneapolis: University of Minnesota Press, 2010 (Aronowitz and DiFazio); Jeremy Rifkin, *The End of Work*. New York: Putnam, 1996 (Rifkin 1996). Each one of these represents different genres within the study of class, politics, and technology but together are also symptoms of a certain invisibility where labor codes are invoked.
9. This is the basic argument of Part One of Marx's *Capital (Volume One)*, but for further elaboration, see also, for instance, Harvey's *Limits* and his *A Companion to Marx's Capital*. New York: Verso, 2010 (Harvey 2010).

10. While the basic argument of Harvey's *Limits to Capital* was composed in the 1970s, its prognosis remains remarkably prescient around these themes.
11. See, for instance, Étienne Balibar, *The Philosophy of Marx*. Trans. Chris Turner. New York: Verso, 2014 (Balibar 2014). Balibar is careful, of course, not to present Marx as a philosopher. To be fair to Piketty he does peruse philosophical texts (he approves of Rancière, for instance), although is characteristically suspicious of Marxism in that regard: "When one reads philosophers such as Jean-Paul Sartre, Louis Althusser, and Alain Badiou on their Marxist and/or communist commitments, one sometimes has the impression that questions of capital and class inequality are of only moderate interest to them and serve mainly as a pretext for jousts of a different nature entirely" (655). Atteint!
12. This is the subtitle to Henderson's aforementioned book on value.
13. See Pierre Macherey, *A Theory of Literary Production*. Trans. Geoffrey Wall. New York: Routledge, 2006 (Macherey 2006). The French text was originally published in the moment of "reading capital," a project in which Macherey was a leading participant.
14. In addition to Macherey's work, see, for instance, Georg Lukacs, *The Historical Novel*. Trans. Hannah Mitchell and Stanley Mitchell. Lincoln: University of Nebraska Press, 1983 (Lukacs 1983); and, N.N. Feltes, *Modes of Production of Victorian Novels*. Chicago: University of Chicago Press, 1989 (Feltes 1989).
15. I tend to differentiate the proletariat and working-class in this way: the former connects a logic of relation vis-à-vis capital's need for labor—to borrow from Hastings-King, capital is always "looking for the proletariat"; the latter concerns forms of social division and identity such a relation actually produces. At this level, class consciousness is both a realization of class identity and a coming to terms with the substance of the proletariat for the reproduction of socio-economic relations. At the moment class becomes proletarian, a specific historical mission is conjoined.
16. In addition to the work of Althusser already mentioned, see Antonio Negri, *Marx Beyond Marx*. Trans. Harry Cleaver. New York: Autonomedia, 1992 (Negri 1992); each work by Zizek is hardly a variation on this theme—one could just as well make a case around Hegel and quantum physics but see, *Revolution at the Gates*. New York: Verso, 2004 (Zizek 2004); and Georges Caffentzis, *In Letters of Blood and Fire*. Oakland: PM Press, 2013 (Caffentzis 2013).
17. Here Caffentzis problematizes the metric of subtraction itself in his Negrian reading. See, "Immeasurable Value? An Essay on Marx's Legacy" in *Reading Negri*, Pierre Lamarche, Max Rosenkrantz and David Sherman (eds.) Chicago: Carus, 2011: 101–126 (Caffentzis 2011). See also, Bruce Roberts, "The Visible and the Measurable" in *Postmodern Materialism and*

the Future of Marxist Theory, Antonio Callari and David Ruccio (eds.) Middletown, CT: Wesleyan University Press, 1996: 193–211 (Roberts 1996).

18. The case studies in this project lean heavily on the worker in her representation and confirm both the compulsiveness of the assumption, "they must be represented," and a displaced responsibility in the production of such representation. The paradox is that once one subtracts the worker from representing labor as relation the notion "the world is labor" (Hardt and Negri) is true. The dialectic between all the stories are about labor and the quandary of representing workers (who embody labor but do not represent it as relation) is a challenge not just to aesthetic history but to a politics of transformation. How can a requisite consciousness be produced if labor is not figured as workers? Surely the narration of labor minus workers is a capitalist fantasy? Indeed, it is against this desire the possibility of representation as intervention is maintained. From this perspective, the figure of the worker is the "labor trouble" of the "world is capital." This is another part of the explanation for "worker of the world(s)." The idea is to make the worker more than the world that is capital and less than one that is always already labor as relation. The gesture toward a singularity of "worker" in a plurality of "worlds" indicates the vexed field of representational aesthetics in this regard.
19. Fredric Jameson, *Representing Capital.* New York: Verso, 2013 (Jameson 2013).
20. See Hitchcock, "Defining the World," 125–144.
21. Karl Marx, *Capital Volume One.* This appears in the first chapter on the Commodity.
22. See Marx, *Capital.* See above David Harvey, *A Companion to Capital,* and Jameson, *Representing Capital.*
23. This is a difficult point since I contend "not working" extends beyond pure unemployment to living outside work. Cultural practices around representing workers focus much more on life beyond the workplace than on the worker working. The absenting of work itself is part of the reification of labor as relation.
24. See Georg Lukacs, *History and Class Consciousness: Studies in Marxist Dialectics.* Trans. Rodney Livingstone. Cambridge, MA: The MIT Press, 2000 (Lukacs 2000). This text occupies a central role in the emergence of New Left Marxism so its articulation of the proletariat is particularly pertinent. See also Lukacs' late and incomplete work, "Toward the Ontology of Social Being," especially the third volume, meant to begin the second part of the project on "The Most Important Problems" titled *Labor.* Trans. David Fernbach. London: Merlin Press, 1980 (Lukacs 1980). Not surprisingly, the latter begins with a notion of labor as a form of social abstraction rather than

the worker as subject. I have also tried to make this distinction around the question of ontology.
25. See Fredric Jameson, *The Antinomies of Realism*. New York: Verso, 2013 (Jameson 2013).
26. Another huge topic that I must bracket on this occasion, but that I have broached elsewhere. See the special issue of *Mediations* 25(1) (2011) that I helped to assemble with Sean Grattan. Jameson argues that affect should be more deeply articulated with the emergence of realism where feelings elude language and emotions are named. Could this antinomy in affect extend to labor, where labor is felt but attitudes to work are described? Here the difference between form and content is the logic of that between the value of labor and its reification in the commodity.
27. See Philip K. Dick, *Do Androids Dream of Electric Sheep?* New York: Del Ray, 1996 (originally published in 1968) (Dick 1996). The phrase Dick uses is "flattening of affect" which is another symptom for the instability of reality, like the reification of labor itself.
28. Fredric Jameson, *The Political Unconscious: Narrative as a Socially Symbolic Act*. Ithaca: Cornell University Press 1981 (Jameson 1981).
29. See, for instance, H. Gustav Klaus, *The Literature of Labor*. New York: St. Martin's Press, 1984 (Kalus 1984); Janet Zandy, *Hands: Physical Labor, Class, and Cultural Work*. New Brunswick: Rutgers University Press, 2004 (Zandy 2004); Barbara Foley, *Radical Representations: Politics and Form in U.S. Proletarian Fiction, 1929–1941*. Durham, NC: Duke University Press, 1993 (Foley 1993); Paula Rabinowitz, *Labor and Desire: Women's Revolutionary Fiction in Depression America*. Chapel Hill: University of North Carolina Press, 1991 (Rabinowitz 1991); Ian Haywood, *Working-Class Fiction: From Chartism to Trainspotting*. London: Northcote, 1997 (Haywood 1997); and John Kirk, *Twentieth Century Writing and the British Working Class*. Cardiff: University of Wales Press, 2003 (Kirk 2003). The place of theory across such diverse texts is hardly uniform but generally they problematize class in a different key than that which confronts the troubled nexus of labor as relation with realism.
30. This is not a small topic for Jameson because it is part of the dialectical claims for a Marxist reading of fiction. See, for instance, Jameson's introduction to Lukacs on the historical novel noted above.
31. The key text here would be Alain Badiou, *Being and Event*. Trans. Oliver Feltham. London: Bloomsbury, 2013 (Badiou 2013). While a distinction between the being of labor and the event of the worker would not hold within Badiou's terms, the historical possibility of the Event remains provocative regarding the absence/presence of labor. But see also, Alain Badiou, *The Rebirth of History*. Trans. Gregory Elliott. New York: Verso, 2012 (Badiou 2012).

32. The novel in question is Hilary Mantel, *A Place of Greater Safety*. London: Picador, 2006 (Mantel 2006). It is a novel, not coincidentally, about the French Revolution of 1789, and one replete with micronarratives of fictiveness in the event itself.
33. David Mitchell, *Cloud Atlas*. New York: Random House, 2004 (Mitchell 2004).

PART II
World(s)

CHAPTER 4

Sensing Class in John Berger's "Into Their Labors" Trilogy

One of the standard ways that you measure class is by investigating the processes of its formation. Proletarianization, for instance, is extremely important in understanding the logic and substance of working-class identification, yet, curiously, much criticism of working-class culture begins from the perspective that the working class is always already formed, and that the forming somehow ultimately detracts from the identification of working-class existence itself. This is, I believe, a mistake not just in understanding class, but in analyzing the experience of class that is vital in cultural expression. The assumption that the proletariat *is*, that it has being, is belied by the process of being that attends it, including the ontology of work to which this project has already alluded. This does not mean that proletarian being is therefore only performative, unless one reduces class to praxis, or action based on being (which tends, inadvertently, to reinforce the manual/intellectual labor split). What is performed in class exceeds the principle of performativity itself, even as it is certainly connected to theories of identity and identity politics. Such a philosophical knot is particularly acute in terms of proletarian being, whose process of becoming leads to self-identity and its annulment in the same instant (although it is true that the revolutionary being of bourgeois subjecthood also suffers from this paradox—the lack in bourgeois subjecthood compels the search for further surplus value extraction, as if this process might allow the nirvana of the completely bourgeois). In the main, the problem of the performativity of proletarian being might best be understood in the moment of passing, a topic I have discussed elsewhere,[1] but the process of class formation does not give up its meanings so neatly to culturalist reaccentuation. To decenter the "is" of proletarian being, either the assumption that class unproblematically maintains subjecthood or the triumph of thingness over relationality (if Marx offers a rule of class, it is that class is a relation, not a thing: it is a social process, not a cultural artifact first and foremost), we might usefully attend to the fictive constituents of the process of class being. This immediately invites the handy interpretive chiasmus in the fictions of class and class fictions reading. For those interested in theorizing working-class fiction, for instance, the consonance of fictive being in class with literary fiction only seems to confirm the incommensurability of socio-economic paradigms with creative writing. But, if the disjunction in disparate discourses must always be acknowledged this does not imply that imaginative work cannot speak powerfully to our understanding of class, precisely because imaginaries are at stake in class relationality. On the one hand, what follows will attempt to clarify the theoretical underpinnings of proletarian and peasant being, as abstractions and as processes; on the other, I want to provide an exegesis of elements of John Berger's fiction in order to elaborate the difference between thinking the process of proletarian being and assuming that class is there, identifiable, and *is* (or was) according to the ideologies of the hour. Reading class in literature in order to fathom the process of class formation is not a shortcut or substitute for political economy, neither is it a noble expression of what is sometimes derisively called a sociology of literature: it is a means to come to terms with the affective nature of social being, to comprehend imaginatively the dynamics of class subjectivity which is a narrative about becoming, not one about presence.

It is interesting to note that Marx's *Capital* crucially attends to the processes of proletarianization rather than a critique of its being.[2] Lest we think that this is some reflection on the particular stage of proletarian class formation against the class attributes of the bourgeoisie one should add that the being of the latter is also conspicuously absent from Marx's most celebrated text. The closest that Marx comes to identifying the bourgeoisie as a class is through a form of personification, either in footnotes about various economists, or in the paradoxically abstract individualism of the "capitalist." It is as if the class attributes of the capitalist are coterminous with capital itself and therefore need no social differentiation. Meanwhile, the class character of the proletariat is never named as such in *Capital* (most tellingly in Volume One); indeed, as Étienne Balibar has pointed out, even the word "proletariat" is barely mentioned and when it is it underlines the tenuous nature of proletarian existence in general.[3] There are theoretical and political issues about this elision that touch on other aspects of the present project (how does proletarianization unite on a world scale?), but my point is that Marx's approach to the problem of working-class constituency, the working class as a subject, has implications for class cultural analysis that prescribe to an extent the kinds of criticism possible. Of course, the nature of culture itself speaks to key issues in class subjectivity which, if it cannot overreach the enigma of proletarian being, still occupies a crucial place in discerning the processes of socialization that produce the riddle in the first place.

If *Capital* is the most forceful demonstration of the process of class formation without a subject—again, because proletarian subjectivity only arrives at the moment of its annulment—it tends to interpellate a subject for that process anyway. Marx projects a history of class based upon the very specific nature of class struggle that forms the backdrop to his intervention (basically, England's Industrial Revolution). In an intriguing way, a good deal of working-class cultural critique performs the same operation, as if historically sedimented class effects are in fact the essence of the social relation so construed. Thus, while culture remains the agonistic unconscious of class and class war, it can stand in for the fabric of political economy about which it has much to say but is not an unproblematic surrogate. The more one analyzes the performance of the term "proletarian" within the theoretical constructs of *Capital* the more one faces the specificity of antinomies in Marx's dialectic which pose process against a monadic subject or a handy agglomeration of identitarian formulae. Rather than disable, in advance, the prospects of class cultural critique, the efflorescence of proletarian in Marxian thought remains a provocative catalyst both sides of the culture/class divide, particularly now, when the ideology of the socialist state no longer masks the concrete existence of the working class as subject. Indeed, as "actually existing socialism" is further problematized or otherwise recedes from quotidian discourse in the present, the prospects for analysis of class process in capitalist societies is greatly enhanced. Without the foil of the proletarian subject, often banalized and reified by projections of "actual existence," the social and economic contradictions of class come much more sharply into view. Yet, if this is the operand in the following argument, it is principally to rethink what counts as a genealogy of the problem itself. This does not mean the present is free from ideology, or even the ideological formations of the Cold War, for instance; nor does it suggest that the historical commitments of millions upon millions to worker states was simply a reflex of false consciousness, whatever the pronouncements of this or that ideological state apparatus. The reconfiguration of the world system by globalization, neoliberalism, and the collapse and/or transformation of socialist states also rearticulates the ways in which labor in culture can be thought, expressed, and the sense of a longue durée in which this is elaborated.

The work of John Berger does not represent the quintessence of this new focus, nor indeed does the criticism that attends to his writing on this occasion.[4] I would say, however, that Berger's imaginary engagement with community life, particularly in his trilogy, *Into Their Labors*, helps us to read the texture, if not the text of class existence as more than its present, or presence.[5] Berger himself has often elaborated a kind of dialectical antinomy, that of culture and nature, that has inspired both his art criticism, his photo-narratives (with Jean Mohr and Patricia Macdonald[6]), and his literary production. I am particularly interested in what I call his "sensing class" as a means to explore processes of class formation, however much Berger and his writing resist sociological schema and, given his biography, any easy consonance with class identity. Yet, the architectonics of class, class making, lies at the heart of his stunning achievements in cultural expression. This is not so much a response to the impasse noted in Marx's concept of proletarian being, but it is certainly an extension of the question of socialization as process. Just as Marx, in the *Economic and Philosophic Manuscripts of 1844*, explains the deformation of human sense perception by the sense of "having" compelled by private property, so Berger writes out what makes a human social in her sensate relationship to work and the subsequent estrangement of labor through proletarianization.[7] Indeed, the suspension of being in proletarian subjecthood is deeply related to what capital does to sense perception, and this realm of the modern is something about which Berger has been consistently concerned (both the 1844 manuscripts and Berger's *Ways of Seeing* are mutually illuminating on the sense of sense[8]).

Berger's writing is thoroughly engaged with the nature of human's social being. Yet, it is relatively easy to dismiss his trilogy of fiction, *Into Their Labors*, on disappearing peasant life versus emerging urban working-class life in Europe as hopelessly arcane. If, as he believes,

Berger has told a story of peasantry and class mobility, not just of Haute-Savoie peasantry, but of world peasantry from within the experience of peasantry being proletarianized, then how much of that represented Being escapes the projection of the urban, modernist observer caught on the barbs of modernity itself? Are his peasants becoming proletarians forged in the crucible of a properly dialectical seeing or are they more literally a projection—that of a deracinated Self who wants to hold on to a putatively centered subjectivity by living it vicariously in the milking, butchering, shit-shoveling, seeding, hay-making, and shepherding of those that "progress" squanders?

No critique of Berger can escape the problematic politics of projection implied in the above: his work, after all, is the scene of this difficulty. The politics of projection is the very stuff of Berger's concern with how stories get told, passed on, remembered. If Berger sometimes seems less concerned with the authority of his narrative voice he does not let go of its gnawing status within his world of seeing. To dismiss or at least quietly compartmentalize the accomplishment of narrating others in Berger's fiction is to underestimate quite seriously the way Berger negotiates the typically incommensurable space between the intensely local and the philosophically global (in my parlance, the worker of the world[s]). Yet perhaps it is symptomatic of the very demise that Berger is addressing—the end of a specific form and forming of Being before the juggernaut of extermination unleashed by modernity. Thus, to consider *Into Their Labors* is already to explore a central dilemma of modern existence: the stuttering subjectivity of working-class urbanization—the one that cannot quite say "I."

These are big issues—big because, as one Berger critic puts it, Berger is intensely concerned with "one big canvas," the big picture of life, death and the struggle between the two in what counts for humanity.[9] However big the canvas is, of course, Berger's vision remains much too idiosyncratic for the universality that implies. As Fred Pfeil has noted, peasant life is deeply differentiated on a world scale (which will become more evident in later examples) and, if only by scratching the surface of peasant existence elsewhere, Berger's peasants of Haute-Savoie are revealed as one special case among others.[10] Again, however, it is easy to sidestep the major concern, the way in which Berger's peasants and proletarians are rendered. How is the content of their experience made a vehicle for an epistemology that goes beyond them, and their putative author? In general, critics are so quick to register the impossible point of view of Berger's engagement they rarely tackle the "way of seeing" that is proposed. I would suggest four ways in which this perception is formulated. First, Berger's portrayal is deliberately partial. Who, after all, must decide when the story is enough? Berger underscores the complex and contradictory relationship between his storytelling and the stories to be told by suggesting that he and the reader will follow the succession of tales "side by side." The reader is not assumed to be a peasant in that exhortation and Berger knows it. Berger's portrait is about framing a cycle that subverts specific concepts of the frame. After fifteen years Berger completes his trilogy knowing that the peasant has not been completed by him.

The second point accentuates the critical apparatus in the first. Berger modestly offers a series of stories in the order that they were written but this convenient chronologism is clearly blasted by the concept of time advanced in the narratives themselves. Events are remembered like yesterday but those who remember often were not alive or "present" at the occurrence. The continuum in which peasant memory is rendered lies outside the chronotope of the urban everyday, and yet it is strangely synonymous with it ("in each time" as Berger puts it in *Another Way of Telling*[11]): the strangeness results from the fact that the reader is never allowed to forget that the time of the peasants has been engulfed by modernity. The strangeness is also a lesson in proletarianization, for peasant memory retains a process of history without becoming a subject of it.

Third, the way of the world for the peasant is doggedly presented through the prism of love, or at least relationships of love (the love story is perhaps Berger's greatest forte). This often provides the pathos of the stories, one which enables sympathy in the reader. Yet despite the intensity of the love affairs (Pépé and Mémé, Lucie and Jean, Félix and his accordion(!), Caroline, Boris and "the blond"—who lost her name in the clearing that signified Boris's grief, Danielle and Pasquale, Sucus and Zsuzsa—normative heterosexual pairs in the main), it is love as a passion for existence that is emphasized. Indeed, the trilogy is an extended love letter from someone who admits that he must always be a stranger to his addressee.[12] While it would be careless to read this only as an allegory of writer and reader, it is nevertheless one of the central tropes of Berger's perception. The difficulty is that the lover's object of love is not the one who receives the love letter. This is the true pathos of Berger's devotion.

The fourth facet of Berger's perception connects to the other three and relates to the impasse faced by Marx in analyzing capital and class formation. Berger argues that work for the peasant is a "constant necessity," one whose routines and rituals are a "conscious experience of survival." For the worker under capitalism that question of necessity is bound to a wheel of fire driven by the sale of labor itself, but obviously this is not the same experience of survival endured by the peasant. The rhythm of work, which is a lot less lyrical than it sounds, is in a much greater state of flux than the rationalized and regulatory time and motion of, for instance, industrialization (and this exists in the trilogy as the most difficult adjustment the peasant must face). The trivial image of the peasant under the yoke of nature does not do justice to the skill with which the peasant applies tension to this necessity. The incongruity of the forms of narration with the "conscious experience" of what is narrated makes work itself a primary scene of perception. In this sense, we are not concerned here merely with "into their labors," but into labor itself as the fabric of peasant identity. How does labor as relation mediate the terms of peasant representation? I read this as an aesthetic commentary on the difference between the proletarianization of peasants and the subject position that the experience of work provides; labor in culture describes what this difference does to aesthetics.

Certainly this is a fiction of identity, a class fiction, although that in and of itself does not negate the truth claims that Berger makes for peasant existence (as Berger puts it, "only in fiction can we share another person's specific experiences"[13]). It does draw immediate attention, however, to the status of the observer and observation in the trilogy, elements that cannot be separated from the nature of work and processes of proletarianization (this, of course, is a problem we have met in the workers' inquiry). If, as I maintain, the problem of the representation of work is a problem of the formation of the imagination (the supra-sensible sense of sense) and is the aesthetic corollary of class formation rather than class subjectivity, direct experience of manual work is not necessarily the key to its expression, but it does play a pivotal role in the conditions of perception, or what Bakhtin calls "sympathetic co-experiencing."[14] This is not a logic that vigorously erases the difference between the observer and observed but traces the passage between the two. How does Berger manage to evoke this relationship without inserting an alibi for the authority that must accrue to the author as observer?

The story "Once in Europa" begins, as others, in the middle of things (perhaps that is why there are no quotation marks at the beginning of the opening paragraph that ends with them). The commentary on the poppy flower mimes the displacement of chronology that many of the narratives enact. We are with the poppy but we are asked to consider how its redness comes about. The narrator suggests that what splits the almond-hard calyx in which the flower forms is the desire of the red itself to be seen. It is as if the story will out not by a recognition of its content, but out of an understanding of the force which gives it form. Of course, the natural imagery is deliberate, but it is not didactic: it asks merely that one sense the process in the production of the poppy. Neither Berger nor the peasant makes the poppy, but they understand the necessary desire. This is how the story is written.

The narrator is Odile, a middle-aged woman who gets perspective on her past quite literally: she tells the story while hang-gliding with her son high above the scene of her life (to acknowledge Auerbach's mimesis from below does not mean that it cannot be coruscatingly panoptic). While bordering on the fantastic of the everyday in magical realism this idea was given to Berger by a peasant he knew, a woman of almost sixty who was indeed taken hang-gliding over the place where she lived. In an interview Berger claims that he had the story of "Once in Europa" a long time but did not know how to tell it so he "waited for the voice of the story."[15] This waiting is an imaginative urge that contrasts sharply with the artifice of expediency. The poppy must bloom according to the time of its desire, its desire to be red.[16] With the extraordinary perspective of the peasant woman in flight Berger now had the requisite voice. Why is this viewpoint appropriate? The position itself is a topography of existence—from that height the village and the factory where Odile worked is "a living portrait of itself." "The question of place" with which Berger begins the trilogy is spread out before Odile, it is the place that she cannot move from, as Berger contends, without ceasing to be a peasant. And, interestingly, from that height it is also a "White. . . . page of the world below": the story will be inscribed on the whiteness of the Alps. But this is only the first stage in the complex process of identification in which the sense of work as proletarianization will become manifest.

In "Once in Europa" Odile and her family are an example of European peasantry still coming to terms with the conditions of its erasure. The symbols of this are unmistakable. Her father, for instance, stands by his house one night staring at the smokestack of the local factory as it spits flame and smoke at its surroundings: "Look Odile, he whispered, look! It's a black viper standing on its tail—can you see its tongue?" (114). The factory is an invader, it takes the space of the farmers, it literally surrounds her father's home. The factory is part of another narrative about which Odile learns as a child at school: the mountains provide the raw materials for industrialization—fast-flowing water for hydro-electricity which in turn powers the furnaces that smelt ore for manganese and molybdenum. From Odile's perspective on the hang-glider, the factory looks like a woman squatting over the river to pee. But the factory is also the place where Odile gets to meet men as well as learns about the different regimen of industrial work. She lives this contradiction differently from her father (who resists it to the end) even though initially her images of the factory are drawn, like his, from the language of peasant existence: "Whenever I went near the factory, I saw the dust. It was the colour of cow's liver, except that, instead of being wet and shiny, it was a dry kind of sand: it was like dried liver, pulverised into dust" (114).

So the place of labor looks different: by itself that is not a knowledge of its difference. This is where Odile's logic of perspective comes in. In a way, she occupies the position of the author (like a god, in Joyce's conception, but with dirt-filled fingernails), yet she knows the landscape from the inside—both the earth of her family's farm and the machines that produce the slag heap burying it. Odile's viewpoint allows Berger's as what he calls "an independent witness." Not that the transferal of experience is ever seamless in its communication—if that were so there would be no such thing as fiction. But this framing, this literal tilt in perspective, is the second stage in ordering the experience of labor in forms that are appropriate if not synonymous with it.

The third provenance in Berger's eye for labor is to evoke laws for the work process that are independent of his interpretation of them. Again, this does not make them universals but it allows a knowledge of work that begins not from abstraction but from the very texture of labor as it is lived, acted. Since "Once in Europa" is primarily about the changed circumstances of the peasantry under the sign of specific form of industrialization, these laws have both the air of capitalist rationalization and the wonder (and dread) of the peasant who internalizes them. Odile, for instance, experiences both sides of the line between the earth and the industrial. As a child she helps her father dig in the manure for the new growing season with a fork that he has made for her. From her father she learns why she should do the opposite of the walnut tree (last to come out in leaf, first to shed them) and why planting proceeds according to the temperature of the earth. When she works in the components factory the basic law becomes time for money. Initially, Odile makes 1,700 small metal plates for radios each day. That is her quota: if she gets ahead of it she can stop for a smoke. What else is there? The monotony of work is accentuated by the emptiness that marks her grief (her first love, Stepan, is killed in the manganese factory). But many worker narratives talk of this deadening emptying out of experience as experience. The manganese factory itself (where Odile briefly lives with Stepan in worker barracks) is a typical symbol of the genre. Odile comments: "There was only one law in the factory that counted: that the ten furnaces be tapped the required number of times every twenty-four hours, and that the castings conform to standard when chemically analysed" (147). That this is an alien concept to Odile is underlined by her description of its dead presence, something that tumbles out in a stream of negative associations.

> Each wall, each opening, each ladder was like the bone of a sheep's skull found in the mountain—fleshless, emptied, extinct. The furnaces throbbed, the river flowed, the smoke sometimes white, sometimes grey, sometimes yellow, thrust upwards into the sky, men worked night and day for generations, sweating, retching, pissing, coughing, the Factory had not stopped once for seven years, it produced thirty thousand tons of ferromanganese a year, it made money, it tested new alloys, it made experiments, it made profits, and it was inert, barren, derelict. (155)

The significance of this is not its similarity to a thousand such descriptions in fiction since the onset of industrialization, nor the stark contrast that Odile will make between this and her fertility (although, of course, this has importance in the story since her relationship with Stepan at the factory will produce Christian, the son who is flying her). The basis of its meaning rests in what one could call the "thereness" of the factory's presence (the deference to Heidegger here is more accurately a measure of difference, for if Dasein is a "thereness" of Being, the "is" of the factory is its automaton). It sits there, solid, unmovable depending only on its original law for its existence which is relentless, seemingly unstoppable in the fact of its utter lifelessness. It is the place where the sense of place itself is expunged. It does not give but takes (and carries away its booty by train every two weeks in the dead of night). It takes Michel's legs, and Stepan's life. There is no Being there except thereness itself as a sense of the incontrovertible, like death.

But "Once in Europa" is a love story that could only occur by virtue of the factory, by dint of the changes wrought upon peasant life, the process of proletarianization in which it is enmeshed. Certainly, this broadening of possibilities does not mean an "escape" from former existence: the sadness in Odile's life is an integer of the limits imposed upon it. What draws the reader in beyond the clichés of everyday worker life are the ways in which resilience exceeds the mere fact of the factory and the thereness it represents. Odile can fly over the factory. Michel can walk with Odile in his arms despite the loss of his legs. And he can take away the pain of burns although nobody knows quite how. This, of course, is a measure of Berger's co-experiencing as humanism—a deeply felt engagement with the lifeblood of his subject, a solidarity that pivots not on slogans, but affect. In a way, it parallels Michel's ability to ease pain, just as his point of view is often at one with Odile's perspective, above and among her peasant community. I will say more about the engendering of work in this identification below, but here it should be emphasized that Odile's story, the "once" that occurs in and around (and above) the factory barracks called "IN EUROPA" (itself a literalism as *deus ex machina*), is of a piece with Berger's original explanation. He does not necessarily seek a peasant essence in the trauma that marks their "disappearance" or inevitable proletarianization (even when Heidegger might provide him with a relevant touchstone); instead, he reveals the power of storytelling as co-experiencing. He cannot be the equal of the peasants he writes about (he remains a "stranger" as he says, a foreigner in French and France), but he does strive for a commensurability in storytelling itself. Berger waits for a voice that he hears in the Haute-Savoie, a sense of "how events fit together" (*Pig Earth* 12). Odile's experience of love and labor is only an approximation, or a fiction, of that voice to the extent that it permits the story to be told. But the story is not *from* labor, it is *into* it and this requires greater elaboration, working out.

The question of perspective is crucial, and one that links each story in the trilogy, particularly in the second volume where point of view shifts in the vortex of transition in peasant life. For instance, "The Time of the Cosmonauts" begins in the third person with a strong authorial voice that sets the scene as if the local community were setting it. All the vital details are there: the place of the story, the time-frame, and the biographical background. But the narrative begins with a warning: "...life outstrips our vocabulary. A word is missing and so the story has to be told" (77). Events are in excess of the words available to describe them, and this wisdom prescribes the storyteller's art. Berger is drawn to the story because it is in excess of his authorial seeing. Storytelling approximates this surplus but cannot name it (this also the representational fix in labor power). The author can pretend (as can the readers) that the eye of observation is all-seeing, all-knowing but this would extinguish the truth of the tale, the answerability that lies between the author and her subjects. Even the sense of sight cannot superadequate class as a relation. In this story, perspective shifts as a register of the truth in its telling.

But that "truth" is also inadequate which is how the story comes to unfold (the desire of the red once more). First, the time of the cosmonauts is not the time of the narrative, even if it is the time that makes the narrative possible. Why does Berger introduce this perspective? The choice of Gagarin circling the Earth is not innocent, although it is understated enough not to displace the actual time of the tale, a quarter of a century later. Gagarin's flight signifies the apotheosis of modernity—the human in space who can now view the people of Earth as they could not view themselves. He flies even higher than Odile as a symbol of technological prowess and possibility. The peasants at the time could look up at the sky at night to spot Gagarin in his Sputnik. He was something separate from the everyday cycles of their existence. Then, the chalets on Peniel plateau in the mountains were full and each family had so many cows the farmers agreed to limit grazing time to spread the wealth of the pastures. Twenty-five years later only two of the chalets are occupied, by Marius and Danielle. Perspective, then, is a measure of the speed of transformation.

Despite their age difference, the common experience of tending animals on the plateau brings Danielle and Marius closer together. The intimacy of everyday farming may shock the reader who does not farm (as the slaughter of the cow at the beginning of *Pig Earth* is meant to do) but it facilitates a more open relationship. There are less and less secrets between Marius and Danielle because that is the nature of the community. Secrets are possible (they are listed in "Once in Europa") but less tenable if one stays within the community. The work itself requires an intimacy, an interdependence between people in relation to the land and their animals. We see this when Danielle helps Marius deliver the calf and, most obviously, when she dresses the wound to the back of his thigh. But their generational difference means they are unlikely to be lovers. History has divided them even as their experiences help bring them together. The old man remains loyal to his oath to restore dignity to the family name and keep herding alive on the plateau. This was the embodiment of his will. Danielle is marking time. She helps her father but knows that her own life is driven by a different fate.

This arrives in the form of Pasquale, an Italian who is among a group of woodcutters working in a forest nearby. Like Danielle, Pasquale is no stranger to working on the land. In this case the labor is measured by its absence, in the space between the woodcutters ascending the mountain and returning in the evening, some fourteen hours later. Danielle watches them come down: "The light was already fading. They were walking slowly, as if they were blind and were forced with each step to feel their way forward with their feet. They had a dog with them whose antics they were too tired to notice. Slowly they approached the chalet, each walking at his own speed, exhausted and alone" (92). The pace of the passage captures perfectly the fatigue that their work entails. Danielle, for companionship or from compassion, directs them to the spring to wash. She heard their saws, she sees the result, and now she senses their endeavor up close: "she could smell the smell of their washing: a mixture of soap, stale shirts, petrol, smoke, pine resin, and sweat" (94). As she watches them stripped down to the waist her desire is piqued ("a man washes his body like he washes down a wheelbarrow; it's not by washing himself that a man learns to caress." [94]). Pasquale and Danielle fall in love.

The smell of work is not the love of it, nor is it the love that may spin around it. But the sense of labor is not to be disparaged.[17] A worker is not a worker by smell alone, but Berger knows how to read these signs into the experience of work as a whole. If the reality of class is abstraction then its concreteness is paradoxically sensate. Sensing class is a way to comprehend what is actually stymied by class as a social division: that is, a human as what Marx calls a "species being," in whom the senses "become directly in their practice theoreticians."[18] Berger's continual exploration of the position of perception, structures of seeing as well as feeling, foregrounds not just what is curtailed in the forming of class, but what persists as a potential in the human sensorium.

But beyond the intimacy of experience as sense there also exists the possibility of deception and/or self-deception. This emerges in Berger's trilogy as the clash of cultures: they represent key ways in which peasant life is being broken up. This is most evident in "Boris is Buying Horses" but it also takes the form of a displacement there, as if the question of peasant disappearance can be settled in the stark opposition between a peasant man and an urban woman, Marie Jeanne. Berger suggests that deception resides not just in the relationship, but also in the narrative voice used to describe it. Is the storyteller Berger? The narrator is a writer whose books are now on sale at the souvenir store that Marie-Jeanne converts from Boris's farmhouse after his death (Boris' passion signs over his property to Marie-Jeanne). The storyteller knows Boris well enough to have bought him cigarettes. If the writer does indeed identify with Boris it is not because of the latter's superior moral position but because the stark acceptance of passion's object erases, for a moment, the distinctions that separate Boris' and the writer's lives on the alpage. The consequences of passion confirm for the narrator the existence of evil in the world, the possibility that, from the height of peasant pride (signified in the triumphal "Boris is buying horses") the peasant can quickly sink into despair and self-destruction (underlined by the equally laconic, "Boris is burning his sheep" [59]). But is this really about the difference between urban and country ways of being? Indubitably. There is no coincidence in the choice of the love interest but the cultural deceit this involves works both ways. Boris deceives himself by believing that Marie-Jeanne would fall so easily for his earthy masculinity, his animal-like sexuality, his brute obviousness. His first gift to her, a slaughtered lamb, garishly indicates the outcome of his naiveté and overblown masculinist pride. Which lamb has gone to the slaughter? Boris thinks he smells a woman of leisure (he does not smell vinegar on her). He is right, but wrong about the consequences of this for his standing as a peasant. The crux of his masculinism lies in class resentment; that Marie-Jeanne represents a bourgeois, or at least a petty-bourgeois, infringement of peasant life and peasant masculinity. And this "smell" is just different enough to be a lure that the peasant male should avoid. In the end, however, the story is not about the tragedy of obsession, nor indeed about the misogyny of Boris' crass depiction of woman as manipulator. About a decade after its central action, the point of the story rests in the souvenir shop that Marie-Jeanne now runs. Pieces of peasant life, and imitations thereof, are offered up for tourist consumption. Boris did not just lose his life: he has had the memory of that way of living packaged (souvenir, of course, to remember). And this quiet victory cannot have escaped the narrator whose stories, after all, are now available in the same store.

These are all stories from *Once in Europa*, the second volume in the trilogy and there is much more to it than the notes here. The final story of the collection, "Play Me Something," features a farmer, Bruno, who has gone to Verona as a tourist and there meets Marietta, the politically conscious daughter of a politically conscious family. Marietta's albeit received political wisdoms are supplemented by her sense of class. Marietta guesses that Bruno works on a farm because she smells the cows. Bruno smells Marietta's scent and she admits that she works in a chemist's shop. Bruno continues: "One look at your hands and I could tell that you didn't work with them." Marietta tells him that such a statement is what her father calls "infantile proletarianism." Bruno's response is classic Berger: "He said nothing. Perhaps it was a Venetian expression" (184). Their political repartée is cast against the background of a festival organized by *L'Unità*, the communist daily paper, and clearly for Marietta this justifies the political nature of her conversation. But, of course, this is just as much a come-on as Bruno playing his trombone even as it emphasizes that another difference between a peasant and a worker is the mode of political interpretation. Bruno declares that he will vote for anyone who raises the price of milk. Marietta replies that is not good for workers. On this contradiction parties have formed and fractured. The love story develops in this vein, as Berger carefully dissolves political platitudes in the intensity of their relationship. Bruno comments, "all our ancestors asked the same thing...you and I will never know in this life why it was made the way it is" (190). Perhaps, but Berger shows in these tales that knowledge of that kind is drawn from the nature of interaction. It is not simply a question of peasant adaptation to the industrialism and post-industrialism of contemporary global modes of living. It is also a problem of openness to peasant existence, something that is rendered palpable in love stories that crisscross the borders of what he perceives as a properly peasant world. But are we "into labor" in the heat of such exchange or is the popularity of these tales based on the fact that love supercedes all else that the "independent witness" sees?

I have been commenting on the middle volume of Berger's trilogy, in the middle of things, yet in the wake, as it were, of peasant labor. But this puts special emphasis on the first volume of the trilogy, *Pig Earth*, for this book, in the specific nuance Berger gives his "chronology," is the test of the labor that is lost. If, as I argue, the core of Berger's trilogy is an attempt to represent the unrepresentable, to give therefore a sense of labor that is deemed beyond the capacity of modernity, then *Pig Earth* is its most dramatic instantiation. Here, in the essays, poems, short stories, and novella of the collection, Berger makes his case for the significance of peasant life. Where *Once in Europa* articulates the dynamic of change in the clash of peasant and urban experience, the first volume accentuates what is sedimented in peasant life, the basic components of peasant social being.

In his insightful reading of *Once in Europa*, Bruce Robbins is struck by the dead-end that Berger's way of seeing creates: "If you look at the endings, the pattern is pretty clear. You have a choice between marriage, which takes you to the city, or death, which leaves you in the country. The city is the future, the country is the past."[19] Or, as Marietta says, peasants will disappear, the future lies elsewhere. Like me, Robbins sees this narrative cul-de-sac breaking down. The peasants in these stories are not consigned to the pattern of Berger's argument. This, I believe, is a further sign of Berger's answerability which, despite the potential for a monologic ordering of perception, allows each declaration to be rewritten under the sign of the Other, the characters who speak back across the authorial divide.

Pig Earth begins with the slaughter of a cow, and its symbol pervades the writing that follows. One is tempted to say that, like the cow, the peasant village was not held together by cement, but by *energy*. But the energy of place that Berger details again exceeds the spirit of rootedness that he ascribes to the peasant community. This is important because Berger claims that the first volume is "set against the traditional life of a mountain village" (this note begins the second volume). The ambiguity of the phrase "set against" nicely captures the tension of Berger's intent. According to one interpretation, the term means that tradition provides a backdrop: it is that which allows perspective on the subjects in the foreground. Second, it can mean that the stories use traditional life as a support, like a pitchfork resting against the side of a barn. A third provenance of the phrase is more confrontational and contradictory; it suggests that perhaps the stories are positioned in contradistinction to the tradition that otherwise gives them life. They are against the tradition implied to the extent that they resist the finality of its consequences. My point, then, is that the extinction of being is not reserved for the moment of transition, when the winding asphalt vines of industrialism creep up the alpage; it is immanent to the peasant's experience of tradition itself. This is the drama of *Pig Earth*, the revelation of an energy perceived even at the moment of death.

The ambiguities of whatever passes for peasant spirit is a clue to the massive paradox of peasant labor: the principle of work they embody cannot be annihilated even if their process of Being can. They have no monopoly on the sign of their labor even as they indicate the substance of its necessity. Robin Lippincott suggests that "Berger *places* us among the peasants" but, for the reasons outlined above, I find this entirely unsatisfactory. If we make the journey that Berger proposes alongside him this is an affirmation of the difference of the reader from the peasant represented.

It is not the action of Berger's placement that is significant but the spirit of place conjured in the alienation between the author and his subject. In short, it is not the author who places us, but the convolutions in the orders of experience that contemporary Being offers. The pattern to *Pig Earth* is formed in the fragments of such complexity. On one level, one can register the everyday components of peasant existence: instruments of being (the ladder or the ladle), constants of being (birth, death, seasons), or the production of being (potatoes, hay, *gnôle*); on another, the juxtaposition of narrative elements themselves recalls the process of shifting perspective to which I have already alluded. The elements of peasant existence are presented in panorama; the substance or texture of peasant life emerges in the mode of juxtaposition. That this pattern invokes the art of photography, and particularly a photographic narrative is deliberate, for Berger's way of writing is very strongly connected to a way of seeing, principally that outlined in his book with Jean Mohr, *Another Way of Telling* (of which more in the next chapter). This pattern is the agon of existence, the struggle in the revelation of being to itself and others. A revelation that is also an impossibility. It is not an essence of an individual character, still less the essence of peasantry, but a pattern from experience glimpsed in the shards of a reflecting subject. This is the pattern in which *Pig Earth* becomes possible, the possibility of labor in culture.

In the "Historical Afterword" (and he does not use that first word lightly), Berger advances the thesis that the peasants are a class of survivors with a specific "culture of survival"—one which sees the future as repeated acts of survival. Is Lucie Chabrol simply an embodiment of this assessment, or does she survive the polemic in a way that sharpens the sense of peasantry beyond the brusque adjudication of the critical eye? Yes, she "disappears" and yet survives but the point of mixing philosophy and history with a work of fiction is to fathom the continuities and disjunctions among the components, not to provide some neat and idealist equivalence.[20] Three elements of desire are crucial in "The Three Lives of Lucie Chabrol." The first is Berger's desire as both a storyteller and social critic. He knows that by framing the fiction with an ardent essayistic defense of peasant existence he risks undermining both his status and that of the narrator as "independent witnesses." The space of the Other has a voice that is appropriate to it, one that, as Berger avers, *speaks to him* and not the other way around. Can the reader trust that one is not simply a mask for the other? To the extent that all fiction is about masking, obviously the question of trust must be operative from a different angle, the responsibility of the writer to her subject. The amalgam of the reflecting subject is an ongoing process of responsibility or answerability tested by the relationship to the Other as a ground of knowledge, not only of herself or himself, but of the author who, for better or worse, enters into this pact. Berger's desire is not for a narrative voice that substantiates the truth claims of his argument by echoing it, like Pasquale's thrush. His desire is, rather, for a voice of the Other that orders or transforms the knowledge that is the supposition of his writing.

The zone of desire is complicated by a second influence in this story by Jean, the narrator. Perhaps he had stopped loving Lucie when they were apart, but who would deny that his little expedition into the mountains for mushrooms was a way to cross paths with a love from the past? In an interview, Berger says that Jean was the voice that he was waiting for, the organizing consciousness for the substance of the tale to congeal (Papastergiadis: 11). There is an awkward parallel perhaps, between Berger's desire to "examine the meaning and consequence" of the disappearance of the peasants and Jean's search for Lucie as the confirmation or denial for his wasted life. In this sense, Jean is a vehicle for the tenor of Berger's argument, but clearly Jean's desire has its own self-consciousness. While he is a bridge between the world of the peasant and the pleasures of existence elsewhere the force of his desire breaks through his meager Being in that equation. What is wonderful about his character is that he is never able to name this desire, only his sense of loss that it was not fulfilled. To indicate that time reveals the naming of desire (the naming and not the name), Berger employs a brilliant (although hardly unique) device. Lucie repeats Jean's name but in the space between he has lived forty years off the alpage. It is as if desire has compressed that moment as a false desire, as a misplaced or misguided attempt to live one's life differently. The fullness of Lucie's second life is a measure of the vacuum Jean has made of his.

Lucie's desire is the most complex of the three. Her will to survive is not in itself a sufficient ground for consciousness of self. Her autonomy is to be admired: the beautiful passages in which she collects berries, cherries, mushrooms, and dandelions are the poetry of life on the land. But there is more to her than that. Her foraging harbors a supplementary desire which is to understand the nature of surplus for her existence, an understanding elaborated in the existence of surplus in nature. Again, on the surface this may sound like Berger proselytizing but in general Lucie's tenacity in her search for understanding is not synonymous with authorial desire.

Her skill in selling her wild produce is a personal lesson in the function of money and difference. In the city markets Lucie learns the secret of money and its function for urban existence; indeed, she knows the city as it cannot know itself.[21] Steeled by the logic of the market, Lucie gets rich on the conditions of its desire. As a peasant, she has worked out a system of dealing with the city. This is why we do not have to wait for *Once in Europa* for the moment of transition. The contact zone of the peasant and modernity is already sketched out in the contours of Lucie's second life. It is no coincidence that a large portion of the money Lucie makes is from smuggling foreign cigarettes across borders (both between countries and the city and the country, practices ameliorated but not eradicated by the emergence of the EU); that is, not at all from the natural surplus she forages. Her desire is to understand the way of the world of money without succumbing to its mystique or becoming merely a cipher of its logic of appropriation and exchange. She faces the lure of commodification but she is conscious of its consequences for her Being, the packaging of peasant memory as object. It is the force that is unleashed in Marie-Jeanne's souvenir shop. It is the force which Lucie's desire is "set against." Perhaps, just as Berger waits for the voice that Jean now represents, Lucie herself bears her loneliness while she awaits Jean's return.

But nothing quite prepares the reader for the wonder of Lucie Chabrol's third life. Like Jean, we have observed her close up in the intricacy of her everyday toil. We have come to appreciate the worldliness of her knowledge in all of its idiosyncrasy. And, also like Jean, we have come to understand the nature of her unpredictability without seeing this as an essence of her as a woman or as a peasant. We share his amazement of her dressing up for him but perhaps are less surprised by her bold proposition to move back to the village and live with him. If this is a fulfillment of desire then for Jean it is a promise that has been lost. It is a hope that has been, as he puts it, dissolved by the actual course of their lives. The clash of optimism and resignation in the moment of Lucie's proposal is further testimony to the ambivalence of experience. Through their mutual encounters with the city and the "world" (a world for each, in my schema) they have not lived the dream of peasant tradition; indeed, they have been "set against" the organic mode of peasant community that Berger ascribes to it. If Lucie and Jean's return to the village implies the dream of "re-becoming a peasant" that Berger explains, they yet contradict the substance of that being: rather than "the constant necessity of work" Lucie wants to live out her days with Jean on her savings. That this is incommensurable with peasant experience is only accentuated by Lucie's murder which is senseless yet somehow explicable as an inherent danger for becoming wealthy in her community.

The odd dance of desire punctuates the last section of the story. At the funeral Jean seems to want to hear Lucie's voice as a sign of natural closure that their relationship had been denied. Her ghost speaks to him as a function of this desire but also of Lucie's whose soul cannot rest while she remembers the living. It is hinted that her brothers may have been responsible for her death, as if they were still too avaricious even after taking her inheritance before. But Lucie's return is not to solve the mystery of her murder. She does want to know, however, why Jean had thought of killing her. The ghost piques his guilt in a way that conscience sometimes cannot. He finally admits that, as before, he feared that she was trying to maneuver him into marriage. She goes but his senses confirm she has been there: "the room smelt of boar" (169). Later, Jean will go to pick blueberries, once more crossing the paths where he would be most likely to meet the object of his desire. Lucie appears to him, and from here the denouement of the story is nothing less than fantastic.

Lucie leads Jean to a place of the dead where they are building her a house. Even in death the measure of peasant community is made by the labor they perform. It is to be her resting place but it is also a rendezvous where Jean admits that he had been mistaken, "Yes, I should have married her!" he blurts, although neither the dead nor the living hear the outburst, or the earnestness in which it is delivered. People he knows are still living appear to help with the building of the house. In this dream state a natural division of labor disappears as if to emphasize the unbending continuum of peasant Being. In the sharp descriptions of the labor they perform it is no longer clear who embodies that toil, although the ghosts are referred to as the "working dead," as an impossibly literal "dead labor." As commentators have pointed out, because of the teleology of extinction that Berger sets up in his "explanation" one could argue that every representation of peasant labor is an example of the working dead, as factory workers must be the zombies of the present. This, however, is not Berger's point in drawing the reverie of the rendezvous. Jean is Berger's example of peasant imagination (the imagination of a peasant, and imagining a peasant: Jean/John). He can imagine the pleasure of being beyond the peasant community but not the places where that pleasure might be manifest. The power of his imagination is therefore *situated*: it is dependent on the spirit of place that attends the alpage. If one wanted a more or less logical explanation for the dreamy scene of housebuilding and the festival that accompanies its completion, one could say that it is produced in the moment of Jean's near death from a fall down the mountain. Yet it is imagination itself that holds Jean's being in place, like the energy that sutures the cow until the moment of its expiration in the first story, "A Question of Place." How can one sense the peasantry if the cognitive ability for that act is tied to the very place in which that experience is lived? The answer to this question is also an answer to Berger's decision to live in the alpage for decades. The demand on the reader is too great, however, and the danger is that the moment of identification will be lost within the pietistic compulsion of that demand. The ghost of Saint-Just calmly tells Jean that justice will be done "when the living know what the dead suffered" (187). Access to such knowledge is a leap of faith, and one that is entirely congruent with the trilogy's religious epigraph. One is asked to be "into" a labor that others have done which, in the Biblical correlative, is a reaping as a form of understanding, a condition of "life eternal." At the end of the story, Jean has reached this understanding, as if Lucie's ghost has shown him the meaning of a life he has otherwise wasted. The twist, however, is that Jean will associate his love of the Cocadrille with the forest in which her spirit lives (the original title for the narrative was "The Forest," one where the ghost of Heidegger is more palpable). The sense of place is what leaves him there and perhaps the reader a little closer than before.

I have suggested that Lucie's "lives" are set against the thesis that powers their creation. Knowing the peasantry, then, is not just about coming to terms with the evocation of their "place"; it is also about the centrifugal forces intrinsic to that sense of place. Similarly, the labor of Lucie Cabrol is not simply the aggregate of her everyday toil; it is also an agglomeration of her being in the world, the way she "wears the world"— and this includes forays into urban life. The essence of labor is actually the fabric of its possibility, not the mere description of it. The difficulty remains whether storytelling can indeed represent this possibility or whether it can only measure the incommensurability between Berger's labor of writing and the writing of labor, the sense of changing peasantry, to which the trilogy is dedicated.

Lilac and Flag deepens this challenge in several interesting ways. First, it must be said that because of its chronology in Berger's writing it bears the trace of Berger's initial insistence, it fits the logic and lament of urbanization. Second, however, while generations might separate Lucie from Sucus and Zsuzsa they share the same episteme as outsiders in the city. This is underlined not by the obvious labels of location (Zsuzsa lives on Rat Hill) but by the fact that the story is told in the musings of an old woman who has never left her peasant village. Just like Jean's rendezvous with the dead, this stretches the tissue of credulity (on this point Pfeil is altogether correct to bemoan the weakness of the narrator's attempt to justify her knowledge). The narrator is a bridge between elements in the same order of experience and yet is as unlike the lovers she describes and indeed Lucie (except perhaps in birthdate and location) as one could get. Here the independent witness is the impossible one and on more than one occasion the reader is left wondering whether Berger might have misheard the voice that he was waiting for to tell his third volume. Why, then, is she so crucial to our understanding of both the story and its function within the trilogy as a whole?

I have tried to indicate that there is a constitutive opacity in the process of peasant Being and peasants being proletarianized that Berger will not elide for narrative translucence: the peasants do not give up *the* meaning to their existence even when Berger might sometimes persuade himself that this is the case. This is another sense of "sense"; that is to say, its indication of approximation rather than truth. Crudely put, to sense is not necessarily to know. Again, we owe this insight not to law, and especially not to the laws of science, but to fiction, to the art of imagination. The contradictions for answerability are at least twofold. The reflecting subject, as Berger calls it, in part suspends the conviction, the force of vision, that he brings to his story. By being answerable to the substance of the peasants' everyday experience his own will is to some extent bracketed by the other components—the reader, the protagonists, the other narrator. Berger does not resign himself to the role of "stranger": the other elements compel it. A second contradiction spills out of the first: to be answerable to a peasant, let us say the old peasant woman who narrates *Lilac and Flag*, is also to answer to human foibles—particularities of taste, memory, experience, etc. On one level, this may still mean that the narrator's defensiveness masks the projection of the author's own. Yet on another level, the same foibles individuate the narrator. Maybe they are her weaknesses, both the digressions and the frankly stereotypic and heterosexist depictions of what makes a man a man, a woman a woman, and desire what it is between the two. The significance of this should not be underestimated, but it is a dangerous gambit in the representation of laborers and their labor. For the author to cede perspective to the narrator intensifies identification at the same time as it risks the admonition (conscious or otherwise) of the other components in the amalgam, the readers and the protagonists. The beauty of many of the passages in *Lilac and Flag* is compensation perhaps for the weakness of the narrator's worldview, but how much does the old peasant woman as "bridge" risk breaking the composite that animated the earlier volumes?

A great deal, but there are several advantages to the role she plays. Like Odile in "Once in Europa," the narrator here allows for complex shifting perspectives (which in and of themselves are no more outrageous than Odile flying over the factory on a hang-glider). If the reader has sensed the fate of the peasantry in the earlier books, then here that sense is sharpened by the volatility (and fallibility) in point of view. The old woman's digressions in the narrative sometimes grate but they alter the pace and accentuate the condition of perspective that threads the tale. Many of them offer echoes of the village life from which Sucus and Zsuzsa are for the most part oblivious in a metropolitan kind of way. Thus, Zsuzsa lives behind the tanneries where Marius once worked (the smell of labor remains central to the sense I am suggesting). If we listened only to Sucus, would we know that his father's uncle was Marcel, imprisoned for resisting the "value" of money? And why shouldn't an accident of memory allow us to learn that, after all, Félix's birthday was June 3 and that, even though he lost his seventeen cows while he was in hospital for jaundice, he bought six more when he recovered? For those who have not read the first two parts of the trilogy, such details need not detract from their experience of the novel on its own terms; but as part of the trilogy, even tidbits broaden our experience of its major characters. Rather than force the overlap between village and urban life, these ghostly echoes of other stories in the trilogy emphasize just how remote village experience has become for the youth who are its offspring.

The rhythms of labor in village life have been almost completely erased. The poor from the countryside have become the detritus of the metropolitan landscape—a waste that washes up in the shanty towns that form its borders. The "lucky" ones secure menial labor (Zsuzsa's mother is a cleaner for IBM). Clement has left the village to work as a porter in Troy's auction rooms but ends up shucking oysters the rest of his life. Most of the peasant poor of Troy seem to live by their wits in the grey or black economy. Sucus sells coffee to men who have just exited the local prison because he realizes that evokes their first "taste" of freedom.

Later he will compete with others in taking people's blood pressure. Both jobs are born of his belief that you survive in the city by satisfying "real needs" (there are no jobs, he tells his father, except the ones we invent).

Troy is an urban composite, and a European one at that, but in how many cities across the world has this logic now come to mold contemporary existence? Berger is not saying that the consequence of the erasure of peasant life can only be this sharp dichotomy of inside/outside, but it clearly represents an extreme narrowing of experience in which the "haves" write off poverty as the natural effluence of affluence and the "have-nots" are forced into ever more ingenious roles to fight this supposed inevitability or fall into more conventional modes of beggary.

Lilac and Flag is a love story, however, one whose movements shift both gently and jarringly between a rhythm of desire in Zsuzsa and Sucus' relationship and the peasant woman's interpretation of it. Despite its status as a novel, its sharp juxtapositions and different narrative modes are more frequent and intense than those which fractured the stories, poems and essays of the earlier books. Again this strains the credibility of the narrative "I" but it simultaneously wrestles the reader into the tone of modernity—its fits and starts, its deadening logic of inconstancy in conformity. When Sucus' father dies (killed by a faulty television!) the one-way street of modernization comes more clearly into view. Clement, who prides himself not just on his oyster shucking, but on his etymological skills (aided by the gift of a dictionary from his wife, Wislawa), tries to instill some kind of order into the experience of modernity he sees in his son. So Clement tells Sucus the history of how the village came to be and thus the roots of their community. Clement thinks he can make Sucus understand by taking him back to the village with the factory that makes molybdenum. But Clement is conscious enough of the realities of life in Troy that the only promise he wants of Sucus is that he get a job on a building site where Clement has a contact. We know what the old peasant commentator would want, but Troy and what it represents closes off this possibility, except in dreams, and in death.

Sucus is made for Zsuzsa because she recognizes the peasant in him and he senses in her, rightly or wrongly, a nature that might embrace him. The peasant narrator tends to read the latter in terms of age-old assumptions about what women are and what men want from them but this "nature" also includes fragments of peasant existence (Zsuzsa was able to milk goats "before she could count" and locals still employ her to kill their chickens). But if the love story is also a tale of what becomes of peasant labor in the cities, the sense of work I have been discussing is conveyed in particularly bleak terms. There is, of course, Sucus' job on the building site, one that he takes to fulfill a promise demanded by his dying father.

The building site offers a stark comparison with the ghostly construction that occurs in Lucie Chabrol's third life. The latter is a product of the community's will, dead and living alike, to provide a chalet for Lucie. It is an act of repentance and memory. The edifice that Sucus helps build is for the Mond Bank (the proximity to world bank and people's bank in the French is clearly tinged with not a little irony), a building almost entirely divorced from the community of workers who erect it, and one whose operations work to exclude them from the benefits of labor they exert. Certainly, the collection of workers itself is a tenuous one—a group composed of migrant labor and temporary hands. Yannis, the crane driver, is from Greece and dreams of home almost every time he views, from his vantage point, the "wine-dark" sea (the allusion is deliberate—at one point his mother says, "you work in the sky like a god, and you are lost!"). Murat, the man in charge of concrete mixing, is from Turkey and firmly believes in worker justice. He tells Sucus: "If we keep the idea of justice alive under our yellow helmets... if we all keep it alive together, one day the world will belong to us" (72). Part of my suggestion in the current project is that this inevitability is overdetermined and displaced by a multiplicity in world that seeks a singularity in the worker. For his part, Sucus points to a generational difference, that men like his father and Murat talk of "us" when he, like Zsuzsa' brother Naisi, only thinks of "me" (which is also a symptom of the displacement noted). His discomfort with Murat's faith in the future is more a comment on the changed politics of class and location. How can you sense this "us" when the city demands that you think of "me" as your most immediate concern? Skeptical or not, when Murat is injured on site it is Sucus who expresses the "us" of others by confronting the foreman for neglecting worker safety. Murat loses his job because of his injury; Sucus for protesting it.

Both Sucus and Zsuzsa decide to play things Naisi's way. They steal passports, new identities for drug couriers, from a conductor's compartment on a trans-European train. Is this the crime that destroys them? Not really. The novel does suggest that in a world that eschews a more complex symbiosis of living and making a living, crime is not an occupational hazard but an imperative. The love that Zsuzsa and Sucus, Lilac and Flag, find together cannot sustain them; instead, it releases a desire for a world that cannot be found in the squalor of Rat Hill or among the "eternal audience of the poor" in Alexanderplatz. Yet it is a world that cannot be found in the money they make from their thievery either. Sucus' desire drives him to rage when he finds out Zsuzsa works in a strip joint: he hits her so hard he believes he has killed her. Zsuzsa's desire is what makes her a survivor even in the face of Sucus' death (he commits suicide because he believes he has killed Zsuzsa, another notable allusion with a twist). As our old peasant narrator puts it, "Poverty, loss, pain, passion, time, or moncy will have marked her eyes, her hands, her mouth, and the way she holds her arms and the way she places her feet... but they will not change her soul" (210).

Once more, Berger employs a fantastic denouement to explode that stereotype and extend his answerability in the sense of peasantry at issue. Ultimately I disagree with the authority of Berger's shorthand judgments on such existence but clearly much of his polemic, his "explanation," is displaced by the quality of narratives that are themselves "set against" the abilities of the critic as observer. Hector wants to go back to whatever he believes the village to be, but cannot. This is the problem of nostalgia, for what he seeks he knows has been lost. This is also the problem of Berger's thesis that the peasant who moves ceases to be a peasant. The migrant industrial worker also dreams of home but floats according to the value of labor ("with these hands," says Stepan in "Once in Europa," "I can work anywhere in the world"). The peasant is hamstrung by the "thereness" of the village; the industrial worker by the "thereness" of the factory. It is not simply the fact of a place, that a factory is there, that dictates necessity and nostalgia but the way that its image scratches itself onto the worker's sense of self. Ultimately, it is not strictly about necessity or nostalgia: a worker must be able to imagine concretely a place in order to labor with satisfaction within it. This is why Hector's heart gives out.

Against the inevitability of imaginative atrophy offered the peasant by urban experience, Berger conjures a world cruise of the spirit, a voyage of the afterlife that takes the narrator, Hector, Naisi, Sucus and all the other lost souls of urbanity back to the alpage. This is not a solution and I do not think Berger intends as much (this is why, for instance, the book ends with glimpses of Zsuzsa still in the city). It enhances the spiritual conviction of Berger's endeavor, for sensing peasantry is not an anthropological curiosity: it is an affair of the soul. If one accepts the role of the old peasant woman as narrator, however, this voyage is very much in keeping with the voice that animates the rest of the tale. Clearly, the plausibility of the old woman's narration is also a question of spirit, of identification, of sense. Does any reader believe that these details emerge from her reading the newspaper, or from the fact that her ears "grow bigger" with age? The ship is her ship, the place where she gives the homeless, the exiled and the institutionalized "a room of dreams." And Sucus' room? It is a stable full of cows, the "question of place" with which the trilogy begins.

The sense of labor in the formation and deformation of class that Berger attempts is contradictory, an imaginative effort that can never escape his position, however sympathetic, as privileged observer, or indeed the truth that peasants and proletarians are highly differentiated on a world scale (each worker in her singularity; each world in its multiplicity). Oddly perhaps, his trilogy incessantly shows the pitfalls of globalization while affirming that imaginative acts of this kind remain imperative.[22] Rational forms of globalization wield reason like a sledgehammer when it comes to the modes of community that precede it (this will be one way to read Jia's *Still Life* in a later chapter). Imagination alone does not rescue peasants from such a process, although clearly there are vibrant peasant cultures that resist and transform the dictates of modernity. The trick to the "old wives' tale" and perhaps to the trilogy, is the role of the reader's imagination in elaborating the sense I have taken as a primary theme. The reflecting subject as peasant is not possible without the reader's imagination, without the cognitive effort of identification yet separation that governs affective modes of answerability. It is not a question of "either you get it, or you don't" when it comes to sensing class. At a basic level, the task is to heighten awareness that a cognitive and imaginative effort is at stake in coming to terms with different orders of experience. This is the difference between sensing as routine, as natural, and sensing as a confrontation with different ways of being, or seeing. In *Into Their Labors* work is made central to such an understanding of difference as Berger details the actual labor processes that his characters live, rather than viewing this as simply extraneous to their existence. The peasant is not identical with her work, but her identity can only be sensed through an effort of understanding her relationship to the labor she performs. One does not have to agree with either the spirituality or the paradigm of extinction that Berger forwards to make this effort. Perhaps the weight of Berger's moral imagination outstrips us all, but he understands that when it comes to peasant stories the reader who is not a peasant must commit themselves to an imaginative sense that cannot be owned, rented or borrowed. It is something that can only be achieved in the fullness and openness of answerability, or the peasant will have already disappeared and sensing class will not have assumed a material force.

Notes

1. See Peter Hitchcock, "Passing: Henry Green and Working-Class Identity," *Modern Fiction Studies* 40(1) (Spring 1994): 1–31 (Hitchcock 1994). See also the essay, "Slumming" in *Rites of Passing: Essays in Identity and Interpretation*, Maria Sanchez and Linda Schlossberg (eds.) New York: New York University Press.
2. It is quite surprising that capital is so "substantial" and class is so ethereal in Marx's major work. See Karl Marx, *Capital*, Trans. Ben Fowkes. London: Penguin, 1976.
3. See Étienne Balibar, *Masses, Classes, Ideas*. Trans. James Swenson. New York: Routledge, 1994: 125 (Balibar 1994).
4. An early attempt to fathom Berger's career is Geoff Dyer, *Ways of Telling: The Work of John Berger*. London: Pluto, 1986 (Dyer 1986). A work that also reflects on his subsequent life (and one heavily dependent on the trope of motorcycling) is Andy Merrifield, *John Berger*. London: Reaktion, 2012 (Merrifield 2012). Needless to say, the capaciousness of Berger's abilities, at mid- or late career, tends to cheat all attempts to encapsulate it. My interest here is to gauge the extent to which Berger speaks to the problems in the cultural representation of labor outlined in other parts of this project. I will indicate other texts, in and around Berger, that are pertinent in this regard, but even then there is much more that could be said. See, for instance, an argument for the influence of socialist realism on Berger in Andrzej Gasiorek, *Postwar British Fiction: Realism and After*. London: Hodder, 1995 (Gasiorek 1995).
5. *Into Their Labors* is divided into three books: *Pig Earth* (New York: Pantheon, 1988, originally published in 1979), *Once in Europa* (New York: Pantheon, 1987), and *Lilac and Flag* (New York: Pantheon, 1990). Page numbers in the text will refer to these editions.
6. Macdonald took the aerial photographs that accompany later editions of *Once in Europa*. Mohr's photography, of course, is integral to the narratives of *A Seventh Man* and *Another Way of Telling*.
7. See Karl Marx, "Economic and Philosophical Manuscripts" in *The Marx/EngelsReader*, Robert C. Tucker (ed.) New York: Norton, 1978 (Marx 1978).
8. If, as Marx maintains, the "forming of the five senses is a labor of the entire history of the world down to the present" then Berger has made significant contributions to our understanding of that history. Of course, the major sense in question is sight and processes of representation. One of the problems that Berger investigates is how seeing includes what is not there, that is, the abstractions that accompany our visual apprehension, including permutations of ideology and experience. Any extensive critique of Berger's oeuvre would

have to come to terms with the innovative and intricate concepts of sight that Berger develops not just for the visual arts but for a philosophy of the human senses. See, for instance, John Berger, *Permanent Red: Essays in Seeing*. London: Methuen, 1960 (Berger 1960); *The Look of Things*, edited with an introduction by Nikos Stangos. London: Penguin, 1972; John Berger et al., *Ways of Seeing*. London: Penguin, 1972 (Berger et al. 1972); *About Looking*. London: Writers and Readers, 1980; John Berger and Jean Mohr, *A Seventh Man*. London: Verso, 2010 (Berger and Mohr 2010); and John Berger and Jean Mohr, *Another Way of Telling*. London: Writers and Readers, 1982 (Berger and Mohr 1982).

9. Robin Lippincott, "One Big Canvas: The Work of John Berger." *The Literary Review* v(35) (Fall 1991): 134–142 (Lippincott 1991).
10. Fred Pfeil, "Between Salvage and Silvershades: John Berger and What's Left." *TriQuarterly* 88 (Fall 1993): 230–243 (Pfeil 1993).
11. John Berger and Jean Mohr, *Another Way of Telling*. London: Writers and Readers, 1982 (Berger 1982).
12. I will remark further on Berger's outsideness below. Nikos Papstergiadis usefully links Berger's observer status to questions of intellectual exile and exilic discourse in general. See *Modernity as Exile: The Stranger in John Berger's Writing*. Manchester: Manchester University Press, 1993.
13. John Berger, *The Success and Failure of Picasso*. London: Penguin, 1965: 129 (Berger 1965).
14. See M.M. Bakhtin, *Art and Answerability*. Ed. Michael Holquist and Vadim Liapunov.Trans. Vadim Liapunov. Austin: University of Texas Press, 1990 (Bakhtin 1990). The term is somewhat freighted by the aesthetics of "sympathy" but is here invoked because of Bakhtin's emphasis on the production of an "outside" in the authorial act.
15. See Nikos Papstergiadis, "John Berger: An Interview," *The American Poetry Review* 22 (July/August 1993): 9–12 (Papstergiadis 1993).
16. It is not an act of fanciful romanticism to hark on Berger's use of red here in terms of political ideology (his book *Permanent Red* deploys the color and metaphor in the same way). Here, the desire to be red in the poppy can be read as a commentary on class subjectivity, something that requires a fullness in time and desire to achieve. That this desire is more abstract than either the poppy or its redness is underlined by a later version of "Once in Europa," the collaboration between Berger and the photographer Patricia Macdonald, *Once in Europa*. London: Bloomsbury, 1999. (Macdonald 1999), where the poppy does not bloom as image until the effulgence of love and class consciousness in the relationship of Odile and Stepan.
17. I have discussed the importance of sense in this regard elsewhere. See Peter Hitchcock, "They Must Be Represented?: Problems in Theories of Working-Class Representation." *PMLA* 115(1) (January, 2000): 20–32

(Hitchcock 2000). In *Into Their Labors* examples are legion. As Odile notes in "Once in Europa," "the men who worked in the factory smelt of sweat, some of them of wine or garlic, and all of them of something dusty and metallic" (114). Or Marius: "When I came back to the village, you could pluck a hair out of any part of my body... sniff it, and say: this man has worked in a tannery" (78). Or Boris, who knows he has fallen for a bourgeois blond when he notes, "She had the smell of a buxom, plump body without a trace of the smell of work. Work has the smell of vinegar" (46). Traditionally, class markers are ascribed to dialects or forms of dress. Here I am arguing that labor can be sense in a much more expansive and provocative way, both for criticism and for politics.

18. Karl Marx, "Economic and Philosophical Manuscripts" in *The Marx/Engels Reader*, Robert C. Tucker (ed.) New York: Norton, 1978: 87 (Marx 1978).
19. Bruce Robbins, "John Berger's Disappearing Peasants," *Minnesota Review* 28 (Spring 1987): 63–67 (Robbins 1987).
20. Berger's most eloquent and elegiac statement on this writing practice is his *And Our Faces, My Heart, Brief as Photos*. New York: Pantheon, 1984. It is a difficult book to read because of the different modes of address that Berger uses. It has a writing philosophy that is about writing philosophy or, as he quotes from Novalis" "Philosophy is really homesickness, it is the urge to be at home everywhere."
21. It is a skill that Berger shares. See, for instance, his extraordinary if all too brief reading of Paris. John Berger, "Imagine Paris." *Harper's* 274 (January, 1987): 72–74 (Berger 1987).
22. This is something of the tack taken in Bruce Robbins' essay, "Feeling Global: John Berger and Experience" in *Postmodernism and Politics*, Jonathan Arac (ed.) Minneapolis: University of Minnesota Press, 1986: 145–161 (Robbins 1986).

CHAPTER 5

A Gift: Workers to Sebastião Salgado

"You photograph with all of your ideology"—Salgado

In a photograph the workers give what they cannot have: the right to be seen. Sebastião Salgado first came to international prominence as a photographer in 1981 when he was assigned by the *New York Times Magazine* to cover the first 100 days of the new presidency and was there outside the Washington Hilton as John Hinckley attempted to assassinate President Reagan. Salgado had already proven himself as a photographer in the previous decade (efforts that led to him joining the prestigious Magnum agency in 1979) but nothing could quite match the buzz of such a momentous event. In a minute and a half he took seventy-six pictures, many of which are considered a definitive record of Reagan's near- death experience that day. While Salgado's career was blossoming without this particular "decisive moment" (to borrow from Cartier-Bresson), one wonders how much the history of the twentieth century would have been changed had Hinckley succeeded in his mad mission? This chapter is not about Reaganism but is certainly attentive to a political and economic history in which Reaganism is but a lasting symptom and against which Salgado's oeuvre continues to stand. His long-term photographic projects, including *Sahel, An Uncertain Grace, The Children*, and *Africa*, have been controversial because they have raised questions about the photographer's relationship to his subjects and whether, for instance, human tragedy should aspire to beauty in the image.[1] Some critics worry that Salgado has aestheticized starvation, for instance, while others see his photos as overtly political, as if he were somehow reliving the photojournalism spawned by the upheavals of the Twenties and Thirties (I will return to these contentions). Still other critics believe Salgado to be a spiritualist who, whatever the assignment, simply projects his religiosity onto his subjects. My interest is primarily in his *Workers* project, a massive photographic narrative that might fulfill, as Salgado notes ironically, a Marxist dream: "the workers of the world, at least on paper, will finally be able to unite before, in their present form, they disappear."[2] The reason they do not unite is not simply a reflection of corrupt communist parties and misguided idealism; it is also a function of regimes of representation to which Salgado's work provides a crucial and glorious commentary, one fraught with material contradiction. Indeed, we could say for something to disappear it would have had to have "been" in the first place, and this is the paradox of the gift in worker existence that Salgado highlights: it is a form of appearance as disappearance that continues to trouble imbrications of labor in/as aesthetics and politics (a particularly provocative impasse as Salgado becomes "the most *visible* photographer of our time"—emphasis in original[3]). Capital gives to the image the language of aphanisis–the subject fades before she has even been brought to focus. This is the "uncertain grace" of proletarian being; this is the revelation of the image for the worker under contemporary capitalism. And this is the moment, the decisive moment, of worldliness in Salgado's art.

It is commonplace to point out we primarily live in a visual economy of difference; that cultures today are dominated by visual representation over and against the claims of the oral or the musical, or the written, for instance. If one considers the explosion of image markets in the twentieth century, inextricably linked to the globalization of capitalist markets themselves, there seems little doubt that the field of vision has a fundamental cultural purchase on the way that lives are experienced in contemporary existence. Indeed, in the twenty-first century, mediatization as image saturation is the very definition of globalization as currently construed. But the era of the eye cannot be separated from the techniques of the observer and indeed how vision has been constructed within a general economy of scopocentrism.[4] Two impulses seem to tug in different directions. First, there is the idea that visuality itself gives us a privileged access to the real, as if the image were a fact of the real's reality (this logic is the basis of authenticity in documentary realism). Second, image markets have always depended on a deferral of this very condition, such that we may "willingly" suspend our suspicions of three-dimensional reality represented in two-dimensional space (3D imaging and "virtual reality" have interrupted but not sublated such conditionality). The optical unconscious oscillates in the conceptual space between two competing orders of knowledge of the real. Does the sense of sight constantly adjudicate this difference and allow us to live "at home" within the internecine struggles that construct sight itself?

Not alone. The power of sight is obviously significant beyond everyday assumptions—especially in terms of those orders of vision we associate with surveillance, as Foucault and theorists since have reminded us—but it is both undermined and overdetermined by a greater power still in its very possibility: the power of the Other. The construction of the sense of sight and its relation to the Other, the Other who gives an "I" its subjectivity, certainly informs the present analysis, but I would hope that in these observations on observation in the work of Salgado one simultaneously engages a concomitant reflection on the power of the Other in predicating the images that constitute Salgado's photo-documentary style, which has specific implications when the subject as worker is presumed. Salgado himself claims that "a photo is not made. It is a gift," a gift of the Other who is the subject before the camera.[5] The nature of this gift depends on the peculiarities of subjecthood, which I have already questioned in terms of labor ontology. The stunning and disturbing images of Salgado's *Workers* project rely, for their effect, on a complex confluence of presence and aphanisis, of tactile "thereness" in the world to borrow once more from Heidegger and a ghostly absence in the manner that Derrida discusses "specters."[6] The revelation of the image is connected to the soul-forming or "inner-exterior" that Bakhtin describes in his discussion of I/Other relations.[7] It is also related to a specific break in the worldliness of the world of appearances and to an interruption of otherness in general in the field of vision. But most of all, the revelation at issue is an integer of the unrepresentable; namely, workers in the international division of labor, the workers of the world. And to image this gift is to come to terms with a way of seeing that is a profound challenge to the scopic regimes of the normative "eye" of contemporary sight. It is because the worker can only offer up her appearance that she is photographed. The power of the image finds its limit in the non-representation of her being, a being as labor she does not have.

But surely, in Salgado's hundreds of photos of manual laborers the worker is before me in *Workers*, imaged, framed, present? How can one write of the unrepresentable when the worker herself is so obstinately there, so passionately figured before the gaze? As I have indicated earlier in this study, the problem is not necessarily in the appearance of the worker, but in the tendency to read this as a metonym for labor, whose being and socio-economic contradictions are simultaneously displaced and resolved in the representational logic of the worker as subject. Rather than being in the frame, labor as relation is more like the "space-off" in an image of a worker, a parergon in Salgado's massive "archaeology," but a supplement that is constitutive of how globalization "works." The appearance of the worker in Salgado's project is simultaneously the preservation of a certain vanishing and an acknowledgment that such disappearance is itself a mode of presence. What is seen to disappear is redolent in appearance, as if photography might perform the paradox of class in the being of labor, that which is privileged to produce its own disappearance (the proletarian succeeds as a class when class as proletarian is made to disappear). This is a "way of seeing" rather than a theory of all eyes or all sight, despite the will to universalism and ineluctable ethics that to some extent compose the images to be discussed. In general, however, black and white photography lends itself very well to the representation of that which would seem otherwise unrepresentable or absent as labor—the worker. Why this is so will inform and structure the argument below. Here it is pertinent to note John Berger's point about the enigma of appearances: that "appearances both distinguish *and* join events."[8] Berger suggests that photography "quotes" from the world of appearances and that ultimately this quotation will constitute a discontinuity from the process of life observed—a break which is the source of the photo's ambiguity vis-à-vis the verisimilitude of its factual source (Kaja Silverman's notion of the photograph as analogy can be linked to this process[9]). A black and white photo announces this discontinuity as a matter of course; it breaks from the continuum of color that gives to the world its customary "appearance." It reduces the subject of the image to emphasize its enigmatic subjectivity. It is the form of this subjectivity that is the major concern here and the answerability that is adequate to it, even as a special effect—elements that may take Berger's enigma in a different direction and Salgado's visualization onto another level of historicity. The gift must exceed the beholder (some of the tension in their senses of sight will re-emerge in my discussion of their documentary together, *The Specter of Hope*[10]).

There are several themes of Salgado's photography that build on the nature of the gift he describes, but here are specifically linked to the impossible representability of the worker under regimes of capital, a conditional limit in labor made spectacular by globalization (coincidentally, perhaps, "spectacular" is a word often used to describe Salgado's art). Despite the obvious sentimentality and overstatement of Salgado's worker project, it marks a crucial moment in the historical ability to comprehend what the worker can mean in contemporary existence. Salgado's work ostensibly tells the story of a worker emptied out by shifts in the nature of work itself, changes profound enough for the book jacket to announce that *Workers* is "an elegy for the passing of traditional methods of labor and production." This would seem to be the desire of another eye than that which looked through the lens at its putative subjects. Salgado's collaborative introduction suggests a much more complex moment, one in which his text interrupts a normative relationship in the discourse between North and South—the former usually benefitting directly from the exploitation heaped upon the latter. The status of the visual is very much at stake in this maneuver, but so too is the question of desire: who speaks for whom, what is the nature of the transaction? I will suggest, perhaps with the sweep of Salgado's photography itself, that the "archaeology" of the "industrial age" is the impasse of worker subjectivity in an economy of visuality, one that necessitates a rethinking of worker representation in worlds that are still made by the worker. Thus, the photographic story is a discrepant discourse on rights—the right to look, the right to give, and the right to other forms of social representation.

Salgado's biography is by now well known. A man who studied economics and the global reach of capitalist expropriation, Salgado discovers photography at the age of thirty and, like the iconic W.Eugene Smith, subsequently uses it as a medium of socio-critique. The conditions of possibility, however, between social documentarians like Smith, Lewis Hine, Walker Evans or Ansell Adams, and the fractured perception of contemporary capitalism depicted or enacted in Salgado's work give to the latter a bizarre beauty caught on the barbs of an effete or highly questionable modernism (we have earlier noted such out-of-timeness in Rancière[11]). The place of each photograph in *Workers* is obsessive enough to make one wonder about the place of photography itself in visual culture. Critics of Salgado's career often talk of the sympathy and dignity his photographs evoke but they do not sufficiently analyze the specificity of this aura. We usually think of this in terms of humanist identification, and it is true that the most ardent consumers of Salgado's images are themselves consumed by liberal empathy, those for whom a human story might yet overcome the socio-economic hierarchies of interest that produce the poor, the hungry, and the overworked precisely for consumption. Yet the truth of that visualization is adequate neither to Salgado's career nor to the prescience of his visual praxis. In an interview Salgado notes that his work in photography began in July 1970, when he took snaps on a holiday with his wife, Lélia, in the Haute-Savoie region of France. He photographed her and "some of the local people. It was fantastic." Let us imagine John Berger in one of those shots.

We have already noted that Berger's strangeness in Haute- Savoie is fundamental to the narrativization he attempts. Here I want to add a further gloss on this imaginary relation for the state of the workers is always already about ways of seeing, about being in place and out of the place of sight simultaneously. We can elaborate the discussion of Berger's trilogy in the previous chapter by articulating conceptual links between Berger's work on photography and Salgado's photographs of workers. Berger's alienation provides him with a window on the plight of the peasants of the alpage and this is instructive about Salgado's introduction to and emergence in photography as a field of vision. In his book with Jean Mohr, *Another Way of Telling*, Berger expounds on an art of storytelling without an obvious story line.[12] In about 150 images he and Mohr construct a tale based on the first principle of photography: that the photo is conditioned by an absent subjectivity—it exists where the subject is not.

This truism of the separation of the moment of the photo-taking and the moment of its viewing is never innocent; indeed, the photographer must always live with the guilt the technology enables—that the subject is presented in its absence. The subject is in the photograph but not as it was in the moment of its apprehension. What is seen is the other moment of the subject's existence, an existence that itself might denote regimes of absent/presence. It is a simple point, that the photo preserves a subject in its image that is not there when it is viewed even, of course, if it is that very subject who is viewing the photo. But what interests Berger is less the separation the technology demands, but the modes of storytelling this "shock of discontinuity" (86) therefore shapes. This is a Benjaminian and modernist move, but one that is not altogether outlived by the social transformations of globalization.[13] Berger suggests that a photograph not only quotes from the world of appearances but constructs its fundamental ambiguity in the form of a "trace." Berger means this literally rather than philosophically in the Derridean sense, but the ambiguity invoked depends on the connection between the trace of the real in the photo and its philosophical correlative. Berger would agree with Derrida that the truth in photography is not the truth in painting, not least because of the status of figuration and time available to the producers of both.[14] The trace of the photo is its dependence on a technology of facticity. Obviously, there are trick photos and art photos that question the status of facts, but this is no less true of the family snapshot in its arrest of time from history. Yet the technology of the trace is something else: it is that process by which what remains affects the status of truth. It is no coincidence that, as Berger points out, the technology of the camera develops coterminously with positivism and empiricism. This nineteenth-century sociological and philosophical precision sometimes promised a utopia on the basis of facts but, ironically, the "progress" unleashed gave the lie to the facticity at stake, and all that was solid has melted into air. The trace of the photo now exists in an ambiguous relationship to the status of truth it was originally held to embrace for now, Berger intimates, it connotes an aura of subjectivity the commodification of people's labor and lives would otherwise deny.

One does not have to agree with Berger's particular argument for the social function of subjectivity (which is really about subjectivism in contrast to subjectivation) to see how the trace might open up an alternative space for the subject. If the photo does indeed free time, then it is a commentary on time's difference from history, on history's different trajectories through time. Berger's thesis suggests that the photograph therefore graphs, or traces, that which challenges the forms of simultaneity produced by capitalism's emptying out of history. What the photograph then foregrounds is its subject's complex relationship to history, which for humans is primarily a condition of memory. In short, the photo is an arena of a struggle over the function of memory. This is the place from which Salgado begins.

Several forms of memory contend in the photograph and, indeed, in the photograph's relationship to other photographs. Roland Barthes usefully suggests that "the Photograph is the advent of myself as other: a cunning dissociation of consciousness from identity."[15] This "disturbance," as he terms it, is about the advent of ownership, about the ways in which the subject becomes an object under capital. But it is also, simultaneously, about the capacity of remembrance and recognition in the revelation of the photograph. Whose memory? Is it the photographer's in choosing the subject? The subject as object within the photo? The spectator who views the photo? Or is it, more controversially, the photo in relation to other photos as part of a possible sequence? The capacity for memory in the latter is not altogether decided by the photographer's choice or the spectator's in constructing a story from the sequence. The space between the photos is an arbitration of imaging itself: it gives to the subject as object personhood by the juxtaposition of singular moments, whether or not the photos refer to the singular moments of an individual person. Photos reflect on the capacity of memory itself, and from this one is drawn to the differentiating claims of one memory to another and the significance of memory in relation to a specific material history. A photo materializes a history.

Memory, memorialization, memorial. What does Salgado remember that catalyzes the elegy he is held to produce in *Workers*? "These photographs tell the story of an era. The images offer a visual archaeology of a time that history knows as the Industrial Revolution, a time when men and women at work with their hands provided the central axis of the world" (7). Salgado's conceit here is quite pronounced for he knows that in conjuring the remembrance of what "history knows as the Industrial Revolution" he is in fact providing a history of the present, a present in which a profusion of uneven modernity exists as an integer of the profound inequalities of the world system (ironically, absolute proletarianization is greater now than at any time during the Industrial Revolution, as ever larger portions of the world population head to the cities from the countryside. The end of work, as Rifkin calls it, appears to entail an inordinate amount of it[16]). While there is no doubt that a significant part of globalization is about "information superhighways" and post-industrial immateriality, Salgado shows worlds still embroiled in the absolute necessity of manual labor, the four-fifths of the world, as he comments, who produce for the one-fifth who consume the fruits of that labor. Now class analysis tells us that this is not simply a division between "First" or developed worlds and "Third" or developing worlds (there are beggars on New York's Fifth Avenue and Mercedes on Broad Street in Lagos) but nevertheless, to foreground this labor at all constitutes a major intervention about what lives in memory as a condition of the present. Part of the difficulty of Salgado's book is that it is impossible to reconcile its substance with its thesis. If its memory is based on a "farewell to manual labor," then how are the manual laborers depicted going to transcend their conditions of manual labor when Salgado avers that "they have no way of achieving equality"? (7). How indeed, when the fact of their labor is actually what helps to drive the post-industrialism and wealth of other parts of the globe near and far? There is no need to end manual labor in those places where the human as machine is cheaper than the machine. And the "developed world" actively seeks out those conditions as a cost-effective way of preserving and expanding its own. You don't need full automation where there are no unions and lots of excess cheap labor, as many a Wal-Mart or Apple executive could explain. But the process of Salgado's story is different from its muddled thesis and here again Berger/Mohr's *Another Way of Telling* proves an important interlocutor.

Once Berger has established that photos quote from appearances rather than by literally representing them, he goes on to consider whether there might be a specific mode of narration common to the photograph. As in every mode of communication, the Other grounds the "I": it is its ontological source of selfhood. Of course, we can suspend this condition of otherness in a variety of ways, but even when we stare into the mirror we are painfully reminded that our vision of ourselves is never the vision of other people as they see us. The Other is the ground of our social being and why our "perfection" rests on the conditions we make for socialization. The expressive photograph, for Berger, is one that gives specific meaning to its otherwise ineluctable ambiguity. The length of its quotation from appearances is determined not by time, but by meaning, which is itself a function of photography's capacity for discontinuity. I will relate this below to Salgado through a discussion of Derrida on the gift and the right of inspection. Here, however, I want to broaden the terms of analysis for understanding Salgado by reference to Berger/Mohr's stunning photo-narration, "If each time."

First, as mentioned, there is no story line to the story-in-photos they present. Berger/Mohr decide not to impose a "verbal meaning" upon appearances because: "In themselves appearances are ambiguous, with multiple meanings. This is why the visual is astonishing and why memory, based upon the visual, is freer than reason" (133). What the photo series does is to present a sequence of "ambiguous appearances" featuring an old peasant woman and what may or may not be her recollections of her life. All Berger/Mohr tell us is that she was born in the Alps, was unmarried, and lived by herself. For a while she lived in Paris as a servant but later she returned to the village. She worked during the day and watched TV or knitted at night. Just to add further abstruseness to their invention, they add: "sometimes she prefers silence."

Indeed, it is the force of this silence that comes so dramatically to the photos themselves, even at those moments when the observer is invited to give voice to her memory. In a way we have met this woman in the previous chapter since she shares something of the characterological features of Berger's peasant community—the magic silence of a Lucie Chabrol is a pertinent parallel. In a perhaps less than ambiguous way, the photos themselves in *Another Way of Telling* provide a commentary on the *Into Their Labors* project, visualizing the unspoken and the unthought in the many otherwise uncertain exchanges of the trilogy. Despite the claims for ambiguity, the photos often de-emphasize the magical realism of the writing and de-mystify the lyrical otherness of narration itself—for instance, in the narrative voice of *Lilac and Flag*. Does the voice which explains silence merely eradicate it? Should the choice of silence be respected? The problem of subaltern subjectivity, for example, is not solved simply by standing in for the silences it may represent. At this level, at least, the fact of the photos already constitutes a violence of representation that sympathizes with yet re-silences the subject portrayed. And there is no suitable alibi for this "being-in-representation," however ambiguous.

Yet how would these reflections on life otherwise be presented? Berger/Mohr fight a certain impossibility in order to gauge the necessity of articulating "a lived experience." As they point out, this does not mean they "document" a life; instead, they explore its texture in all of its fabula possibilities.[17] This includes "moments and scenes which she could never have witnessed" (134). If we are never fully present with that which constitutes our being, clearly we must begin with the willing suspension of disbelief accorded fiction because whatever the lived experience, the articulation decides. All of this, point of view, articulation, presencing, and voice will have special relevance to Salgado's workers.

What is the story in the 150 photos of "If each time"? It begins with hands, the hands of a manual laborer to be sure. This is the most conventional of all synecdoches of the worker of the world(s). They are hands that make, hands that have made from the gnarled surfaces they now represent, the ragged and dirt-filled edges of their nails. These hands are knitting, a conventional sign of female dexterity but one that now signals the centrality of women's labor in globalization as a whole. Berger's fictional old women have always been essential to his art but they are also significant as the backbone of the world who labors. The black and white photos emphasize patterns, patterns of knitted wool, patterns of wood, patterns in the snow, patterns of everyday peasant existence, and, most importantly, patterns drawn onto the face by the texture of a life. Where there are no words there are always patterns which will form them. And, for those who labor, patterns in time are the first lines of experience, the grammar of an existence in labor—the texture of a gift given freely.

The hands of labor are always doing—they are uncomfortable at rest not because rest is not desired but because their motion is the kinetic process of survival. Berger/Mohr convey this not just by showing hands at work (dozens of the photos feature work in this way) but by the act of photography itself. Berger's point about the photo's relationship to time is crucial, for it is by isolating the moment of hands in motion that the imperative of their motion is depicted. Of course, the grammar I have invoked is also a product of another pattern, that of the photo selection and ordering (which is also important to understanding Salgado). Not surprisingly, some of the meanings of the narrative are produced by montage, by the juxtaposition of photos that produced a third meaning independent of their content. For instance, one photo features a Russian folk painting of a peasant woman breast feeding (144–145). The face is impassive, a fact emphasized by the general lack of perspective in the style. The disclosure of the breast is a facet of the banality of the everyday: it does not seek, for instance, the recognition of a desiring male observer (Berger's analysis of the nude in *Ways of Seeing* remains a touchstone in this regard[18]). The painting, however, is set alongside another photo, this time a close up of a standpipe with flowing water. The close-up is of the second photo of the collection, where we see that the standpipe feeds a tank for doing laundry. Is there a meaning here to which the storytellers, the peasant woman, or anyone else need adhere? On a basic level it says merely that the woman gives life as much as the water. But the nature of this life-giving affirmation must be different for the woman depicted than it is for the flowing water. The assumption of their correlation is just that, an assumption. Even what may be harmlessly elemental is still a construction, and this is why Berger is careful to emphasize the ambiguity of the project as a whole. There is always a danger that if the quotations from appearances cohere then the possible meanings of the juxtaposition can be limited to authorial intention. As Bakhtin reminds us, the monologic lives on in every utterance in which the author drowns out the voice of the other, as "hero," as subject, as possible interlocutor.[19] The montage reminds us that the third meaning is always already an authorial will as much it is the observer's projection.

But this is not cinematic montage and so, as Berger points out, any intention is not determined by expectation (what comes next) but what has been—what the conditions were that produced the moment for the photo in sequence. Here then, the ambiguity is intensified by a necessary shortfall in context. This is not memory as the peasant woman remembers it, nor even as Berger/Mohr articulates it, yet it is hard to imagine that memory could be anything else except the form of this juxtaposition of different times, of different images, of different modalities and syntaxes of experience—as quotation. Consider a later example in the narrative (176–177): on the right-hand page there is another Russian folk painting, this time of a woman in repose—again staring impassively at the observer. Mohr emphasizes that this is a photo not just through the absence of color, but by allowing the frame of the picture to enter the photo (with the top edge of its title appearing at the bottom). Here, it is the abstraction of the image that is most evident, for despite the conventions of figuration, the woman's pose is not realistic, the woman's body is stuck on its side. She is not preparing to sleep, still less rest, especially not with her shoes on and a bird perched on her left shoulder! On the left-hand page is a photo of a painting by Holbein. If the folk painting could actually adorn a peasant's house, Holbein's classic portraiture, even in facsimile, appears more abrupt. And yet, there is a similar look to the woman depicted with her two children. If anything, their demeanor is dour and inconsolable. Why has Berger, the renowned art critic, featured this in the narrative? Certainly, it does not exist to emphasize Holbein's artistry in contrast to the Russian painting, although, as with most Holbeins, there is a fascination with its quasi-metaphysical elements: the line on the woman's face suggests a face that has been cut-away to reveal the one the observer now sees. The younger of the two children looks off canvas, and the effect is to send the observer's eye in the direction of her gaze. Of course, in this example, it is to the photo *above* that of the Russian painting on the right-hand page: the hands of the peasant woman once more. Again one is confronted with the patterns of work drawn across her palms—the hands, indeed, have been worked upon by labor. Yet here is a reminder that the photo was posed, or rather the subject resists the idea of the pose that the photographer desires. Are the hands being shown to the photographer so that he might see their work-worn striations or are they raised to deny the eye the chance to see the face? The fact that the hands are in focus whereas the face obscured is not would seem to support the former rather than the latter but here I think the general point is about the status of the observer in photography alongside that of art. The photos of paintings de-emphasize the artistry of painting and accentuate instead the immediacy and ambiguity of photography. The conventions of woman as mother and object are problematized by her laboring otherwise. While the hands are themselves conventional (the synecdoche referred to above) they compel a different set of associative effects. They cannot stop objectification but they can interrogate the logic intrinsic to it.

A similar point is made elsewhere (the juxtaposition of a sculpture of trousers with a peasant farmer who is actually wearing trousers [208–209]; Millet's nude bather alongside two old Yugoslavian peasants sharing some humor [218–221], etc.) but the rhythm of the sequence is broken in other ways. There is the shock, for instance, of close ups of pig innards, or of a carcass cut in two, or of a pig hooked through the snout to a beam. One is reminded that this "shock" is how Berger draws the reader into the everyday experience of the peasant in the trilogy. All that romantic imagery about farmers raising animals is summarily displaced by the brute reality of farmers killing animals; indeed, for Berger this is part of his take on the different experience of death and spirituality in peasant existence (beliefs that we have noted he may share with Heidegger with his views on organic being). The prominence of death is also signified by somewhat bizarre imagery, sometimes humorous, sometimes macabre. There is the photo of a stuffed fox regaled in glasses, a walking stick, and panier. There is a photo taken at the same cafe which features a close-up of an eagle's mouth with a baby doll in it. But most striking of all are the images of charnel houses where the bones of the dead are piled high as the most blatant reminder of death's omniscience. If there is an enduring after-image of "In each time" it is that these photos advance an argument for a different experience of time in the peasant imaginary. Whether or not the peasant woman "J" (for John and Jean as well) can embody these time cycles of birth, death, marriage, planting, harvesting, breeding, and slaughtering is not the major issue; it is, in event, whether or not photography is an adequate expressive form for the appearance of such experience.

We have noted that Berger sees in photography a specific out-of-timeness, an effect achieved in the shock of discontinuity. Berger/Mohr demonstrate this in the fictional depiction of a peasant woman's memory. The conceit here is that all memory is discontinuous, but that it is cast against the flows of peasant time (for the most part, these are European peasants although Berger wants us to generalize from this). I would argue, however, that the lived experience Berger/Mohr quote is actually achieved more successfully not in the sequence of photos, but in their composition. Mohr's photos identify with their subjects through methods of composition. Generally, his close-ups do this more effectively by focusing on detail, the aforementioned patterns, or the play of light and dark on peasant implements or clothes. Sometimes, however, he does this in medium shots by leaving a surprising detail relatively understated (a cross on a barn door, a child appearing in what initially seemed only a cow-filled shed). Then there are Mohr's veritable "still lives": the milk churns turned upside down (160); the back of a chalet in Haute-Savoie (222–223); a pair of tree trunks blasted by snow (250); and the last photo, the entrance to a farm house in Haute-Savoie (275), a place that the old peasant woman might otherwise call home. Does memory "see" in these details? Sometimes the same image recurs but its compositional effect is altered by cropping or by reducing its size relative to an adjacent photo. This emphasizes memory as a shard, not perhaps as a pre-existent whole that photography redeems, but as a condition of being that actually allows a narrative to be told. One has to add, of course, that Berger/Mohr are not proposing a reflection on the composition of time as time; rather that the "each time" of each photo speaks to a thereness, a being-in-the-world that has for its memory a syntax of images that may or may not give substance to the subject remembering. But every step of a story, as Berger reminds us, is a step over "something not said," and each time I "read" the photos of "In each time" I am struck by their ability to question what constitutes the substance of a life. That they intimate the lived experience of a peasant woman is itself a major intervention, for how often are such lives considered worthy of sustained deliberation? Berger opines that the peasant woman of "In each time" is defined by "the way she wears the world"—a narrative "sewn" together by her experience, but also, of course, sewn together by photographers, storytellers, critics, and observers of various kinds. What are the lessons then to be carried forward as a reading or observing apparatus for Salgado's workers? Do they live similar modes of discontinuity? Do the workers he portrays now wear the world of globalization? Is the latter in fact de-natured by the "in each time-ness" of worker singularity so that the worker wears the world, but many more of them than that of globalization?

I do not believe that Berger/Mohr would have us believe that theirs is not the organizing consciousness of "In each time." This is evident not just in the selection and organization of images but in the logic they reveal. Where is the woman's desire in these photos? Who has she loved and what have her hands embraced besides the knitting needles and the plough? Such comments are never far away from a discourse of desire itself, one where the viewer would hardly be surprised by the effacement of woman as desiring subject. In the Lacanian mode, the story becomes the scene of demand and need where the demands of photography require presence or absence but at any rate an Other that might satisfy these needs. I am not saying that in the field of the Other desire simply accrues to men who, in a moment of masculinism, suspend the question of the desiring subject. I am interested, however, in whether photography itself can do anything else but reproduce the cruel conditions of such effacement when it aspires to a language of the unrepresentable. Desire is an effect of the Other but has no language that would be adequate to it because of its relationship to the unconscious—precisely to the non-said of interpersonal relations. It can be like a language, just as a photograph can be graphed for its likeness, its appearance.

Berger himself suggests that photography provides a "half language," silent connections that allow a narrative to form a field of memory. The sequence he and Mohr offers trigger a montage of attractions in which one memory is broadened and contextualized by another. The photograph is inspired by the Muse of memory to the extent that it seeks revelation in the instant: that which stands against the homogenizing drive of time. Yet by the end of the *Another Way of Telling* Berger has become less equivocal. The placement of photographs in artful discontinuity has restored them to "a living context" and "their ambiguity at last becomes true." Thus, "appearances become the language of a lived life." (289) Again, these appearances, however, are *like* a language, not a language, for surely memory cannot quite separate itself from the unconscious suppressions that provide its very possibility? The lesson of photography is not that photos quote from appearances but that photos "appear" to quote, and what appears like a language calls attention to its process of materialization. It is this process of materialization and its relationship to a desiring subject that will help articulate how workers "appear" to Salgado.

Like "In each time," Salgado's *Workers* is significant merely by representing workers who labor, for work is so consistently and insistently banished from the field of vision in contemporary cultures (places of work are envisaged, but narrative seems to work around work rather than through it). Like Berger and Mohr, Salgado is a leftist who believes that the social being of humans is the key to the most progressive form of their socialization. Like Berger, Salgado also contradicts this view in a fiercely individualistic way; for both men, their personal vision ultimately transcends (or rejects) any more conventional organized collective that might embody their leftism. For Berger this is clearly an experience of the

New Left and laborism in Britain; for Salgado it is a reflection on big government as bad or corrupt government which, while not a monopoly of Brazil, complicates Salgado's North/South identifications. Both men tend to sentimentalize and romanticize the poor and the oppressed and accusations of piety or sanctimoniousness offer their detractors the first line of attack. Yet it seems to me that if their reverence is sometimes misplaced or misguided, they have both produced bodies of work that are a resource of hope in addressing the mess of human organization: a world that feverishly produces obesity in some parts while emaciating life to the point of extinction in others; a world that rewards the greed that produces scarcity while punishing others for not indulging in the same form of progress; a world that passionately pursues longevity for humans while enthusiastically destroying an environment that might justify living longer. Their art is infused with the conscience of great human contradictions.

Unlike Berger, however, Salgado is not a theorist in any rigorous sense, not a thinker whose aesthetic articulations exist much outside the evidence of the photographs themselves. This may be considered a distinct advantage, but it has opened up his work to some fairly traditional artist bashing, especially where ideas are concerned. The absence of a more fully articulated position means that critics can zero in on the obvious, like the rather glaring contradiction between a coffee-table book of photos for $100 and the poor and penniless subjects who feature between its covers. Or they might focus on Salgado's star status and the packaging and tours that celebrate and gird such a position. The deeper questions, political and aesthetic, about the conditions of representation themselves are often passed over or, as in Julian Stallabrass' otherwise extremely insightful essay, put down to academic browbeating.[20] For Susan Sontag, however, the problem is in the pictures themselves: "their focus on the powerless, reduced to their powerlessness."[21] Parvati Nair, who has produced the first book-length study of Salgado's oeuvre, takes the position there is no correct view of a photograph, and extends this to the competing aims of argument around Salgado's work.[22] There can be no doubt that such an approach is warranted, for in her detailed exegesis of Salgado's life and work (however held back by the fact that his signature *Genesis* project was defiantly in media res at the time) Nair understands well that the sheer global ambition of Salgado's art can only intensify disputes about the form in which globality itself is imagined. Given the scale of Salgado's projects, Nair tends to read their ethical or political contradictions as inevitable:

they describe a "circle of polity," as she puts it. Whatever Salgado's laudable compassion and commitment, however, his worldliness and the world as such have their distinctions, even in their multiplicity; indeed, it is precisely in the ideology of the multiple that the foundation of globalization can be found, and to photograph with all of one's ideology can never meet such a dominant structure of worlding halfway.[23] As Salgado suggests in his preface to *Migrations* (about which I will say more below): "Globalization is presented to us as a reality, but not as a solution."[24] There is no art that can bridge this gap, for the answer to a deleterious socio-economic system must take the form of a specific politics over and above the otherwise unimpeachable largesse of polity. On the one hand, there is an undeniable imbrication of the workers, the landless, the migrants, in what constitutes the ideology accompanying Salgado's art; on the other hand, the actual challenge of each to globalization lies in the specificity of their claims and not simply in their glorious agglomeration, even if they sometimes share the same body. This is why, for instance, I argue that the more we understand the logic of the image in Salgado's work, the more we comprehend the constitutive fix of worker representation to which Salgado's *Workers* is a highly nuanced and developed rejoinder.

Where does the narrative of Salgado's work begin? At first glance, the scale of the book would seem to militate against a syntax of the image (a syntax that is *like* but not a language). What Berger/Mohr often achieve by repetition, juxtaposition, detailing, and discontinuity, Salgado seems to sacrifice in the grouping and size of his photos. The logical explanation for this emerges from their exhibition quality. Indeed, for those who are astounded by the size of the book's images, the exhibition proportions of the photos must seem nothing less than epic.[25] Each image stands by itself as an auto-referential piece that defies one to articulate it as anything else but the substance of its individual view. And yet there is a narrative—both in the sequence of images, their grouping, and in the captioning that accompanies the book in the form of a pamphlet. The latter is particularly effective because it separates word from image and allows the collection to be viewed in a variety of ways (which is where Nair's critique begins). The weakness is that the important context the pamphlet provides can remain separate, one which might usefully emphasize the art of the book or undermine its browse-me coffee table pretensions. The photos are grouped in six sections which correspond to work associated with: crops, meat production, transportation and heavy industries, mining, the oil industry, and large-scale infrastructural development. Again, if Salgado wants to capture these images before the "end of manual labor" the sheer number of examples underline that manual labor is going on in prodigious quantities wherever and whenever it is cheaper and/or not possible through automation. Every highbrow pronouncement about the end of work and the jobless future might wonder how so much of the world is so reprehensibly stuck with forms of labor that Marx would easily recognize. This is not so much a memory caught in the moment of imminent extinction, but a question about the obstinate persistence of exploitation, one that has intensified within a globalization obsessed with growth and modernization.

The large monochrome format and natural lighting suit the subject very well. On the one hand, the chiaroscuro can emphasize detail in what might otherwise be a drab place of work; on the other, the play of light can draw attention to conflicts that are barely pronounced. The latter, for instance, can define the confines of labor, the workspace that is an economic calculation and the poorly lit corners where work is expected to be done. We are not surprised by this, especially in representations of mines—and Salgado includes a poignant section on the coal mines of the Dhanbad region of Bihar, India (which, because of India's immense power needs, still has over a hundred working mines)—but we are disturbed by this sense in car factories or sugarcane fields, which equally seem to imprison their laborers. The majority of the photos are unposed which again is a useful reflection on the work process—especially where machines do not have time to stop and look (Salgado himself has argued against posed photography because "you see the photographer inside the frame rather than the subject"). Even with those photos that are posed or where the subject is aware of the camera and faces it there is little sense of intrusion. I believe this is testimony to Salgado's work habits, in particular the long time he usually spends familiarizing himself with those he would like to photograph. Salgado estimates that of the forty or so stories in *Workers*, he spent a minimum of two weeks on each one and often much longer. Such an engagement included conversations where possible and sometimes he would send prints to those he had photographed. In the factories such familiarity is uneven, since both management and labor are not prone to accept the presence of a non-worker for a long period of time, however benign his explanation might be (a worker inquiry is simultaneously about the resistance to inquiry). The worker in the motorcycle factory in Madras, India, on 150–151 carries both an air of surprise and suspicion at the presence of the photographer, and this is an entirely natural reaction from someone caught working the line.

What most of the pictures feature is action: that labor for the manual worker is kinetic and works the body. Workers are bent by labor into shapes that connote ardor. Their hands and faces are transformed by the activity—their physical being is literally made over. Photo after photo emphasizes both the skill of the worker in what she does and that this work is regimented, it is a task that must be done. Some photo stories emphasize community (the tuna fishing in Sicily, Italy, for instance) while others accentuate work is often segmented and separates worker from worker as a very condition of production (as Orvell points out, the air of nostalgia for line work is not much of a critique[26]). Like Berger/Mohr, Salgado is able to capture the patterns and textures of work and working conditions, designs that give his photography compositional solidity and documentary heft. It is Salgado's eye for this kind of detail in the workplace that creates the narrative tension in the book, between the artistic vision for composition and what that composition actually implies for the workers within it.

In a sense, photography is perfect for the representation of work because its discontinuity has a form of negative capability in connoting action and process; it is also silent, which allows for a visual attention that is often subverted by sound in the workplace itself. Indeed, in Salgado's photography silence underlines the reverence of his act and subjects; the religiosity, spirituality, and lyricism of his work builds on the fundamental soundlessness and stillness of the work as portrayed. It is as if the positive image of the photos is actually the negative of the real in the photos. Where is this moment of stillness for the worker working, and is it ever the crude equivalence of the photographer or observer who later pores over this moment? Salgado's photography confirms what is and what has been in its matter-of-factness; its silence is a comment on the tangible thereness of the image depicted. Its truth is in its furtive contemplation but this mode of reflection is a refraction of the worker's own relationship to work. The workers think more than the silence bestowed upon them and Salgado obviously knows it. It is really only in the documentaries about Salgado where this is made evident, not least because workers sometimes talk about their work, they speak.[27] If photography nevertheless can confirm this aspect, then it comes with the liability of erasing it. Yet this is not the point of photographing workers. In the silence and compositional richness of Salgado's images he wants to draw attention not to the transparency of sight in its seeing but to the abstraction of the worker's being in process. The disturbance in the field of vision is precisely the advantage of the book's grandeur, for whose vision is most likely to be destabilized by the silence of worker's desire, by their non-linguistic relationship to the act of work itself?

Just as "In each time" is contextualized by a thesis on photographic narrativity that cannot be identical to the subject of the narration, so Salgado's *Workers* strives in its form and structure to undermine the tidy impossibility that desire is silent because it has nothing to say. This is usually the point in critiques of Salgado that one begins to talk of "dignity," of "grace," of "empathy," and enduring "humanity" in his representations of labor. All of these elements are relevant and not only because Salgado has emphasized them so often himself. But I wonder whether there is a political and theoretical valence to such pronouncements exceeding the author's confirmation that this is indeed the case? Could the logic of grace or empathy for instance be part of a narrative context of desire that can never quite find a language to speak, a language of and by the Other? Before exploring this scene of the Other through Salgado's belief in the nature of the photo as gift, let us remark further on narrative sequencing and the importance of history to Salgado's project.

Like much of the labor presented, the final form for the book was collaborative, as Lélia Salgado, the project and exhibition director, details in her acknowledgments. Beyond the categories already mentioned, what other narrative meaning might emerge from the ordering of Salgado's compositions? The book begins in Brazil, appropriately, and documents the labor intensive and demonstrably arduous work of the sugarcane industry. The history of cash crops and their location, of course, is a history of colonialism and Western expansionism, of slavery and brutal subjugation—a legacy that Salgado learned about as an economist, and must have been reminded of again when he worked for the International Coffee Organization (interestingly, Salgado photographs the tea industry, rather than coffee, despite his expertise in the workings of the latter, although this shortfall has recently been remedied by Salgado's *The Scent of a Dream: Travels in the World of Coffee*).[28] What has changed these industries is not just the retreat of colonialism in their operations but the rise of agribusiness and global capitalism. Just to underline Salgado's understanding about how these First World economic relations redraw and absorb the Third it is worth quoting from Eduardo Galeano's impassioned introduction to Salgado's collection, *An Uncertain Grace*:

Salgado is a Brazilian. How many does the development of Brazil develop? The statistics show spectacular economic growth over the last three decades, particularly through the long years of military dictatorship. In 1960, however, one out of every three Brazilians was malnourished. Today, two out of every three are. There are 16 million abandoned children. Out of every ten children who die, seven are killed by hunger. Brazil is fourth in the world in food exports, fifth in area, and sixth in hunger.[29]

The international commodity markets are not interested in these statistics unless they threaten the price or circulation of a particular commodity itself. But this opening section also emphasizes that the fate of the so-called Second World was always dependent on the economic machinations of the market in the First. As Salgado's accompanying pamphlet to *Workers* points out: the Brazilian sugar market received a boost when Cuba's industry was isolated by the boycott of the USA. The Soviet Union did not save Cuba from the deprivations that accrue from the international market but replayed them; that is to say, the Cuban reliance on sugar and tobacco exports intensified its dependence on a vast range of imports just as it would have under the beneficence of American capital. Now, Cuba is continually berated by the international community for the abject poverty of its citizens as if (a) this might not have something to do with the collapse of the Soviet Union and (b) this might not be coterminous with one of the world's longest economic embargoes. Would history find the day to day toil of these laborers different now? It would be interesting for Salgado to return to Cuba. Its growth industry today is tourism, an economic necessity that marks the transition to another stage of Caribbean postcolonialism with all of its attendant precarity (and more so given the warming of Cuba/US relations and the opening to capital).

The question of history here is not a small one. Salgado's dedication to his subject, the long-term nature of his projects (*Workers* was a six-year effort), throws into relief the movement of history. Far from isolating and dehistoricizing the worker her fate is entirely enmeshed in broader and specific historical conditions that go well beyond volition. One thinks here for instance of Salgado's section on the Rwandan tea industry, shot in 1991. The Rwandan business of tea was brought to a virtual standstill by the events and aftermath of 1994 in which hundreds of thousands of Tutsis were massacred by Hutus and millions of refugees flooded in all directions. As I look at these workers I wonder not just about their working lives, but whether they survived the subsequent genocide. Berger's point about the function of photography for memory seems justified by these sequences because however much the image is out-of-time it demands a memory of its relationship to a time, or at least a history that would texture its very possibility.

This is evident again in Salgado's photographs of the Chinese bicycle industry. Having owned and ridden bicycles in China I am certainly drawn to this part of his project. But timing here is problematic. The images were taken in 1989 and one assumes it was before the Beijing Spring which culminated in the massacre of June 4. Surely a foreign journalist could not have taken these photographs later that year? In fact, Salgado claims because he is Brazilian he was not restricted in his project. Yet why would Salgado's political perspicacity have allowed him to produce this very benign view of Chinese industrial production? There is no discussion here, for instance, of the idea of autonomous unions (that featured strongly in the oft-misrepresented "democracy movement"). In addition, the focus on the bicycle industry gives a rather quaint view of the massive industrialization and technological transformations of Chinese manufacture under the Four Modernizations. Salgado's notes claim that bicycles have resolved some of China's more pressing problems with employment and transportation and have also provided the Chinese with a continuous form of exercise. This may be true, but one should add that this was always a function of economics and when Salgado returned to China for his *Migrations* project he must have noticed the major cities are inundated with cars (and traffic jams and pollution). Many people still ride bicycles but if disposable income allows Chinese will, like many people, opt for less strenuous forms of transportation. The ecological and geopolitical consequences of China's economic expansion are writing a history well into this century (which we examine in more detail in the next chapter). Meanwhile, this section of *Workers* also reminds me that captioning does not necessarily verify the truth of the image (the "bar" on 140–141 is a tea room).

The state of the workers in what is putatively a worker state is a study in its own right and it is only the scale of Salgado's project which minimizes what would otherwise be essential to an analysis of work in the world system (on this point, the fiction of Berger/Mohr's work recommends itself over the photojournalism of Salgado). The same is true of his photographs of car production in Ukraine, Russia, India, and China—for it is clear to Salgado in the second half of 1991 when these photos were taken that great changes were already occurring in the production processes at issue. The "shock therapy" of the world market long ago emptied these factories of much of their labor force. In India, that for so long pursued a non-aligned independent industrial policy, the "market" has assumed unprecedented proportions. The Hindustan Ambassador car featured, long a symbol of national independence, could not possibly compete with the Asian and European car makers now operating in India and its production was ended in 2014 (there is considerable investment in new Indian and/or joint venture car production, and Tata, of course, owns Jaguar). Again, much manual work will disappear for these workers but it is the cost of their labor that has figured most prominently in the logic of globalization.

The section on coal mining is particularly evocative of this process. It is only relatively recently that, with the full weight of transnationalism, appreciable modernization has occurred in the Indian coal industry. As Salgado's captions explain, during the British colonial period "gallery mining" was the chief mode of extraction because it minimized expensive mechanization and maximized large quantities of cheap manual labor. When the British were expelled (the notes suggest they simply "left") they abandoned an industry radically ill-equipped to utilize India's coal resources. They also bequeathed to India a rash of problems with underground fires that continue to burn even now. The mines of Dhanbad provide work for 400,000 people but Salgado wonders what the new market forces will do to them (as I have suggested, the increasing demands for energy in India has, for the time being, largely protected its coal industry; globally, coal remains the chief energy source for the production of electricity, and a major component of ecological disaster). In Britain, the coal industry was eviscerated under Thatcherism to kill what was that country's strongest pro-labor union, the National Union of Mineworkers (it survives, of course, but with a much depleted impress). Most of the mines were closed not modernized because Britain found it cheaper to import coal from non-unionized or otherwise "passive" (read, "exploitable") enclaves of the world's coal industry—including India, where Britain has invested heavily in the industry it once exploited under the mantle of colonialism. Salgado comments, "This modernization process is not without problems, among them the enormous investment needed and the drive for profits. The new goals could be achieved with the exclusive use of machines, but what would become of the hundreds of thousands of workers who depend on coal employment to stay alive?" (170).

This represents a classic fix in Salgado's narrative: on the one hand, his photographs show how people endure some horrendous working conditions in order to provide a means of subsistence; on the other hand, he genuinely fears that although further modernization would improve working conditions it would also create massive unemployment. In this case, what capitalism desires is an expansion in production more than labor contraction (the latter occurs locally rather than globally). But there is another level to this argument that has everything to do with the function of the image for Salgado and apparently has much less to do with the function of labor for capital. It would be incautious to separate out these levels of analysis in understanding the pertinent achievements of Salgado.

The caption to 270–271 reads: "Workers (women and men) under contract to truck owners load trucks with coal. A dirty and exhausting job, it is badly re-numerated with a maximum daily salary of only twenty-two rupees (U.S. $1.30). Dhanbad, Bihar State, India, 1989" (17—the same work today in the same place garners 130 rupees, or approximately $2 at contemporary exchange rates). Interestingly, the photograph does not show truck loading; indeed, there are no trucks in the image. What we do see is a stunning photograph of three workers with one in particular occupying most of the frame and its focal point. It is this image that also adorns the cover of the book both because of the worker's expression and because there can be no doubt that labor has drawn his face, which is covered in coal dust. The importance of this image for Salgado is further underlined by the description he provides in his introduction[30]:

> A miner's face is permanently covered by tarry dust, all except for a small area around his eyes where the movement of his eyelids keeps away the dust, and his mouth, which he keeps clean with his lips. He emerges from the mine transformed into a specter of black dust, only eyes and lips shining out.
>
> But his eyes also carry a burden of fatalism, a burden shared by coal miners throughout the world. He lives with the constant threat of death in the heart of the earth. And he knows that the same fate awaits his son just as it had done his father. These miners are forever tied to coal; they belong to coal. (15)

Here Salgado's comments seem to fight his caption, just as the photograph battles the sequence it punctuates. Death certainly threatens the miner but if the context is to be believed, the greater danger is unemployment which will effectively nullify the lineage of labor to which Salgado alludes (again, the greatest danger is the compulsive use of fossil fuels, whose implications signal a rather more permanent mode of unemployment). The photograph itself is monochrome photography at its best—the exposure, high contrast, and focal distance capture appropriately the otherworldliness of a worker who works in the other worlds of labor. The difference in texture and shade between his coal covered skin and his eyelids and lips is a measured study in detail. The lines of his turban only accentuate the line of shadow from which emerges his eyes, and an expression that is as intense as it is impassive. But other questions quickly begin to arise. There are coalworkers in the "developed" world (even now) so why might this image stand in for them? Could it be that the exoticism of a brown man doubly othered by black coal dust is emblematic of the worker's abstraction for the observer (or even the photographer himself)? Is this, like all attempts to figure labor in globalization, an allegory of racial capitalism?[31] If photography preserves the Other what aspect of otherness is being maintained here? What is the question in the worker's eyes and does Salgado's answer, in the form of an image, not text, articulate its import? Given our earlier comments, to what extent is the worker indeed a specter and how does this spectrality occur? And why, under global capitalism, should a worker "belong" to coal which still kills extraordinarily well (both the worker and the natural world)? If indeed we are at or close to the end of the age of coal, then what function does this image serve except to remind us that so much of modernity needed power more than life itself?

To begin to answer these questions much depends on Salgado's aesthetics as much as it does on the international division of labor, which is where the image is actually inscribed. At the center of this aesthetic is the concept of the gift. Salgado has been quite adamant that he does not take photographs, but that they are given to him as a gift of the subject photographed. He explains this in several ways:

> Of course, you're a photographer, and you take pictures. And you'll probably arrive at the same point as the guy who takes things from the outside. But now you touch it from the inside. And then the photos have another reason, another meaning. Because in the end it's not really the photographer who takes the pictures; it's the persons in front of the camera who give the photos to you. (*Rolling Stone*)

> Photography is 100% human relationships. You need to be accepted and respected by the people you photograph. I need to go to a place and learn

about it, not to judge it. If a photographer comes with the "superiority" of his culture, it will be hard for him to have the opportunity to get good pictures, because the strength of the picture depends on the connection between the photographer and the subject. There is a moment when the subject gives you the picture. (*Photography as Activism*)

[The idea is to] "create a relationship that doesn't disturb the people that you are photographing. And this relationship sometimes is so strong that it's not anymore that you are taking the pictures, it's the people in front of you that are giving the picture to you, like a gift, you know. It's the truth, it's a whole relationship." ("A Lecture")

It is not you with the camera that makes the picture. The picture is a gift. (*New York Times Magazine*)

My photographs are all a gift from the person you see. It's when you establish a relationship with them that they really have the power to offer you something. (*British Journal of Photography*)

A photo is not made. It is a gift. (*Other Americas*)[32]

There is much that is laudable about this concept and the conviction with which Salgado espouses it. He knows, for instance, that in photojournalism assignments are often parceled out as relatively brief excursions pinned to news cycles. When he was documenting the extreme famine in the Sahel in the Eighties he saw countless photographers of this kind, professionals who took moving pictures of the dead or dying but brought back only what they brought with them. Salgado wants something else, he does not want to "complete" an assignment in the accepted sense; he wants the photos to emerge out of the relationship that is established between the subjects and him. This is something of co-experiencing, an empathy that depends first of all on an outsideness, that indeed you are not the suffering person, or the coalworker from Dhanbad.[33] Your exotopy, your outsideness, however, can only produce a subject through identification, in which you "touch" the other being as a condition of your selfhood in relation to theirs. Obviously, there is a way to do this purely as a function of guilt (and I will comment further on this below) a guilt that cannot be denied because of the relative position of the photographer to his subject. But the inevitability of inequality in the relationship between photographer and subject does not in itself negate the prescience of Salgado's belief. It certainly explains a will to heroicize his subjects, again in the Bakhtinian sense, a desire to enable the subjectivity of the subject to determine the narrative beyond the authorial or pictorial "I." It also lends itself very well to forms of spiritualism which are an almost constant theme in Salgado's work and this too, is entirely relevant to the nature of the gift, to the spirit of a certain grace. If in the following discussion theory seems to weigh too heavily on Salgado's conviction it is out of a belief Salgado has discovered a central dilemma in worker representation: if you have given all what more is there to give that might deny the object that you have become for capital?

First, one must say that Salgado is wrong to describe the image he takes as a gift of the other. He is mistaken not because of the patronizing privilege that allows his pronouncement (however long he stays, he does eventually leave—a contrast here with Berger) but because it promotes a misunderstanding of the worker's relationship to the gift in exchange as image. There is a philosophical disposition to the gift that is entirely elided by Salgado's appreciable populism, and one that also challenges his materialist understanding of how workers come to be. Thus, if the Indian worker gives, the recognition of the image as gift annuls the very possibility of giving. What does this mean? Surely there can be a common sense notion of the gift that would govern the moment that Salgado describes? To recall the discussion of Berger, the meaningful experience of the photo cannot reside in the photo alone, nor in the relationship of the photographer to the subject. If we merely depend on the photographer to announce the moment of the photograph as a gift, where is the desire of the other in this process? The appearance of a gift to the photographer does not make it so, just as the perception of gold for the miners of Serra Pelada does not turn clay to precious metal. No. The force of Salgado's identification alone does not produce the gift of image in his pronouncement. And again, to utter, "this is a gift" is to cancel the status of gift in the moment of giving.

Let us consider the gift, and then work our way back to the image of the worker. The philosophical discourse on the gift is immense, particularly as it relates to anthropology and sociology—of which Marcel Mauss' *The Gift* is an obvious and influential contribution.[34] Rather than summarize this long tradition I want to use a philosopher whose idea of it is every bit as idiosyncratic as Salgado's photography; Jacques Derrida. This choice will seem anomalous, since one of the most incisive and attuned essays on Salgado's art is by Julian Stallabrass who explicitly rejects just that kind of "postmodern" thinking to which Derrida's work is (often misleadingly) attached. Indeed, it is on the nature of the gift that Stallabrass presents Salgado's work as a riposte to avatars of the postmodern condition with their "absolute respect for the discrete nature of the 'Other'" (152). Nair, by contrast, carefully situates Salgado's photography within the reflexive postmodern critique of modernity, as symptomatic of modernity's broken discourses of progress, growth, modernization, and global integration under the sign of capital. This is certainly connected to "alterity and the Global South," although theoretically and politically it might usefully be triangulated with the distinct projects of postcolonialism and post-structuralism, which are by no means simply commensurate with a postmodern episteme. Despite such caveats, Derrida here productively alters the perspective of the image at issue.

A gift is not impossible but thinking the gift certainly represents a philosophical knot in Derrida's schema. In *Given Time: 1.Counterfeit-Money*, Derrida lays out the problem quite succinctly:

> For there to be a gift, there must be no reciprocity, return, exchange, countergift, or debt. If the other *gives* me *back* or *owes* me or has to give me back what I give him or her, there will not have been a gift, whether this restitution is immediate or whether it is programmed by a complex calculation of a long-term deferral or différance.[35]

At this level Salgado's thesis appears secure for it is quite possible to imagine that in a $100 book of photography he has given nothing back to the workers. It is not a counter-gift to the extent that the workers do not receive Salgado's work in return: the status of the image as gift is secured by this patent lack of reciprocity. But I do not believe this (and not just because Salgado has in fact given photos to his subjects) and, for other reasons, neither does Derrida.

> For there to be a gift, *it is necessary* [*il faut*] that the donee not give back, amortize, reimburse, acquit himself, enter into contract, and that he never have contracted a debt. (This "it is necessary" is already the mark of a duty, a debt owed, of the duty-not-to [*le devoir de-ne-pas*]: The donee owes it *to himself* even not to give back, he *ought* not *owe* [*il a le **devoir** de ne pas **devoir***] and the donor ought not to count on restitution.) It is thus necessary, at the limit, that he not *recognize* the gift as gift. If he recognizes it *as* gift, if the gift *appears to him as such*, if the present is present to him *as present*, this simple recognition suffices to annul the gift. Why? Because it gives back, in the place, let us say, of the thing itself, a symbolic equivalent. (13—emphasis in original)

If Salgado has been given a gift he has annulled that gift by recognizing it as such, for acknowledgment itself is a form of giving back: it is a symbolic equivalent. Therefore the gift did not take place and however Salgado rationalizes the image he took as a gift it does not cancel the nature of the impossibility it represents. If the workers did provide a gift to Salgado then he is a charlatan who took his image and gave nothing back; yet if the workers provided a gift that was recognized as such then no gift was involved. This is a classic deconstructive aporia, but it is not only that; indeed, if it were only that it would remain merely a theoretical curiosity (and a fading one at that). Materialism too is full of aporias, or within Marxism constitutive antinomies, the most relevant here being the impossibility of reconciling the difference between class consciousness and proletarian being. The being of a proletarian is annulled at the very moment of its realization for it effectively destroys the class relations on which its possibility is based. Marx knew this very well as he wrote *Capital* (in which, significantly, gifts only occur among capitalists) where proletarian being is simultaneously trapped and energized by circulation and the extraction of surplus value. There is a history of the Left that tried to short-circuit this dilemma by propagating a being in advance of revolution, sometimes known through what was called "proletarian ideology." The aporia was deferred, but in the new millennium it has returned for the workers of the world who no longer have a state that lives in the name of their subjectivity (and for some never had it even then). And no amount of regressive dogma or liberal democratic handwringing will *give* back to the workers the history usurped by the assumption that the state itself was the solution to the problem of proletarian representation. Yet workers who live this contradiction are still patronized, as if images, for instance, were the key to the redistribution of wealth.

What is the use of Derrida's counter-concept of the gift to our discussion? The advent of a gift cancels its status as a gift; its appearance is a phantom, its operation, a simulacrum (14). The significance of the gift is not its appearance as an image, as a photo for Salgado, as a "specter of black dust," but as a principle of the quotation that is lived experience–a principle that, as Berger understands, must be unrepresentable. We see the worker therefore, but not the principle of the gift that allows the image to appear. This connects to the out-of-timeness of the photo discussed earlier. Interestingly, Derrida describes the moment of the gift as a "gift event" (événement de don): "something must come about or happen, in an instant, in an instant that no doubt does not belong to the economy of time" (17). Could the moment of a photo be a gift in this way, not as an object but as a modality of the photo's relationship to time?

Barthes, always sensitive to structuralist classification, distinguished between the *studium* and *punctum* of the photograph.[36] The *studium* is a kind of enthusiastic commitment to the image by the observer, a cultural identification with the subject of the photo. The *punctum*, however, interrupts this process and proceeds from the image itself: it may "prick" the conscience or may wound it more significantly. The *punctum* is often a detail, a "partial object"—"hence, to give examples of *punctum* is, in a certain fashion, to *give myself up*" (43–emphasis in original, "me livrer"). Barthes does not use "give" innocently in this phrase. He goes on to suggest that the detail perceived is "in a sense the gift, the grace of the *punctum*" (45, "le don, la grâce"). Here the gift exists for the observer in a way that it cannot exist for the photographer because the latter cannot provide the image *and* its gift as an observer (the name for this image device is perhaps the mirror, and it remains problematic). Here I am running two senses of the gift at one another: the first says that no acknowledgment of a gift as a gift by a photographer in the form of an image can in fact constitute a gift; the second says that the sense of a gift may exist for the observer in the form of a disturbing detail within the image (with the qualification that this gift is a product of the detail, not the subject of the image). There is a way to reconcile two seemingly contradictory notions of the gift in what is already a phenomenon of incommensurable proportions. This will draw attention (a punctum, indeed) to the significance of Salgado's images of workers, both in terms of subjectivity and in terms of grace or forgiveness.

Desire is unspecular—it cannot be seen as such but seeing itself can cause it. This is an oversimplified point regarding Lacan's thoughts on the gaze, particularly with respect to the Other as a function of desire. Nevertheless, the principle of the gaze allows for the idea that when one is seeing, one is also seen; or, as Lacan puts it, when I see at the same time, "I am photo-graphed."[37] Lacan invokes the photo precisely because it freezes looking out of time; the camera, at this level of generality, is the very instrument of otherness (otherness itself is a structure of modernity). And not—which is only to say that a desiring machine cannot be an object as machine. How does the gaze function in Lacan's project? Since we focus here on the worker of the world(s) Lacan's explanation is provocative:

> We are beings who are looked at, in the spectacle of the world. That which makes us consciousness, institutes us by the same token as *speculum mundi*.... The spectacle of the world, in this sense, appears to us as all-seeing.... The world is all-seeing, but it is not exhibitionistic—it does not provoke our gaze...not only does it look, *it* also *shows*.... It shows—but here, too, some form of "sliding away" of the subject is apparent. (75)

But if the gaze is outside the subject's control, even one who opens and closes a shutter, then where does it reside? The gaze emanates from the field of the Other. The object of the gaze produced is not an object per se, but closer to an *objet a*, that detachable part of the subject which floats between self and other. To the extent that the subject desires this *objet a* of the Other, Lacan suggests that the Other is the cause of desire, even though what is desired is always an imaginary object (there is nothing actually floating here except the signifier). The subject's demand is displaced but "demand constitutes the Other as already possessing the 'privilege' of satisfying needs, that is to say, the power of depriving them of that alone by which they are satisfied."[38] The reason the Other is privileged becomes evident in Lacan's subsequent comment: "This privilege of the Other thus outlines the radical form of the gift of that which the Other does not have, namely, its love" (219).

Why invoke Lacan's theorization of the gaze and gift when Salgado's understanding of the gift focuses on solidarity over separation, on exchange over appropriation? Because it troubles the logic of the image of labor if Salgado's acknowledgment of the gift effectively annuls it; it is significant if the gift in the photograph may emerge as a partial object for the observer that may or may not derive as an effect of the photographer's desire; and it surely matters if the photograph re-establishes that objectification (sans objet) of the Other through a gaze that desires a love that the Other, as worker in this instance, does not "have." The deconstructive, structuralist, and psychoanalytic correlatives here do not mix and match in any formulaic way since they all derive their premise of the gift from different theoretical models that announce their own alterity. But we need to raise the stakes on Salgado's belief because there has never been an artist who has methodically tried to represent the "workers of the world" like this, or claimed it as a gift of the same, or is one who has so persistently and dialogically negotiated the fraught relations of the global south and north as a matter of course in that endeavor. The problem is this: the image's status as gift is not the same when the subject is a starving Ethiopian in the Sahel as it is when the subject is a mineworker in Dhanbad, India (although there are comparisons—the basic problems of sustenance for the latter are also substantial); I would press the issue, however, that if Salgado's solidarity is a moral imperative that cannot but reflect on the forms of the political in our time, there is a necessity to be precise on the nature of the gift lest it confirm to those who economically exploit workers (and who may consume expensive glossy photo books or exhibitions) that this gift cancels or defers a debt that has yet to be paid, a debt that only expires, in this case, with the capital relation itself.

And thus, the second point: that Salgado is absolutely right to characterize the photo as a gift. How can this be if, for instance, he has annulled the gift by acknowledging it? Derrida's polemic is not out to cancel the idea of the gift but to underline its crucial role in understanding being and time. The out-of-timeness of the photograph does not confirm its universality (although Salgado often believes that it provides the scene for universalism) but the material possibility that a time has been given by taking it. The uncertainty of the gift connects to its complex etymology, that it can provide both pleasure and poison, and to its incongruous relationship to circulation and exchange. The gift of the photo lives out these uncertainties, and the "uncertain grace" that must accompany any ambivalent sign of death. But more than this: if the acknowledgment of the photo as gift annuls its status as gift this is only for Salgado a mark of its objective materiality. Thus, this photo before you is what was given. But he knows it was not given; the Dhanbad worker no more gave Salgado the photo than he did a bucket of coal to keep Salgado warm. And yet in an important sense he did. The convolutions of the gift in Derrida's argument point to its position not as object but as "a condition of a present given in general" (54). In English this may be easier to understand than it is in French (or Salgado's Portuguese) for a gift is a present (a gift gives a time) and its doubled nature gives a transcendental perspective on what time is to presence (presents). This not simply a conceit of deconstruction, or a witty extrapolation from that fascinating story by Baudelaire, "Counterfeit Money" that is the occasion for Derrida's philosophizing—"to look for noon at two o'clock" (55). The gift of the image is the time of work, not the photo as object acknowledged.

Consider the image of the Indian coalworker once more. He and the two workers behind him are not working at the time of the photo even though everything about their faces tells you that work has been done. Work as time is absent from the photograph. Time must always be invisible to be time (rather than its representation), but the evidence of the worker's face is irrefutable: time has been given to work, and not just any old time, but labor time. Labor time is not visible except by its effects: what it does to the body, what it does to social relations, what it does to personal welfare. The lie of labor time under capital is that it cannot be given freely, it must be acknowledged in the form of the wage as an exchange (which in itself represents the presence of time for labor). And yet, of course, the capitalist does receive a gift, for in giving the wage the capitalist does not restitute labor in full and has therefore extracted value from the present of labor, labor time. In this sense, what must be absent from the frame is the condition of its very possibility.

Labor time under capital is counterfeit: what it purports to be it is not: it annihilates what it claims to represent, time for labor. But surely a photograph of workers does not demonstrate this cruel imperative of capital for labor as relation? Is this really the unacknowledged gift of the image for Salgado—the underside or the invisible of that which was annulled? Workers are not often seen; it is a profound embarrassment to the capitalist that profit needs workers at all (automation is the ultimate humanism). But work must be done and capitalists will do their very best to make sure that their exploitation of this necessity is not rendered visible in what is done or made (hence the contrast, however anachronistic and ironic, of Salgado's photo of "the heroes of socialist production" in Chimkent, Kazakhstan, which features a long line of photographs of workers that celebrates their productivity under a mural of Lenin giving, or demanding, socialist inspiration). Thus, it is not necessarily the case that the counter-argument is to put a worker in the frame; the gift of the image is the attention to time, that work is being, has been, or will be done. The gift here is an effect of work, not necessarily its concrete image. The sign of work is its relationship to given time.

But doesn't Barthes focus on what is visible in his analysis of photography, on the actual image within the frame? Barthes is interested in the structural components of the photograph; that it conveys a message without an apparent code (and therefore it messages constantly—it is "absolutely analogical"—as Silverman reminds us, however, the relationship between the analogical and the representational in photography is not contiguous[39]). The image sits still but is constantly seeking contexts and this is the source of its rhetoric. But the gift in Barthes' critique is explicitly visual which means that it cannot be the question of time that we have drawn from Derrida. Not quite. Recall that the *punctum* itself is visual but its effect is emotive; the gift is not the image itself but the effect of the image on the observer. The *punctum* as gift in the photograph of the Indian workers is what they have kept for themselves and yet have shown. Again, this is most often described as "dignity" (by Salgado, and by many of his critics) but this projection is not the vital issue (the recognition of dignity is often an alibi for more contentious ideologies of identification). The *punctum* depends upon a more amorphous sense for detail, nebulous because it cannot guarantee a specific effect, only the principle of visual interruption or disturbance itself. Much depends then on the context that the observer provides because this disturbance cannot be interpreted in any unitary way. Our photo contains a *punctum* based on what remains for labor from the process of work. It is not necessarily that the workers' dignity is made visible but that they live on in labor. The disturbance in the field of vision here is also connected to the trace of labor and the workers' action to it. This is the dust-free area of the lips and around the eyes. What may eroticize or objectify them to the observer is also the grace of their being, what remains in excess to the process of value extraction itself. The lids and the lips deny the omnipotence of work as conditional. They are the marks not just of surviving work but signing a principle of irreducibility. We give so that we and others may live.

Derrida draws back from the psychoanalytic function of the gift because it implies exchange, but this image in particular wants us to understand the role of desire in the photographic representation of workers. We have noted that the lack of coal dust of what remains may eroticize the lips and eyes. They are the partial objects of the workers' being here. They are certainly the most blatant cause of desire that is the gaze for this photo, which perhaps explains its prominence of position and its extensive caption. But of course the gaze is returned, the eyes of the workers stare intently back at the instrument of looking. But if the eyes of the "I" desire the workers' love, is this in fact given? Do those who want to look at these photos also want the desire of those photographed? Who would want the love of a worker as a worker and for what reason? Again, the intention here is not to play down the substance of Salgado's long-term solidarity but is to emphasize the gift of the photo is not his to acknowledge. If the worker is the Other of a capitalist's existence the worker is also the Other that is the foundation of the voyeur's scopic drive. The capitalist does not seek the presence of the worker in this image but his or her manifest absence. The eyes remind capitalists that they are seeing themselves being seen, and the lips encase the organ of sound that the photo cannot speak. The eyes and the mouth are separated off as *objet a*, as signifiers of absent presence or, more precisely, present absence. The gift here is not named, the time of the worker is not detailed or described but it has been given nevertheless so that the capitalist might *be*, so indeed that the capitalist has the right to look, the right of inspection, as Derrida puts it.[40] The image of the worker, then, is a divergence for the capitalist, an image in which capitalist desire (which is primarily the desire for capital, although not only that) is displaced. Its challenge is its metonymy; its gift is that its presence lies elsewhere, in a relation that is, by definition, invisible. There could be no such thing as capitalism were its barbarism simply representable; so much is true for the posited being of the worker, whose presence must be absent in the field of vision, and especially where the worker herself is photographed (the presence elsewhere is the sign that being itself is elsewhere than in presence).

Fred Ritchin has suggested that Salgado does not work from an "intellectual analysis of the other." He continues:

> It is from a personal warmth, and an extraordinary reverence for their essential dignity. His approach at least begins, in its respectful empathy, to approximate Martin Buber's sense of the relationship between I and Thou, where the other momentarily becomes one's whole world. His point of view is also motivated by the sentimental, populist embrace of a Marxist-influenced economist. "You photograph with all your ideology" is the way Salgado has put it.[41]

On the contrary, the idea that you photograph with all your ideology is the direct product of intellectual analysis (in the documentary, *Looking Back at You*, Salgado declares again, "I take photographs with my ideology"). But Ritchin provides an interesting qualification through his reference to Buber. This concept of momentary identification from Buber is what inspires Bakhtin to elaborate exotopy, that fundamental reaching out to the other by an author or artist that is the hallmark of aesthetic activity ("It is about the other that all the stories have been composed"[42]). It is important, however, that this describes the relationship of Salgado to his subjects and not necessarily to the observer. If the otherness of the author/hero relationship (as Bakhtin puts it) were transparent to the observer then surely there would be no need for the image; there would certainly be no need for something as luxurious as the aesthetic. Whatever the empathetic co-experiencing of the photographer (which is appreciable), this cannot be identical to that of the observer of *Workers* whose "ideology" might make Salgado cringe. Is it not possible, however, that whatever the position of observers vis-à-vis work and workers, they might appreciate from Salgado's vision the extraordinary labor of manual labor (which has always disappeared in the commodity before it disappeared in post-industrialism)? Would this not encourage a broader, more empathic understanding of the contributions of labor in making the world (or making worlds, as I prefer)? Yes and no. Ritchin, and for that matter, Salgado, know that the photographer has grossly simplified the difficulties of everyday existence in the lives of the workers depicted. This is inevitable of so grand a project and in itself does not constitute a substantial criticism of it. Yet the agon of Salgado's art, however we surmise the ideology that "intends" it, is its sideward glance at those who are most likely to observe it–who, again, are highly unlikely to be the manual workers depicted on these pages. As I have suggested above, the achievement of this work is not simply the desire to photograph workers on this immense scale but the conviction that their display within this context might disrupt a certain logic of desire—a logic that has traditionally been secure in the knowledge that what it surveys it owns, what it sees are symbols of its own inheritance.

If, as Berger argues, photographs bear a special relationship to memory, whose memory is being served in Salgado's *Workers*? This is also part of the other logic, or the logic of the Other in the gaze that surveys the "beauty" of manual labor. Most critics believe that Salgado pricks the conscience (the *punctum* again) of those whose lives are guaranteed by the sweat of someone else's manual labor. Stallabrass comments:

> The book reminds its readers that every time they buy a jar of coffee, strike a match or climb into a car they are participating in the running of a global economy in which their wealth and comfort is founded upon poverty and pain among people distant and near. Through *Workers*, the golden billion may look on the grey eyes of these nameless workers upon whose shoulders they stand. (154)

Such a reading might also work for Salgado because, although he must return to himself, his exotopic experience of the workers, his reaching out to their lives, has certainly made him more aware of how the world works. I am less sure of the effect described for the "reader," for whom friendly reminders may only be the prelude to some ephemeral and diversionary act of charity. The memory at issue does touch on the question of what reminds, what remains: here the status of the gift is its revelatory sense, the grace it provides as memory.

For the observer to be reminded is to cancel the gift because this exchange ("Those poor workers") is an acknowledgement of something given. But what if the grace of the image was something not given in its reminder, not offered up in its salutary nudge that the bourgeois, the capitalist (and the academic who may be both), live off the given time of the worker? The gift provides an aporia for the narrative of the worker's image since it underlines that what is given in a visual economy of difference, what can be seen of the worker, is in itself not the challenge that worker representation represents. There is always an intention in giving, but what the workers give to Salgado is not the image itself but, "in all of his ideology," the revelation of grace in their giving. True, in the Judeo-Christian tradition, this can be a transaction, and indeed the Church has been able to accumulate much capital in this way, but the calculation in the gift from the workers does not accumulate in the same way as capital. This is the specter of the image, for the worker can give in a way that capital cannot. The grace of the worker is her sign of non-accumulation, a revelation that questions objectification in the image itself.

There is much religious iconography in Salgado's photography, whether one considers *Other Americas, Sahel: L'homme en Détresse*, or *Workers*. But the "uncertain grace," as one collection is called, is not altogether the embodiment of a religious act, a contrition if you will. Let us consider one of the most famous sequences of Salgado's photography—the project around the gold miners of Serra Pelada, Brazil. The Serra Pelada mine in the state of Pará operated from 1980 to 1986, and at times featured up to 100,000 workers (mostly would-be miners hoping to strike it rich) scrambling up and down steep, muddy slopes with sacks full of dirt. Officially, almost forty-five tons of gold were extracted, although given the lawlessness of the operation this is considered a conservative estimate. The mine has entered popular folklore and has also been the subject of documentaries, including one called *Gold Lust*, narrated by Orson Welles. A feature film, *Serra Pelada*, was released in 2013 and struggles mightily to recreate the phantasmagoria, or hell, that was life in the mine (the location today is marked only by a polluted lake).[43] The moment of Serra Pelada is the obscenity of capital writ large for workers. Gold is the necromancy of capital, the magic that aspires to give without return and yet sucks dry whatever makes a human, human. It is, after all, merely a metal. As Salgado notes, the gold rush in Brazil was a scramble of epic proportions, with recent discoveries catapulting Brazil to number six in world production. Yet, he continues, it provides barely a fraction of the repayment of interest on Brazil's foreign debts. This is something of what Baudelaire and Derrida mean by "counterfeit." Salgado shows the daily ritual at Serra Pelada: streams of men descend into an open mine each day and clamor in the mud for gold. Those who dig and carry the mud are called "mud hogs" and Salgado's panoramic photography brings this animal status into perspective. Reviewers have often described these photos as if the workers were ants but the comparison is misleading: the ant's nest is a paragon of rational design and their industry embodies this will. Even though the mine is indeed organized, its madness is, on one level, its "reminder" that humanity's claims to advancement are contradictory. Thousands of workers descend into the pit, and thousands ascend with sacks of mud across their backs. The sequence alternates between portraits of individual workers and those wide-angle representations of the mass—an uninterrupted flow of sacks spiraling upward and a line of bowed heads on their way down. There are inserted flaps in this section of the book and when opened out one sees nineteen highly detailed photos all at once. The immediacy of the aggregate is certainly a *punctum* in its own way but there are individual photos that stand out. One is of a security guard who has been pistol whipped on the workers' day off (the workers at play can also play revenge—this is also featured in the films). Gold provides specific forms of justice. Above this is the image of a one-eyed worker staring directly at the camera. Hands on hips and with pursed lips this returned look says: you judge me? In the background there is the furtive glance of another worker getting into the shot, and over the right shoulder of the worker we see a supervisor with clean clothes and a clipboard for whom the observer simply is not there. But does this worker with his muddied shirt tied into an umbilical cord really demand or provide forgiveness for the madness he lives day to day?

Perhaps it depends on which eye you look into. His right eye is accusatory and reverses your judgment, just as his t-shirt is reversed because it doesn't matter: it is a reversed world that would sit in judgment of this look. His left eye, however, is just as intent but sees nothing; in the field of the Other it is here literally the eye that can only be seen. The observer as observer can no more give sight to this eye than the observer's alms would transform the conditions of workers' existence. Symbolically, this is the eye of the gift, that which, by virtue of its sightlessness, provides a grace in excess of the visual, the image given to Salgado. But then such grace is not just a metaphor of the useless organ of inspection. It is a principle, an uncertain principle to be sure (by which I mean it is never certain as an image, and here Nair's claims for the ambivalence of the image are tangible[44]), but one that gives in the relationship of the worker to an exploiter. Grace from this perspective is a responsibility toward death, and the worker must surely assume it in order for capitalism to gracefully die. This, I would argue, is how Salgado's spiritualism throws light on his otherwise stubbornly materialist inquiry.

Of course, Salgado can be more figural about the image signifying grace. In the same sequence he includes a photograph of a mud hog who has just reached the edge of the crater. His hands clasp a wooden post which is the top of the ladder. But this, coupled with the rope around his forehead that holds the sack in place (a crown of mud for a crown of thorns) does not shy from allusion. On 312–313 the image is repeated with another worker, this time including the top rung of the ladder which crosses the beam held. Importantly, the gaze of the observer is not returned by the look of the worker. Instead, you are confronted with the principle of sacrifice and the worker's will to motivate it. Salgado takes a photograph but only the worker can take responsibility for the forgiveness and death which is its agency. In his book on Patocka and religion, *The Gift of Death*, Derrida provides a pertinent corollary:

> What is given—and this would also represent a kind of death—is not some thing, but goodness itself, a giving goodness, the act of giving or the donation of a gift. A goodness that must not only forget itself but whose source remains inaccessible to the donee. The latter receives by means of a dissymmetry of the gift that is also death, a death given, the gift of a death that arrives in one way or another. Above all it is a goodness whose inaccessibility acts as a command to the donee. It subjects its receivers, giving itself to them as goodness itself but also as the law.[45]

While one must remain circumspect on Derrida's special claims for text in this argument (and those made in *Given Time*), he nevertheless enables an understanding of the grace at issue as abstract, as a gift that does not compose itself as image, but for whom image is the possibility of registering, inscribing almost, its presence. The law here is not a religious command on the role of death but an economic one about the function of the worker in the survival of capitalism and capitalists. Of course, this is never the only relationship at issue in imaging workers but it is a paradigm of the gift that might allow for a more conflictual and active connection between the observer and observed. I do not think Salgado cares much for the guilty conscience of those who add this book to their library of looking. It is important for him, however, to convey a deeper understanding of the way a worker "wears the world," and if that means shifting such a gift to the observer as the worker's gift to him then so be it. But does he smother this sense of conflict and struggle by displacing it, or indeed by not representing it at all?

For a photographer who shoots with all of his ideology it is surprising how little conflict emerges in his representations of manual workers. This is one reason why many of those who observe his photographs see dignity and beauty where polemic might be. It is only in another photographic project collected in *Terra*, about Brazilian peasant struggles over land, that a more engaged element of his documentary art is more evident; indeed, the proceeds from *Terra* are going directly to the peasant organizations involved (this is only marked in relation to *Workers*, not to charity). Of course, Salgado does not have to be an overtly political photographer to be a politically significant photographer, as the above notes have already attempted to suggest. There is a political unconscious in his images of workers that works to challenge certain normative notions of what labor should be (including, most importantly, the place of manual labor in actually existing globalization). This right to be seen is freely given; it is a gift in excess of his desire. It is motivated in a moment of co-participation which, rather than reveal an essence of labor, labor as object, maintains a conspicuous invisibility about worker identity. There is no exchange of image for object, and that is a grace that is the sum of the relation, not necessarily a calculation of observation—how many workers are enough workers for a representation of workers of the world? Or is it the singularity of the worker that annuls such representation at the very moment worlds of labor (here, worker of the world[s] rather than workers of the world), is cognized? Is this any more possible than the conscious gift?

There are many moments of resistance in *Workers*. Some of these constitute the sideward glance of a worker questioning with her eyes (I will refer to one of these appearances below). Others are resistance rituals that are a commonplace in the workplace, and these provide a touch of humor. In the section on the French railway system a caption reads: "At the main control unit of the Acheres sorting yard, the cabin squeezed between the tracks is so narrow it is impossible to open a newspaper." Of course, the cabin is not there for reading newspapers, but the worker does it anyway, and yes, the paper is open! Similarly, at the car factory in

Ukraine we see the feet of two workers who are clearly in repose inside the car they are working on: "Rest moments are relatively short, but very frequent" the caption reads. That this occurs under communism in 1987 might say something about the role of the state vis-à-vis the workforce (if the state is seen as the boss, it is treated as the boss), but all of Salgado's ideology will not seem to let him explore that in his photos of workers under socialism.

Sometimes the sense of conflict comes through in other compositional elements. On 204–205 for instance, we see a shipbreaker in Bangladesh bent over inside a piece of metal he is working on. With the shape of the hole and his extended leg he forms a question mark. In the background are the remains of a Russian ship. Why are foreign ships broken apart here? It is a question about the international division of labor within globalization that crops up time and time again in Salgado's book: these images are not about the end of manual labor but globalization's survival by its displacement. The organization of the sections within the book can make similar points: the sequence on shipbreaking in Bangladesh follows a sequence on shipbuilding in Poland and France. Salgado has noted a particular interest in ships because they allow him "to get an idea of a world so vast, but in the end so united." Salgado's narrative features the movement by ship of raw materials to the steel furnaces, the making of steel, the making of ships from that steel, then eventually the transformation of ship's steel into knives and forks, etc., after being broken up in Bangladesh. The meaning of labor to the life of steel is also punctuated in the final section where again, in seeming contradiction to the disappearance of labor, the photos ask how does the logic of globalization proceed when premised on steel and concrete? Thus, there are several sequences on large scale infrastructural projects. Salgado includes a spectacular series of photos on the construction of the Eurotunnel, a project that employed 20,000 people and used state-of-the-art cutting equipment. Some of the Yorkshire miners involved were those who had been made redundant under Thatcherism (most of this occurred in a massive downsizing after the miner's strike of 1984–1985). In one image we see a public relations photo of jubilant workers after their cutter has burst through and completed one section of the tunnel. On one side a worker stands behind two others who hold a sign saying "Hello Mam." His arms are crossed and he stares down the cameramen. Why is he so pensive and downcast? What will the miners do when the digging is finished? Globalization here affirms its ecumene of just-in-time precarity and the pivot of reserve labor, the skilled in waiting, the idle hands before the priorities of price points and political/economic exigency. If Salgado, the former economist, refuses nostalgia about the world of work, he yet reveals the conundrum of labor power within contemporary capitalism, where ships unite the world but not necessarily those who make them, break them, and transform them. The photos themselves constitute a question mark that has not dissolved in the years since their taking: how do you frame a living antinomy?

The sequence of images that follows the series on the tunnel is similarly interrogative, for there the inequalities of the world system surface once more by stunning contrast. Immediately one turns the page from the happy (and not so happy) First World workers celebrating the completion of a massive work program you are confronted with the other reality of similar work in the "developing" world. This considers the extraordinary labor effort to build the Sandar Sarovar Dam and Rajasthan Canal in India. Whereas the surreality of the Serra Pelada gold mines is created by a sheer mass of humanity scrambling in the mud for fortune, these photos record a more basic struggle for reliable water sources. The Sandar Sarovar Dam is a controversial project that has been met with protest from environmental groups and religious communities regarding the various kinds of destruction that the artificial lake produced can cause. Again, Salgado does not show the protests partly out of the belief that the overall benefits of the project outweigh the particular criticisms made (the claim it will provide irrigation for food production over an area of 44.5 million acres). As writers like Arundhati Roy have stressed, water projects in India often foreground the "power politics" of globalization that, in the case of the Sandar Sarovar Dam, often leave local populations displaced, uncompensated and, ironically, short of water.[46] Here Salgado records how manual labor is central to the project and, in the case of the Rajasthan Canal in particular, the significance of women in its production. While women workers often feature in other parts of the book, in general the gendered division of labor is quite conventional, with women providing men with strength enough to expend at someone else's profit. If unwaged social reproduction has been central to capitalism's expansion and survival *Workers* tends to show it without problematizing it. Here, however, the labor project is a family affair (much like the early factory system) with as many people as possible being brought into the construction process. Without the hi-tech equipment available to their counterparts in Europe, the project is long term, indeed generational for those families involved. It is important to note that the images of women in these sequences raise a multiple conflict with the book's observers. The Indian workers are not just a "reminder" that labor is being done but that women, whether in traditional, religious, or modern dress, have been working all along.[47]

To some extent, answerability, as guilt, as liability to blame as Bakhtin puts it, helps to compose the force of the images. There also remains the danger that the Western gaze may displace its role in the production of labor conditions in other parts of the world. Yet again, I would argue that this gaze, if not absolutely sublated (an absolution that will take more than religious observance) is challenged in the field of the Other. The images on 382–383, 386–387, and 392–393 are typical of this. While not identical, each photograph features a Muslim woman working (carrying, digging, carrying and nurturing), but each woman's face is shielded from Salgado's Leica. On one level, one would have to account for Salgado's fascination, his desire for a look that is returned but not seen. Within conventional analysis of orientalism there is a strong tendency toward objectification here—not just once, but three times around the feminine as Asian worker. Yet this propensity seems overdetermined by other elements within the image, here in particular the act of labor itself. This apparent incongruity, a quotation on appearance, complicates the possible meanings for these images. Will the end of manual labor "free" these women, will it allow them to see themselves being seen in a non-hierarchical logic of I/Other? Does the inscrutable and unscrutinizable nature of their look ensure objectification or challenge its founding myths? Perhaps their gift is a promise yet to be articulated in the field of vision—a gift for which the photograph is not an acknowledgment but an effect of the Real as absence. The eye of labor can be photographed but cannot see; or rather can see but cannot be seen seeing. The photograph cannot supply this vision but only reflect on the necessity for the transformation of vision. And this time is given by labor.

In her comments on this sequence, Lélia Salgado points to the art of labor in the women's work that constitutes a veritable ballet in moving and placing irrigation pipes. Part of the fascination with this dance, however, is that many of the women are veiled and perform their labor with their heads and faces covered. The "givenness" of appearance is complicated here by a bar on a specific visuality. The politics of the veil exceed the frame of labor yet point to how labor is also in excess of its vision and indeed of its visual archive. Several of the women workers are photographed not only veiled but with their dowry bracelets prominently displayed.

While the captions note the women are paid less than their male counterparts for the same work, the veil and bracelets deepen the contradictions because they signal the ambivalence of power in transaction, one that extends to the moment of exchange in photography itself. Salgado sees the women in their labor and as a problematic subject of objecthood (within Islam, patriarchy, capitalism) but again, is it their work that speaks of such injustice or the look of their unseen eyes? A woman digging the canal faces Salgado's camera but her veil conceals any facial expression, indeed any obvious comment beyond the implement she carries and the labor she performs. This is not only an image of the transnational and gendered division of labor that structures the world system, but is also a comment on the logic of visuality that attends it. The "must be seen" of labor that can be objectified in the woman worker is simultaneously the "never be seen" of her subjectivity (as an individual and in all of the mediation that makes her so). Here, in the Lacanian sense, she is photo-graphed. If she gives, moreover, the photo cannot capture all of her giving and that gap here purports to take what is irreducible in her constituency, what makes the subject of labor. Like the Serra Pelada mine, it is an endeavor of labor intensity, but also of global disparity. This would suggest there will be plenty of space for manual labor in the future—again, as long as it is cheaper than "labor saving" capital equipment.

The wonder of Salgado's photography is its partial image, its partial object in the visualization of a partial subject, the worker herself. It is extraordinary that a photographer could provide a sense of the world historical experience of labor at this moment in history, but that attempt itself marks a crucial juncture in the narrative of worker being. However much one might decry the generalizations that accrue in imaging workers from different parts of the globe in a continuum of visuality (the narrative of *Workers*), one must ultimately marvel at the fractured logic of unity this provides. There is no knowledge of the everyday practices of the worker offered in toto here, but the passion is for the act of labor itself, processes that suggest that a form of unity is still at stake, even if workers as subjects remain divided from one another, and divided within themselves. The achievement of Salgado is not that these photos were taken or given, but that they ponder a task to be done. Again the photos cannot articulate this act in any formulaic way; indeed, they can only show that workers can be shown. Yet this limit points to an excess in worker representation and the forms of its globality which Salgado's photography can indicate without naming or seeing. If the workers are impossible subjects what makes them so? The answer to this question requires a revelation even greater than the evidence of sight.

In *A Specter of Hope*, the documentary assembled from a conversation in May 2000 between Berger and Salgado about the latter's *Migrations* project, an alternative vision of worker possibility emerges. Obviously, Berger is interested in the poetics of the image and, like Salgado, elaborates a deep sense of ethical responsibility. In the six years of the *Migrations* work, Berger underlines Salgado "took pictures of the face of globalization."[48] If one can certainly deduce this from the images, nothing can quite match the eloquence and seriousness of Berger's tone in the film that acknowledges a kindred spirit in capturing the great human and planetary calamities of our time. But Paul Carlin's film and its haunting soundtrack (music by Dan Jones) also "make" the photos by accentuating specific areas of the frame (via close-ups, pans, fades, and dissolves) that tend to interrupt the viewer's experience of the photograph or otherwise substitute for that relationship. It is a fascinating process in which the form of appearance appears otherwise, producing a visual precarity that at times comes close to speaking the precarity of migration itself. "This is our reality and we must assume it," says Salgado. One of the achievements of *A Specter of Hope* is not only to define globalization as a system and human process (including the migration of the peasants from the land to the city—a topos we have discussed in terms of Berger's trilogy and will continue with my critique of Jia Zhangke) but is to see imaging as an interrogative context for itself within globalization. Globalization is a "view of the world" as Berger puts it, "an opinion about man [sic] and why men [sic] are on the world." The subheadings of the documentary complicate any shorthand for globalization, since a title like "Rwanda 1994–1995" would require a much more rigorous historical sense of what conditions might catalyze a catastrophe of this scale, many of which are only obliquely the substance of its logic. There is no easy equivalence between those who flee the horrors of violence and those who migrate principally for economic well-being, even at the expense of the violence of the wage. Yet the proletarianization of the peasantry is in many ways as traumatic as the ethnic and national struggles that produce the refugee, and that structure the new world order. Together they constitute the central pivot of human movement across the planet.

Photography's place in such movement is at once contradictory. Each of Salgado's photos is a still of the dynamic, a distillation of great change

(Salgado notes that all of the photos in *Migrations* amount to a second, which is about the same for *Workers*; indeed, if we measured Salgado's entire archive—published and preserved—by shutter speed it would come to less than an hour) and throughout the documentary Berger attempts to convey the power of such immensity in the minute, in something otherwise as "brief as photos."[49] He quotes Simone Weil (a philosopher but pertinently once a worker in a Renault factory) in this regard: "There are only two services which images can offer the afflicted. One is to find the story which expresses the truth of their affliction. The second is to find the words which can give resonance through the crust of external circumstances to the cry which is always inaudible: 'Why am I being hurt?'"[50] Salgado himself qualifies any misunderstanding this might imply, for the answer to the question is not compassion for what is depicted in the image but the responsibility of sight that makes from images an active engagement, one that would diminish hurt as manifested in the frame. Speech and action from the silence of the still is how photography has always achieved its social impress, its documentary impulse, but here it is the folding of this imperative within cinematic codes that makes its meaning for Salgado explicit. True, these are still two aging white men illuminating each other but, like the hope Berger discerns in dark moments (a hope that is the light of Salgado's images), theirs is a conversation that exists beyond them, as spectral as the migrant laborer herself in the current conjuncture.

Migrations exists as a poignant bridge to the dilemmas of the global worker today, who often cannot rely on laboring locally for sustenance. Migration, obviously, is much more than this and for all the talk of a borderless world, the travails of the migrant stand as an indictment on the ways in which sovereignty and state relations are conceived. As in *Workers*, *Migrations* is more about symptoms than solutions yet both intimate how imaging refracts the conditions of thinking globality as such. For Berger/Mohr, storytelling in the images of "In each time" is about the singularity of temporality; for Salgado the impasse in narrative derives from the spatial scale of the subject. One does not find the worker by coordinating these aspects although the conversation of these images is no less profound than that witnessed between Salgado and Berger in the latter's kitchen. The dialectic of the dialogue is caught on the barbs that mark the difference between what makes their stories real and how what the image tells is not necessarily telling. But the documentaries about Salgado, including the sumptuous sweep of Juliano Ribeiro Salgado (Sebastião's son) and Wim

Wender's *The Salt of the Earth*, remind us of a further problematic in figuring labor: what if the image moves, cinematically?[51] We know that Salgado's photographs are moving, but what happens to the image of the worker in film narrative? Does the kinesis of the form crack the representational dilemmas of labor as relation? But before I elaborate on image movement as labor movement in the next chapter I wish to close here with some thoughts on the prescient limits of Salgado's photography as both more and less than the limits of photography itself, especially where labor is concerned.

Orvell believes *Workers* is caught between an ideology of progress and one of romanticism which, although a standard critique, accentuates the complex transitions of form and content in what labor might otherwise represent. Salgado is of the Left, but a Left that is, like its political subjects, transmogrified within the terms of globalization. If earlier I noted a concern for the bourgeois eyes that might eye a project and book of this proportion and quality, globalization has also reconceptualized that situatedness, that way of seeing, which is not to say the bourgeois does not exist, but that such class vision does not easily shape consumption marked by price, taste, and location. A Marxist critique of Salgado must appreciate his genuine concern for the poor and the oppressed—which comes both with his art and his economics (and "all of his ideology")—but still have deep reservations about who speaks for whom in that endeavor. Nair, much like Berger, finds it easier to shift the questions Salgado poses onto a different plane, one saturated with an ethical imperative drawn to the global south rather than from it. While not incompatible, such an emphasis circles the essence of photography more than it frames workers under the sign of globalization (this is particularly jarring with Berger since, as I have suggested, his understanding of the peasant and the proletarian shapes the ways in which narration is composed). Nair accepts on faith that *Workers* is an "archaeology" with images that "aim both to affirm the indomitable spirit of human labor and to mark the irrevocable phasing out by technology of traditional methods of production" (68). If the subject is photography, one could just as easily say *Workers* affirms the indomitable spectrality of photography and marks the irrevocable phasing out by technology of traditional methods of imaging. Neither emphasis is wrong, but it is the tension between them that constitutes Salgado's critique of globalization, if not his story of the fate of labor.

This difficulty can be accentuated by considering the photo-documentarian or photojournalist as a professional. Photographing labor over six years is itself a labor that must be sold. Few are surprised Salgado's photos of commodity production and circulation are themselves commodities that are produced and circulated, but this can lead to some extensive handwringing over the credibility of the project's stated aims. Accepting that Salgado's images are not outside the logic of exchange globalization nurtures, how is the line between resistance and complicity adjudicated? In a highly influential essay on Salgado, "Good Intentions" (the reference is to a creed of W. Eugene Smith) which first appeared in the *New Yorker* in 1991, Ingrid Sischy asserts that since the sharp professional divisions between fine art, commercial, and news photographers stand firm, Salgado is at once an anomaly.[52] The question for her is not in fact this division of labor (and how it gets paid) but what happens if such specializations are luridly combined. Sischy is clearly irked by Salgado's prominence (references to "this photographer," Bertolucci's *Sheltering Sky* [!] and descriptions of photos as "stagy" clearly intend to put Salgado in his place) and she is disturbed by the "promotional tone" of his exhibitions (in an article that is, while not promotional, originally flanked by "promotions" for coffee and teak furniture). His work is "weighty" yet "sloppy with symbolism," and even the captions are "pseudo-educational." Frustrated that Salgado is neither El Greco nor Goya (who are referenced in the text), Sischy nevertheless returns us to a key difficulty in Salgado's representational claims: "Salgado is far too busy with the compositional aspects of his pictures—and with finding the 'grace' and 'beauty' in the twisted form of his anguished subjects. And this beautification of tragedy results in pictures that ultimately reinforce our passivity toward the experience they reveal. To aestheticize tragedy is the fastest way to anaesthetize the feelings of those who are witnessing it. Beauty is a call to admiration, not to action" (92). Of course, because tragedy is simultaneously an aesthetic and a popular term for cataclysmic destruction and suffering it is a complex form of anesthesia, featuring a "terrible beauty" synonymous with modernity, caught between a living resource in Nietzsche and a dead one in Steiner. Sischy's general point is that Salgado is wrong to portray distress beautifully and, although here one may wish to cleave more closely to Kant's distinction on the sublime, or the problem of aura described by Benjamin, the idea implies Salgado inspires sentiment more than struggle, sales more than social change.[53]

In a no less polemical vein, Orvell picks up on the problem or "seduction" of beauty in Salgado's art. He agrees with the comments on the consumerist aura of Salgado's projects but pushes this further in relation to what this might mean for workers in particular. I have suggested the worker can hardly be outside the fetishistic propensities of the commodity (an attachment with all its contradictions that some workerism replays). In Salgado's photos this is underlined rather than distanced because of his insistence the pictures are given. In this exchange, as Orvell reminds us, elements of the worker's position are spoken for rather than said (although, as I have pointed out, the quality in such difference is complex even if this can make the documentaries on Salgado pertinent, for his subjects speak beyond their photos and sometimes comment on his work directly). There is a politics of silence that undoes this fix, just as any number of eyes within the frame can disrupt the axiomatic compulsions of the gaze. Similarly, the aestheticization of the worker is not simply the product of individual technical virtuosity but has a symptomatic specificity within the history of labor itself. In an earlier chapter we noted the differences between Marx's *Workers' Inquiry* and those projects that sought to emulate its spirit in the twentieth century ("The American Worker," for instance). Here the beauty that Sischy and Orvell bemoan is also a measure of the schism between the documentary realism of the inter-war years and a time of transition in which the collapse of worker regimes of truth is active in the efflorescence of globalization as also, whatever else it is, a *dispositif* of beauty.

The logic of beauty in distress, the creative destruction of beauty, cannot be separated either from Salgado's achievement or his ethics. They are not consistent but the appearance of consonance is precisely where the problem of imaging workers begins. The fact that Salgado occasionally supported his career with advertising shoots has only deepened this sense of contradiction and cynicism in and around his art. Even Nair, whose critique of Salgado is overwhelmingly positive, comes across Salgado's work for a Silk Cut cigarette campaign and is forced to ask: "How could Salgado, who in *Workers*, takes us to the tobacco fields of Cuba where men and women engage in the painstaking labor of preparing tobacco, now promote the very brand names and products of consumerism that leave such workers unrecognized?" (152–153) Given her access to the Salgados in the course of researching her book, it is interesting Nair does not pose this question directly but instead quotes the non-response given by Amazonas (the agency Sebastião formed with Lélia after he left Magnum) to Matthew Soar about this issue to the effect that Salgado does not believe it is a "good example." Soar and Orvell both excoriate Salgado for the Silk Cut collaboration (and for another with the cookpot maker Le Creuset, shot at the same time Salgado was photographing steel workers in France and a project that uses the same stylistic features).[54] Like Nair, however, they also acknowledge a degree of complicity, as critics and viewers, among the commodity relations in play. Soar believes, nevertheless, that Salgado bears a greater responsibility in the matter because his "seriousness" permits the advertiser a patina of the same regarding the status of cultural capital. Two further points need to be stressed however, and they both relate to subjectivity in objecthood.

First, the shock of the Silk Cut shoot is less about the exploitation in tobacco production (although this remains significant) and more about the suturing of an ethnographic eye. In the most stark image, Salgado uses the mudmen of Papua New Guinea to frame a screen of purple silk with cuts in it, the latter a singular subtlety of the ad campaign. Since the screen bears no relation to the mudmen's culture, the conceit rests in the juxtaposition which says, quite blatantly, the context of the shoot does not matter except as the meeting point of two brands, the cigarette and Salgado himself. For the viewer the Salgado reference is not as alarming as the self-congratulation about the conceit, which presumably the mudmen are not meant to understand. Nair argues that the masks of the mudmen accentuate levels of masking in the photograph, including those that mark the authenticity of the tribe and the one that makes the product unique. Pointedly, whatever Salgado was thinking, the photo never actually ran in the campaign because it was prohibited by the Advertising Standards Agency which said it was "offensive to ethnic minorities." Yet the mudmen cannot escape their primitivism and the lure this represents: they reappear in *Genesis*, Salgado's "love letter to the planet," as "the most striking figures of the imaginative world" and are as other worldly as the "mud hogs" of the Serra Pelada.[55]

The second point relates to the first and the construction of imaginary relations. In *Ways of Seeing*, Berger famously elaborated on the thin lines between fine art and advertising (or "publicity" as he called it).[56] Just as his thoughts on how photos narrate throw light on the appearance of labor in *Workers*, so Berger's commentary on the language of advertising remains pertinent in understanding the figure of the worker in Salgado's Le Creuset shoot. Not only does Berger make a basic point that ads must generate desire and fear (desire for the object and fear of lacking money to obtain it) but that such a way of seeing is itself a process of production (of objects, meaning, styles, differences, etc.). For the most part, the advertising of products has worked hard to efface the labor that participates in their production (this magic of the commodity is, as Marx reminds us, as old as capital); yet one wonders now when the image of the worker is untied from a politics of production whether messaging is less constrained and that the worker can increasingly sign an authenticity every bit as primitive as the mudmen in their finery (or the "mud hogs" with their gold)? In most of Salgado's worker photos the process is reversed: it is the product at the moment of purchase or consumption that is offscreen or is otherwise an abstraction. In *Ways of Seeing* (the BBC program) Berger shows both the ad in which a perfume is featured and the factory where women fill and package those bottles. The temporality of the women workers is described as "an interminable present." The difficulty of Salgado's commercial photography is not how close it comes to his art but that it refuses to engage that proximity in presence so that the reversal, while crucial, merely replicates the abstraction rather than socializing its conditions. That Salgado has remained silent on this constitutive antinomy does not necessarily diminish the power of his worker photos but tends to forestall the knowledge that attends them.

If Salgado's *Workers* is one of the great works of art of worker culture of the twentieth century it is because it speaks not just to a logic of representation but also to technological reproducibility itself (the complex cultural relations manifest in Benjamin's famous essay[57]). In a way, of course, it is precisely that Salgado's life as a "manual" worker, as an artist and as a photographer, does not calibrate with the real of *Workers*' six sections that gives one a sense of the extraordinary work of the imagination and commitment at its base. As Nair points out, Benjamin is useful to a reading of Salgado because of the former's theorization of aura as mystical, theological, and magic. Given Benjamin's debates with Adorno and the latter's alternative reading of the persistence of aura in the aesthetic, one might fashion a dialectics of seeing from a combination of the two so that here the worker is imaged at the point the real and reproducibility are engaged. Yet it is one thing to note the confluence of the elite and everyday in photography, as if aura is simply a problem of technological composition, commodity aesthetics if you will; it is another matter to make workers the scene of this contradiction and this adds another critical caveat to the politics of the gift. As labor continues to change and is changed by globalization, manual labor appears to persist offscreen. Salgado's greatest gift is the one he shows being denied, the chance to compose labor in its difference from the composition given to it.

Notes

1. The most comprehensive analysis of Salgado's career to date is Parvati Nair, *A Different Light: The Photography of Sebastião Salgado*. Durham, NC: Duke University Press, 2012 (Nair 2012). The present critique is more selective but will connect several Salgado projects to my central concern. See, for instance, Sebastião Salgado, *Africa*. Cologne: Taschen, 2007 (Salgado 2007); *The Children*. New York: Aperture, 2000 (Salgado 2000); *Sahel: The End of the Road*. Berkeley: University of California Press, 2004 (Salgado 2004); and *An Uncertain Grace*. New York: Aperture, 1990 (Salgado 1990).
2. Sebastião Salgado, *Workers: An Archaeology of the Industrial Age*. New York: Phaidon, 1993 (Salgado 1993b). I had hoped to include several examples of Salgado's project in this text but licensing issues precluded that desire. Fortunately, Salgado's work can be found all over the internet and some in particular, like http://thephotographersgallery.org.uk/sebastiaosalgado, feature the very photos to which I refer in this chapter. To purchase such prints, the site reminds us that prices start at £4,500 + vat. The documentaries discussed below also feature Salgado's photography. The question of the price of worker representation sits close to the following discussion.
3. Miles Orvell, "Documentary and the Seductions of Beauty: Salgado's Workers" in *After the Machine*, Orvell (ed.) Jackson, MI: University Press of Mississippi, 1995: 98 (Orvell 1995).
4. For a historical critique of modernity in this regard, see Jonathan Crary, *Techniques of the Observer: On Vision and Modernity in the Nineteenth Century*. Cambridge, MA: MIT Press, 1992 (Crary 1992).
5. Sebastião Salgado, *Sebastião Salgado: Other Americas*. With Claude Nori, Gonzalo Ballester, and Alan Riding. New York: Aperture, 2015: xv (Salgado 2015a). Originally published in 1986, this project is surprisingly lacking in context which further problematizes what is given in its images.
6. Da in Heidegger's Da-sein is not quite "there" and especially so with Being. Here I am interested in "thereness" as a tangent to the real rather than its pure expression, somewhere between being in its ontology, and factual existence, the ontic. As Derrida acknowledges, much of Marx's invocation of the specter concerns the ghostly presence of the commodity and, to some extent, communism (the famous opening of the Manifesto). The point here would not be to overlay such critique in terms of the worker (there is little solace, politically or culturally, in worker haunting) but to think of this around the problem of cultural presence and meaning, a genealogy not just "after" worker states but coterminous with capitalist subjectification. See Jacques Derrida, *Specters of Marx*. Trans. Peggy Kamuf. New York: Routledge, 1993 (Derrida 1993).

7. See, M.M. Bakhtin, *Art and Answerability: Early Philosophical Essays*. Ed. Michael Holquist and Vadim Liapunov, trans. Vadim Liapunov. Austin: University of Texas Press, 1990 (Bakhtin 1990); and *Toward a Philosophy of the Act*. Ed. Michael Holquist and Vadim Liapunov, trans. Vadim Liapunov. Austin: University of Texas Press, 1993 (Bakhtin 1993).
8. John Berger and Jean Mohr, *Another Way of Telling*. London: Writers and Readers, 1982: 113.
9. See Kaja Silverman, *The Miracle of Analogy, or, The History of Photography*. Palo Alto: Stanford University Press, 2015 (Silverman 2015). While here I do not argue that the worker is analogous to labor in Salgado's photographs, there is a provocation in its meaning for historicity and temporality.
10. *The Spectre of Hope*. Dir. Paul Carlin. Netherlands: Minerva Picture Company, 2002.
11. I have earlier suggested Rancière makes a virtue of such out-of-timeness. There is truth to the temporal discrepancy of the proletarian in this regard, so that the worker can more easily appear with the vanishing of the worker state. The "workers of the world" is a shibboleth for capitalism; whether the fragment within fragmentation (the worker of the world[s]) is a greater threat is less the issue than the political and cultural possibilities it provides.
12. John Berger and Jean Mohr, *Another Way of Telling*. London: Writers and Readers, 1982 (Berger and Mohr 1982).
13. I refer here principally to Benjamin's use of shock in the title essay of Walter Benjamin, *The Work of Art in the Age of Its Technological Reproducibility, and Other Writings on Media*. Eds., Michael W. Jennings, Brigid Doherty, and Thomas Y. Levin, trans. Edmund Jephcott, Rodney Livingstone, Howard Eiland et al. Cambridge, MA: Harvard University Press, 2008 (Benjamin 2008).
14. See Jacques Derrida, *The Truth in Painting*. Trans. Geoff Bennington and Ian McLeod. Chicago, IL: University of Chicago Press, 1987 (Derrida 1987). For his part, Derrida is less sure the problem pivots on the question of technological reproducibility, although even the "simulacra of fetishes" (179) owes something to the automatons of modernity.
15. Roland Barthes, *Camera Lucida*. Trans. Richard Howard. New York: Hill and Wang, 1982: 12 (Barthes 1982).
16. See Jeremy Rifkin, *The End of Work: The Decline of the Global Labor Force and the Dawn of the Post-Market Era*. New York: Putnam, 1995. Obviously, a key point is the intensification of automation but the "end" and "decline" described is not disconnected from the fate of the worker state (which had promised just this kind of transformation).
17. I mean this in the sense of story over ingenuities of plot, or what the Formalists might refer to as device. The Bakhtin Circle, for instance, thought fabula possibilities might slip the stranglehold of Formalist

aesthetics. See, P.N. Medvedev, *The Formal Method in Literary Scholarship: A Critical Introduction to Sociological Poetics.* Trans. Albert J.Wehrle. Cambridge, MA: Harvard University Press, 1985 (Medvedev 1985).
18. John Berger et al., *Ways of Seeing.* London: Penguin, 1972 (Berger et al., 1972).
19. See M.M. Bakhtin, "Author and Hero in Aesthetic Activity" in *Art and Answerability: Early Philosophical Essays,* Michael Holquist and Vadim Liapunov (eds.), Vadim Liapunov (trans.). Austin: University of Texas Press, 1990 (Bakhtin 1990). Bakhtin's essays at this time were tinged with not a little Neo-Kantianism but are a useful aesthetic counterweight to the psychoanalytic divisions also active in representation.
20. Julian Stallabrass, "Sebastião Salgado and Fine Art Photojournalism," *New Left Review* 223 (1997): 131–162 (Stallabrass 1997).
21. Susan Sontag, *Regarding the Pain of Others.* New York: Picador, 2003: 62 (Sontag 2003).
22. Parvati Nair, *A Different Light: The Photography of Sebastião Salgado.* Durham, NC: Duke University Press, 2012 (Nair 2012).
23. This is not an argument against multiplicity, but the ways in which it has been reified within globalization. Shifting the "s" from worker to world is one way to mark and defamiliarize the actual homogeneity often at stake.
24. Sebastião Salgado, *Migrations: Humanity in Transition.* New York: Aperture, 2000 (Salgado 2000).
25. My comments here focus on the books rather than the exhibitions, although the links between the worker on the coffee table and in the museum says a great deal about the political unconscious of globalization, where every sign of critique is just another commodity event. The experience of scale is also significant. Having recently seen Salgado's "Genesis" exhibit in Berlin I am reminded that the logic of the worker monument in the "Workers" tour intimates a complex process of objectification and disavowal facilitated not just by place but by the massive proportions of some of the photos. Whereas commodity fetishism works against the origins of art, scale appears to conjure a discrepant aura in labor, despite the fact Salgado himself is often read to occupy this position.
26. Orvell, "Documentary and the Seductions of Beauty," 105.
27. See, for instance, *Looking Back at You.* Dir. Snell, Andrew. BBC. 1993. The "Workers" project is prominent in this documentary because it so proximate to its production. There is an intimacy in the film that is more obtuse in *Workers.* Salgado, for instance, is shot working on his photographs in juxtaposition with workers he is photographing. Sugar workers speak directly to the camera. Steel workers engage in conversation with Salgado and he gives them prints, sometimes of themselves. Workers are named. While all of this seems to detract from the status of the photo as art, it serves

as a commentary on the limits of labor in culture as a dialectic of representational codes. The examples I detail in this book are therefore not meant to be definitive in any way but attempt to be demonstrable, of key antinomies in the cultural representation of labor.
28. Sebastião Salgado, *The Scent of a Dream: Travels in the World of Coffee*. New York: Abrams, 2015 (Salgado 2015b). Work has the smell of coffee, as well as vinegar. My reading of Salgado's contribution here will be part of another project. For my previous work on coffee, see Peter Hitchcock, *Imaginary States: Studies in Cultural Transnationalism*. Urbana/Champaign: University of Illinois Press, 2003 (Hitchcock 2003).
29. Eduardo, "Salgado, Seventeen Times" in *An Uncertain Grace* Sebastião Salgado (ed.) New York: Aperture, 1990 (Eduardo 1990).
30. It is also important for Aperture and is available in a limited edition on their website for $10,000.
31. There are ways in which Salgado's project is a surrogate for the collective impulse of the *Communist Manifesto*, the exhortation for workers of all countries to unite. Yet it could just as well be interpreted as a displacement for such unity when it comes to the racial coding of capitalism from its inception. Salgado displays the racial differentiation of workers without necessarily addressing the logic of this differentiation in labor's role for capital. For a longue durée on this and formations of Black radicalism see, Cedric J. Robinson, *Black Marxism: The Making of the Black Radical Tradition*. Chapel Hill: University of North Carolina Press, 1983 (Robinson 1983).
32. See, in order, Jonathan Cott, "Sebastião Salgado's Visionary Light," *Rolling Stone* 619 (December 12, 1991) (Cott 1991); Michelle Bogre, *Photography as Activism: Images for Social Change*. Burlington, MA: Focal Press, 2012: 64 (Bogre 2012); Sebastião Salgado, "A Lecture," Ed. Stephen Perloff. *The Photo Review* 16 (Fall 1993): 10 (Salgado 1993a); Matthew L. Wald, "Sebastião Salgado: The Eye of the Photojournalist," *New York Times Magazine*, June 9, 1991 (Wald 1991); Amanda Hopkinson, "Interview with Salgado," *British Journal of Photography* 6762(29) (March 1990): 12 (Hopkinson 1990); and, Salgado, *Sebastião Salgado*, xv.
33. Outsideness or exotopy (Russian "vnenakhodimost") is borrowed from Bakhtin although I tend to push against his particular interpretation, however useful. For more on the concept, see my "Women, Men, and Exotopy: On the Politics of Scale In Nuruddin Farah's *Maps*" in *Masculinities in African Literary and Cultural Contexts*, Helen Nabasuta Mugambi and Tuzyline Jita Allan (eds.) Boulder: Lynne Reinner, 2010 (Hitchcock 2010); "Exotopy and Feminist Critique" in *Bakhtin: Carnival and Other Subjects*, David Shepherd (ed.) Amsterdam: Rodopi Press, 1993 (Hitchcock 1993b); and, most pertinently, *Dialogics of the Oppressed*. Minneapolis: University of Minnesota Press, 1993 (Hitchcock 1993a).

34. Marcel Mauss, *The Gift*. Trans. W. D. Halls. New York: W.W. Norton, 2000 (Mauss 2000). The influence of Mauss' text on all subsequent theorizations on the topic from its original publication in 1925 cannot be overestimated. The question of how gifts build (or deracinate) human relations is a primary subtext of this reading of Salgado on labor in culture.
35. Jacques Derrida, *Given Time: 1. Counterfeit Money*. Trans. Peggy Kamuf. Chicago: University of Chicago Press, 1994:12 (Derrida 1994).
36. Roland Barthes, *Camera Lucida*. Trans. Richard Howard. New York: Hill and Wang, 1982: 25–28 (Barthes 1982).
37. Jacques Lacan, *Four Fundamental Concepts of Psychoanalysis*. Trans. Alan Sheridan. New York: Norton, 1998: 106 (Lacan 1998).
38. Jacques Lacan, *Écrits: A Selection*. Trans. Alan Sheridan. New York: Routledge, 2001: 219 (Lacan 2001).
39. Silverman usefully points out that there are other possibilities here, one signaled by Benjamin's essay "Little History of Photography" in which Benjamin suggests that the photograph may seek its look in the future, a look that is both redemptive and accentuates a condition of impossibility in the photograph's present. See, Kaja Silverman, *The Miracle of Analogy, or, The History of Photography—Part One*. Palo Alto: Stanford University Press, 2015 (Silverman 2015); and Walter Benjamin, "Little History of Photography" in *Selected Writings Volume Two, 1927–1934*, Michael W. Jennings (ed.) Cambridge, MA: Harvard University Press, 1999 (Benjamin 1999). Such ideas will later inform and consolidate Benjamin's reading of history.
40. Jacques Derrida, *Right of Inspection*. New York: Monacelli Press, 1998 (Derrida 1998). Derrida's collaboration with Marie-Françoise Plissart, a leading Belgian photographer, is an extended rumination on the right to look, droit de regards, which connects to many of his other thoughts on observation and the observed. Does the worker selfie seize this right and effectively cancel the problem of the gift in exchange where capitalism is concerned? Certainly self-expression and self-representation problematize some of the contradictions I have laid out so far. Who is photographing and to what end remain paramount in the "rights" arrayed, but I am attempting to think of this in terms of a structural logic of visualization between labor and capital where certain rights are overdetermined.
41. Fred Ritchin, "The Lyric Documentarian" in *An Uncertain Grace*, Sebastião Salgado (ed.) New York: Aperture, 1990: 147 (Ritchin 1990).
42. M.M. Bakhtin, *Art and Answerability: Early Philosophical Essays*. Ed. Michael Holquist and Vadim Liapunov, trans. Vadim Liapunov. Austin: University of Texas Press, 1990: 111 (Bakhtin 1990).
43. *Gold Lust*. Dir. Neil Hollander. Adventure Film Productions, 1985; and *Serra Pelada*. Dir. Heitor Dhalia. Paranoid, 2013 (Pelada 2013).

44. Parvati Nair, *A Different Light: The Photography of Sebastião Salgado.* Durham, NC: Duke University Press, 2012: 229–247 (Nair 2012).
45. Jacques Derrida, *The Gift of Death.* Trans. David Wills. Chicago: University of Chicago Press, 1997: 41 (Derrida 1997).
46. See Arundhati Roy, *Power Politics.* Cambridge, MA: South End Press, 2001 (Roy 2001).
47. This has been noted earlier in the book but bears special relevance to Salgado. If indeed culture facilitates an understanding of worlds of labor and the worker in her singularity, it also comes to terms with the offscreen presence of women's role in the production and reproduction of the social. To a certain degree globalization has depended on this continuing marginalization of the margin, or accumulation by dispossession, and it remains a primary arena in which, for instance, neoliberalism can be opposed. As Silvia Federici puts it: "Reproductive work is undoubtedly not the only form of labor where the question of what we give to capital and 'what we give to our own' is posed." But the nature of that "gift" is, as she notes, "a ground zero for revolutionary practice." This gift must also be problematized in the worker's image. See, Silvia Federici, *Revolution at Point Zero.* New York: PM Press, 2012 (Federici 2012).
48. *The Spectre of Hope.* Dir. Paul Carlin. Minerva Picture Company, Netherlands, 2002.
49. I borrow from the title of John Berger, *And Our Faces, My Heart, as Brief as Photos.* New York: Pantheon, 1984 (Berger 1984). Berger notes, "The visible brings the world to us" but that "the visible with its space also takes the world away from us" (50). In examining this dialectic in terms of labor the unity of the world itself is made strange.
50. Simone Weil, "Human Personality" in *Simone Weil: An Anthology*, Sian Miles (ed. & intro.). New York: Grove Press, 2000: 67 (Weil 2000).
51. *The Salt of the Earth.* Dir. Juliano Ribeiro Salgado and Wim Wenders. Sony, 2014.
52. See Ingrid Sischy, "Good Intentions," *New Yorker*, September 9, 1991: 89–95 (Sischy 1991). Reprinted in Liz Heron and Val Williams, eds., *Illuminations: Women Writing on Photography from the 1850s to the Present.* London: Tauris, 1996: 272–282 (Heron and Williams 1996).
53. Although in many ways Sischy replays a critique of art and the market from the early days of modernism she also underlines that merely accepting its doxa, as postmodernism is wont to do, seriously underestimates the contradictions in the challenge of Salgado's representational claims. Even an offhand comment, "since when did being a Brazilian qualify someone as the voice of Africa or Asia?" (95) goes to the heart of the cultural representation of labor as "workers of the world." No single example, by any author, artist, or director, can possibly stand in unproblematically for workers or the world

as such. The point, however, is not to cede the grounds of representation themselves to the cultural logic of globalization, which has no problem voicing any part of the world as its reflection. Salgado does not speak for Africa or Asia (still less Brazil) but to the world as a representational impasse. True, he is not a passive medium in his art but if there is a symbolic function in his representations of global labor it is not as a metonym for its meaning, or as some abstruse ventriloquist for all workers in their difference. It rests, rather, in addressing labor mimesis as both more and less than the reality of copied appearances. It is against the certitude of globalization's world that Salgado's photos are arrayed.

54. See, Matthew Soar, "The Advertising Photography of Richard Avedon and Sebastião Salgado" in *Image Ethics in the Digital Age*, Larry Gross, John Stuart Katz, and Jay Ruby (eds.) Minneapolis: University of Minnesota Press, 2003: 269–294 (Soar 2003); and Orvell, "Documentary and the Seductions of Beauty."
55. Sebastião Salgado, *Genesis*. New York: Taschen, 2013. Caption to 208: 8 (Salgado 2013).
56. John Berger et al., (1972) *Ways of Seeing*.
57. Benjamin, *The Work of Art in the Age of Its Technological Reproducibility*. One of the questions that Salgado's worker project poses is whether Benjamin's critique is itself "reproducible" in the twenty-first century.

CHAPTER 6

The Paradox of Moving Labor: Workers in the Films of Jia Zhangke

However one sets about an inquiry of worker representation in culture, the difference of work, worker, labor and capital inexorably undoes or undermines individual cultural claims. Salgado's photographs might accentuate how Muslim women played a significant role in constructing the Rajasthan Canal in India, but this cannot possibly stand in for women's labor in general, Muslim labor, Indian labor, and all of the moving contradictions between capital and labor as relations in such specificity. If the earlier chapters on theory look at several vital symptoms in linking the worker to the world (or worlds of labor as I would have it), the case studies complicate rather than carry the burden of cultural exegesis. The point is not to provide a neat typology for the study of labor in culture, but is to elaborate a lexicon of labor that might more fruitfully address the meaning of the worker for what we think of as globalization. Shifting the scale of worker understanding to the world tends either to intensify abstractions of labor or else facilitates summary assessments that, after all, the workers of the world are "so nineteenth century," or at best a phantasm of the twentieth century before the collapse of the Socialist Bloc. Pluralizing the world is a different scale again that, if it does not categorically refuse the dialectical impulses of totality, nevertheless emphasizes the ambivalence of the worker (as subject, as a ground for contemporary capitalism) and is a way to come to terms with constitutive contradictions in histories of cultural representation that lead to the present. Despite the immensity of the project, Salgado's *Workers* does not "unify the workers of the world on paper," as he puts it, yet that is not a failure of imagination but a provocation about the necessity of imagination in challenging what globalization (and its various attempts at worldliness) has become. Berger's emphasis on intimacy and locality, the intense circumstantiality of the small world, is a different approach to the same problem—an extended reflection on the structural antinomies of the world system as such, one that places a bar on a kind of Auerbachian mimetic faculty commensurate with reading worlds of workers in cultural expression. But what if the scale of apprehension is both proximate and global simultaneously? Would this permit labor in culture to appear as at once globalization's effect and the cause of its disambiguation as a properly planetary project? Rather than unify around a set of economic compulsions, could the worker of the world(s) offer the parameters of a different logic of integration, one in which the platitudes and homilies of a "one world" thesis are dissolved before a socialization freed from the universalities of the capital/labor nexus?

This chapter extends the dialogue with these concerns while focusing on a key component of globalization as currently articulated; namely the intense modernization of China since the inauguration of the Four Modernizations program by Deng Xiaoping in 1978.[1] Again, however, one is forced to confront the very particular circumstances of this compressed modernity in which a state and party once committed to an alternative to capitalist globalization have proved to be a robust combination in making such globalization come true. Chinese workers are as differentiated as workers in other parts of the world, but their massive proletarianization in the last quarter century poses a question to globalization in a way that is pivotal to a working knowledge of worker knowledge in general: does this transformation signal a worldly integration of a different kind than what has been given to the worker in her name, one in which work is not just a rational means to an end, but a means to an end of the banalization of work itself?

Part of this project is not to resuscitate long dead ideologies or propagate nostalgia, in true postmodern style, for a worker state that has not been; rather, I have been trying to elaborate the ways in which the worker subjects our aesthetic categories, including that of the subject itself, to a dissembling critique—one that, if it cannot simply undo a mode of production that is now our first not even second nature, offers alternative imaginaries which would indeed necessitate social transformation. Just as there are material reasons why the workers of the world will not unite, so there are imaginative demands that presage and pivot on precisely this perceived impossibility. This might be read in the spirit of Spivak's "finding feminist readings."[2] To rephrase the quote she takes from Derrida's *Glas*: "when it comes to the worker, it is a marriage of a limitation with an opportunity." How might cinema meet this dialectical challenge in the cultural representation of labor?

If, for instance, we understand the worker under capital as a condition of modernity as such, cinema is part of the cultural production of that effulgence: it is its expression, not its sublation. One recalls the prescient film by the Lumière brothers', "Workers leaving the Lumière factory" (*La Sortie de l'Usine Lumière à Lyon* [1895]) which, in any of its three versions, sutures labor to a specific logic of visuality (the fractured symbolic of the film will reappear below). As we have noted, when Marx theorizes the value of labor, the great unseen of capital as relation, he asks us to visualize its substance in the form of its dialectical impasse—"put out of sight" he says, the product's physical qualities and see instead what cannot be viewed, "human labor in the abstract."[3] Yet, we could argue, the critique of capitalism begins in this desire to make us see (what the workers are doing, what they are doing around work), and cinema traces the movement of labor in its abstraction by enacting such capacity from the Lumières' film onward. Anachronism, at this level, is about the techné of the sensorium; whether indeed our sight is the measure of the mode of production we have created. One could argue "out-of-timeness" is seeing's genealogy so that "perspectivo," for instance, is the Quattrocento's vision of spatial relations to come, the immanent geometry of globality (a world or "globalizability" according to Raphael perhaps). In brief, capital makes labor the central vanishing point of modernity, the arché of its composition, the absence that must make its architecture stand. This is not simply a comment on the structure of our built environment (a house, an apartment, a room does not "appear" by itself) but a story about the imbrication of political economy with what Marx referred to as the "formation of the five senses."[4] The wonder of cinema is its elaboration of that narrative, and its making and unmaking of work in the Lumière's sense of sight derived from their "Cinematographe." While Méliès, who attended the Lumière's first demonstration of their instrument, would invent the dissolve, labor as relation is the always already dissolved and the worker remains only in her representation, the figure for what cannot but must be seen. If the dialectical image is, according to Walter Benjamin, an awakening,[5] the revelation in its moment springs from the movement in which it congeals, a congelation that here I explore as the paradox of moving labor.

Chinese modernity is the quintessence of moving labor. Since the Seventies, moving labor is both a literal and a symbolic substance of capitalization in the Peoples' Republic. On the one hand, it represents a massive migration in human history, the proletarianization of hundreds of millions of Chinese peasants, the *dagong*,[6] who have moved to urban areas and have created over 600 new cities into the bargain (and, in the Foxconn factories of Shenzen, a large proportion of Apple's stock value).[7] In the Eighties migrant labor in China was sometimes referred to as "waidiren" (outsiders) and those working to rebuild Beijing in the image of Hong Kong, Taibei, Seoul, or Singapore first had to build their own houses (the construction companies "lent" them the bricks for their makeshift dormitories, but often with no cement so they kept the walls low and virtually windowless). But on the other hand, the out-of-timeness of moving labor created deep cultural correlatives and disjunctions, serious questions about whether the state of the worker in the putative worker state had an active cultural presence in the new old China (new in its difference from Maoism, old in its willingness to unleash labor power as it had since even before the fall of the Qing in 1911). This is a history much too expansive for the current analysis which will focus only on its meaning for Chinese cinema and Jia Zhangke's ongoing contribution to it.[8] I have four modest claims that together constitute a way of seeing about a way of seeing the worker.

First, the worker appears in her movement, but since the focus on this labor is classically the scene of its critique (in fiction film examples might include *Metropolis, Modern Times, Saturday Night and Sunday Morning, Blue Collar, Norma Rae, Blind Shaft*, etc.) the problem of representation is broached allegorically or metaphorically. In the Chinese context, this movement is figured into migration itself (the work of moving as displacement, a doubled displacement): work is situated and modernity is the drawing of the worker to it. It is a paradoxical movement to immobility (a situatedness overdetermined by the place of the factory in circuits of capital, for instance). Second, in the compressed modernity of creative destruction, Jia often visualizes the destruction (the term "chai" for demolition appears all over the place in *Still Life* as the local town is prepared for sacrifice to the Three Gorges Dam) and complicates the creativity. Not only do we register characters' individual dissemblance to the destruction and aphanisis they are invoked to perform (marked in *The World, Still Life, 24 City*, and *A Touch of Sin*, but not outside the narration of *Unknown Pleasures* and *Platform* too[9]) but that film form itself is precisely Jia's contradictory disarticulation of what modernity hath wrought. Third, and following on from this, whatever the fictions of labor (and we must play on the material variations of the term), we have stressed that labor is difficult to fictionalize and in part, Chinese cinema documents this shortfall, this constitutive gap in what "makes" the People's Republic. Here the impact of the New Documentary Movement on Jia's art cannot be overemphasized: it is a kind of archive in silence, the continuing unspoken of the '49 revolution.[10] But fourth, Jia has learned from Bresson's "cinematography" that cinema is at its purest even in its impurities when it is polemically obtuse and, while nothing in Jia's oeuvre is as stripped down and opaque as Bresson's films (which are a sort of Catholic obscurantism riddled by predestination), it can be argued that in moving labor Jia has discovered his own sense of "cinematographic film": "where expression is obtained by relations of images and sounds, and not by mimicry done with gestures and intonations of voice (whether actors' or non-actors'). One that does not analyze or explain. That re-composes."[11] In recomposing moving labor, Jia asks not what will become of the Chinese worker under capitalism (he is, after all, much more of a humanist than a socialist) but what remains for cinema if this story cannot be told?

Born in Fenyang, Shanxi, in 1970 Jia was a *child* of the Cultural Revolution but not a *student* of it, in the way we associate this with Scar Literature, or particularly the Fifth Generation of Chinese filmmakers, directors like Zhang Yimou and Chen Kaige. Raised less in the turmoil of the Red Guards and more in the trauma of modernization itself, Jia's understanding of revolutionary change is not ideological but always interrogative—a questioning that provides his filmmaking with a creative edge immediately discernible among transnational art-house fare. He is not an urban filmmaker in the way we think of Zhang Yuan or other prominent directors of the so-called Sixth Generation (this designation is basically effete since, while the aura of the Beijing Film Academy remains, the regional studio system that coalesced in the PRC under Mao has disappeared in a rush of niche marketing, trend cycles, and, most importantly, privatization). Jia has described himself as a "migrant-worker director" (minggong daoyan), which has particular relevance given the movement of labor in contemporary China. As critics like Wang Xiaodong and Zhang Xudong have argued, the core of Jia's films is "the not urban" and "the not quite countryside," the *xiancheng,* or "the county city"—these are not small by standards elsewhere but are sharply different from the modern Chinese megalopolis like Shanghai, Beijing, or Chongqing, municipalities that have swallowed county cities by rapid expansion.[12] Zhang suggests a *xiancheng* like Fenyang or Datong is an appropriate space to explore the mix and decay of socialist modernity with the entrepreneurial maelstrom of the Reform era. Part of the interest in Jia's films emerges from recomposition in decomposition, a process of imaging that, far from endorsing Dengist homilies about getting rich and privatizing everything, implies it is a peculiar kind of entropy, one that fragments families, communities, cultural and political discourses, and of course the frame in ways that reward their affective embrace with passionate detachment, ironizing, and arid humor. Whereas a Fifth Generation director might address history in order not to have to handle correctly the contradictions of the people in the *present*, Jia revels in the inside/out of present emptiness, perceiving a narrative that eerily reenacts the recent past of socialism by excluding the worker in her name, even as she becomes more visible and more proximate. Mao believed that the countryside surrounds the city (a point about empowering the peasant); modernization means the peasant is in the city as labor power and assiduously dissolves provincialism. To this extent the *xiancheng* is the dialectical space of Chinese modernity, where all that is solid not only melts into air but pollutes it, rendering the modern itself glamorously unlivable, a kind of carbon nightmare. It is a place where the past is easily torn down but is not cleared away; where quickly poured concrete never seems to set; where new roads abruptly stop or turn to dust; where bridges are half built pending further funds; where speculation builds new towns of residential tower blocks that stand empty; where everyone seems to run their own stall or kiosk but have lots of things nobody wants to buy (an improvement on the state stores that had few things to sell that nobody could afford); where people live in the dormitories of closed factories and forget to even fantasize about work; where the corruption of the cadre has been replaced by the corruption of the manager (often the same person); where the tannoy that announced production quotas or empty slogans of proletarian esteem now reminds denizens to play the lottery or to drink local baijiu; where noise itself is the new narrative and pop songs are the cherished respite from it.

Xiancheng allows Jia to blur the lines between country and city the way his films mash up documentary and fiction, but obviously this works for his Fenyang/Datong films in a manner that does not line up easily with *The World, Still Life, 24 City, Useless*, and *A Touch of Sin*. Jia's familiarity with the *xiancheng* Weltanschauung means the camera is visually at ease while the cinematography itself is kinetic. Even if this might be a phase more than a signature, the space of *xiancheng* permits a kind of tracing of the worker rather than a more fully embodied picture and this is fascinating for more than perhaps Zhang allows. In fact, Jia is not only addressing the spatial problematic in which a vast movement of labor will become precipitate but also some poignant and provocative existential knots in the temporality of Chinese modernity. This does not mean Jia offers any kind of treatise either on Chinese time or the worker as such, but these exist as composites that reveal Jia's importance in another register.

Time becomes involuted as space is fragmented and commoditized. Rather than the Fifth Generation's contrasts of sumptuous historical allegories and the blank spaces of peasant abstraction (*Raise the Red Lantern* and *Yellow Earth*), Jia frames the present in its own detritus, in its own instant decay, a palimpsest of productive inertia and idle potentiality. The immateriality of labor exists not simply in its individuation or characterization, but precisely in its lived contradictions, the materialization of surplus as non-labor, as "hanging out," as petty crime, as pretending to be employed, as hawking bootleg dvds (including, humorously, those of Jia's films[13]), and as waiting (the keyword of post-industrialism in Philip Levine's elegiac "What work is"[14]). Involution is the emptying out of work's intimacy: there is only the time for making money, or for worshiping its symbolic form. In *Unknown Pleasures* money hangs over all sense of activity. The film (strictly speaking, DV, but Jia plays between the media, as *Mountains May Depart* plays with aspect ratio—it's about an appropriate language of transition), makes way for money's cloying omnipresence. As one character, a sage of worn-out slogans, puts it: "Art sets the stage. Let the economy perform on it." This is the time of debates over the WTO. "The WTO is just a money thing" says one character to another as they watch a cartoon "Monkey King" on television. When this deep vein of Chinese culture is opened one can only laugh at the everyday: "The monkey king doesn't give a shit about the WTO" the conversation concludes. Xiao Ji's father gets a US dollar and there is humorous speculation about its value: "You're rich, an American dollar" (Dollar will appear as a fully fledged character in *Mountains May Depart*). This dollar is thought to be worth a thousand yuan (at that time it would have been closer to eight) but it principally exists as a fetish of China's new internationalism (as one character humorously puts it, "international trade means buying rabbits and selling them to the Ukraine"). The temporal collapse is marked by the shadow of suffocating stasis. People want to get out (Bin Bin's girlfriend does, by going to business school in Beijing) but caught between the dying of the *danwei* system (communities organized as socialist "units") and the ministrations of the free market, Datong and Fenyang seem to be running in place. One can only breathe the present through connivance, corruption and cunning, for what can labor sell if not itself? Critics often refer to Jia's hometown trilogy, *Xiaowu, Platform*, and *Unknown Pleasures* as paeans to wandering or disaffected youth (this is hardly surprising since this is in part Jia's upbringing and experience of living in Taiyuan). Equally remarkable, however, is the inspiration and aspiration in play that Jia works off, mixing found sound, pop songs (reproduced through poor or over amplified speakers), common fads and expressions, with long takes, natural light, and silence. If this is a world of irony rather than outright cynicism it seems to emphasize persistence over blanket transformation. This is one way to read the difference and the concept of difference between postmodernism and postsocialism: it is much harder to let go when style is not its own reward.

The Chinese title for *Unknown Pleasures* is *Ren Xiao Yao* from a song by Richie Ren. A loose translation would be "roam free" or "let's roam free" or "unconstrained" (not quite consonant with the darker reference to Joy Division's album title in the English version, although the children of Thatcherism might be equally wan in their seclusion. "Unknown Pleasures" was probably suggested by Jia's cinematographer and close collaborator, Yu Lik-wai—who directed his own film called *Love will tear us apart*). The other reference for the title comes from Zhuang Zi's "xiaoyao" or philosophy of carefree wandering (Xiao Ji's girlfriend, Qiao Qiao, invokes this connection during their rendezvous in a hotel). Again, the narrative tension in the film is not just between the stylistic poses of the young characters and their outlook ("there's no fucking future" says one), but in the difference between DV's carefree versatility (and economies of scale) and the broken time capsule it represents. Indeed, the antinomy at work, its visual dissonance, might best be described as *dereliction*. Jia is less interested in dereliction as a moral flaw (although in truth it could be read into his critique of youthful aimlessness as much as it can be into the moral universe of the Party under actually existing capitalism) but as a visual quandary: how can so much socio-economic dynamism produce so much wasting, so much leaving, so much abandonment? How can this picture be moved rather than simply documented, captured? Much of the answer seems to be in Jia's own inventiveness. He is not just riffing on Italian neo-realism (deigning to be de Sica of *Bicycle Thief*, etc.) or close-reading Bresson (the film *Xiao Wu* is often referred to as *Pickpocket*), or emulating the long take of Ozu or Hou Hsiao-hsien—although like many students at the Beijing Film Academy, he has made copious use of its archives and Beijing's less official resources—but instead he is trying to find a grammar adequate to their contemporaneousness when so much of current Chinese vicissitudes are rendered off-screen. Put another way, if Maoism posed the impossible template for the model worker in Lei Feng, what is the visual economy of the worker within compressed modernity? The model worker is mentioned in *Xiao Wu*, whose lead character exists as its embodied ironization. In the opening sequence Xiao Wu takes a bus ride. While we are offered a close up of a Mao talisman hanging from the rearview mirror (cab and bus drivers often carried such tchotchke for good luck well into the Nineties, some with captions like "We miss you Chairman Mao"), Xiao Wu helps himself to a wallet. If the cadres "serve the people" by stealing from them why not cut out the middleman and have the people rob each other? In *Unknown Pleasures*, Bin Bin and Xiao Ji spontaneously decide to rob a bank (earlier the coffee shop scene from *Pulp Fiction* has been referenced) but their idea of using a fake bomb vest goes horribly wrong. Bin Bin is arrested and accused of a capital crime while Xiao Ji escapes on a motorbike only to be marooned in a storm when it breaks down. This still leaves room for moral approbation of course, but I think the dereliction is manifest both in their relatively unreflective hopelessness and in the wasted or wasting landscape against which they are cast and effectively immobilized. If the social safety nets have been shredded by economic margin calls (in the film a hospitalization now means cash up front) then taking care of oneself has not been structurally or sufficiently overdetermined. In the move from Lei Feng to *Leviathan* the question of a social contract has been rendered obtuse.

    The palimpsest postsocialism represents is not visually unique but Jia presses its implications from multiple perspectives as a work, if not worker, in progress. From the early films, *Platform* (*Zhantai* 2000) does this most insistently not because it wants to explain worker discourse but because it fathoms its disorientation among or within the actual existence of people for whom Chinese history has urged a problematic incredulity. *Platform* opens with a model play, and the viewer is positioned some way back in the audience (an effect rendered real as found footage and enhanced by including crowd conversation, coughs, etc., on the soundtrack). At one point the drama features taking the train to Shaoshan, Mao's birthplace, and Jia's composition here, frame within frame, underlines a performance out of time (in the present, not its present). Rancière argues that viewing Godard's *La Chinoise* is like "watching Marxism." Indeed, he suggests,

"Godard puts 'cinema' between two Marxisms—Marxism as the matter of representation, and Marxism as the principle of representation."[15] In *Platform* we see Chinese cinema between two realisms. Jason McGrath offers these are the postsocialist realism of independent cinema of the late Eighties and Nineties and the realism of the international art house circuit that came to prominence in the late Nineties and early Noughties.[16] It is true Jia's films exude an easy dialogism for film festivals; that is, this is not only what China is like, but it is the China you like to see (unlike those Mainland populist films, the New Year's genre, or endless iterations of *wuxia*, and certainly eons away from any Party line productions). While certainly not Marxist, however, Jia's opening to *Platform* accentuates a realism snared chiefly between the Party alliance with the peasantry (the very reason for the traveling song and dance troupe) and a realism that fathoms the equally vexed relationship of the intellectual to the state (often expressed through the identification of a character as an "art worker"). Two Marxisms are implied, Maoism and a kind of Chinese New Leftism (not coincidentally, Wang Hui, a significant figure within the latter, is a big Jia fan[17]). The tension is historicized between the present and its present (a gifting of the present we have explored earlier), but Jia continues to doubt whether its resolution is epitomized by the bright new Chinese megacity (Shanghai, for instance, the subject of his 2010 documentary, *I Wish I Knew* that, rather than celebrate Shanghai's contemporary billionaire gloss, follows filmmakers like Antonioni filming Shanghai's much more contestable history). Obviously, one cannot choose a Maoist realism, although elements of its Marxism remain interventional in China as a punctum of the present; instead, Jia stages this irresolution of the real through a stripped down transitionality. In the dialectics of such (sur)realism the problem of the worker in postsocialism is not suspended, but articulated in her fading or dissipating presence, or "falling." Falling labor is both a process of desubjectivation in China's cinematic unconscious and a rather literal index of contemporary Chinese labor strife (for instance, in the Foxconn suicides). Falling labor represents another paradox: the peasant moving to the city is simultaneously the worker standing up but also the worker immiserated by strict calculations of uneven accumulation. The antinomy of realism is, therefore, also about whether the "is" of Chinese modernity can be visualized otherwise. It is not about reality as metaphor so much as realism as absence, including the absenting of the worker, or work itself as absence. Here then I would also differentiate the realist question from simply replaying elements of *xianchang*, or "on the scene" realism often cited by younger filmmakers, including Jia (it is a break from the past but elides its dialogue with it). This is not Jia's only dilemma (and certainly not his alone), but we should be careful not to displace it immediately onto Jia's foreign appearances or the strength of applause at the New York Film Festival.

After the opening sequence in *Platform* we're back on the bus, which is as underlit as everything else in China at that time (around the beginning of the Four Modernizations the 25 W bulb was de rigeur). It is a long scene but finally the acting troupe leader tells the driver, "Let's move." Quickly we understand that while the troupe may be moving it will struggle hard to keep up with the script of the new economy. *Platform*, from a song about waiting on a platform, tells the story of the reform period from the view of those being taught to respect its passionate if sometimes bizarre logic. Jia is fairly certain China is not on the train to Shaoshan, although the post in postsocialism is simultaneously an end and an engagement (Jia's aesthetic often hinges on the question, "what is it, exactly, we are after?"). Paradoxically, freed from the workerism of authentic proletarian subjecthood, Jia's films are therefore positioned as authentic by Western observers, but Jia appears less disposed to appease this metonymic authenticity. It is not just the slide between realism and the real he resists but the idea the answer to authoritarian populism lies only in art-house fare for the transnational set. Perhaps this leads to indecision, and not just by the acting troupe trying to find its elsewhere, its new vocation. Sometimes, indeed, *Platform* merely extends as if, for all its transience, duration itself might be some form of safe haven from the ravages of the market. Although it was edited down from its original three plus hours in length it still feels ponderous in sections, particularly where slow pans only seem to be exploring the possibilities of 35 mm equipment (it was Jia's first film in this format).

What holds the narrative together is the change experienced by the ensemble as revolutionary songs are replaced by the personalized pop of Deng Lijun, and Mao suits are switched for bell bottoms and other items trickling up from the special economic zones in southern China (the measure of change also extends to how bodies move, how the troupe dances, for instance). To emphasize the disjunct time I have mentioned, they sing "We'll meet again in twenty years—when city and village alike will glow." This, of course, marks the time of *Platform*'s release and the viewer is immediately asked to measure the reality of such claims. Time passing is also accentuated by shooting much of the exterior shots in Pingyao, a rare example of the classic four-walled town that has rapidly become a living museum, but whose architecture is exquisitely photogenic and allows for all kinds of interesting perspectivo. By 1984 the troupe votes for privatization (as if echoing the mantra of neoliberal globalization): the commune divests itself of its artistic commitments by selling the troupe to itself and the performers become independent contractors (this notion, along with that of the stakeholder, are significant pillars in neoliberal rationality). Earlier in the narrative, Cui Mingliang's mother had argued with him about making dinner to which he responds, "If you won't feed me, the Party will." Privatization ends that relationship of the state to the artist as worker and facilitates, for instance, the emergence of the privately funded independent film, of which *Platform* is a stunning example.

But what of other workers? Wenying's brother, Sanming (Mingliang's cousin), will work in the mines but will not earn enough to keep Wenying in school (the fees are another sign of privatization). The mother explains they are almost starving in the village and if they cannot raise money to support Wenying she will have to come home to work (besides the mine, the other choice is the field). While investment is being discussed a man arrives to install electricity and one is reminded that although this is the mid-Eighties electrification in the countryside still represented an event. Mingliang accompanies Sanming to sign up for work at a privately owned strip mine. Because Sanming is illiterate (he, like other workers, signs with his fingerprint) Mingliang reads the contract out to him: "Life and death are matters of fate. I am willing to work in Gao's mine. Management accepts no blame for accidents. In cases of death or accident the mine offers 500 yuan compensation to families [about 45 dollars at the time]. Daily wage is 10 yuan [a dollar and change]." As the manager says, "We're not responsible for anything." When the troupe leaves the area Sanming runs after their trailer. He gives 5 yuan to Mingliang. "Give this to Wenying" he says, "tell her never to come back to this place." It is a poignant scene that comes halfway through the film and pivots on the new social and economic relations of modernization. It is worth remembering that China's transformation is primarily coal-powered (and is one of the reasons for the abysmal air quality in many of its cities—the other being the advent of the private automobile). While Jia's critique never reaches the level of Li Yang's in *Blind Shaft* (although *A Touch of Sin* comes close, about which more below), it is clear modernity also means the super-exploitation of miners for whom the Dengist exhortation "to get rich is glorious" must seem as stupefying as Mao's "educated youth re-educated by the peasants."

Jia keeps these sharp experiential shifts close to home, not just to Fenyang but to his sense of their meaning for art. This is not only registered in the joy of dancing to popular music but in the ways the troupe has to adapt to the market (there is a particularly comic scene where they believe they are auditioning for a local official but it turns out he is just a friend hanging out in his office). In general Jia resists the lure of direct cause and effect in his storytelling and allows the references to build and overlap more spontaneously in mixed temporalities. The repeated shots of entering Fenyang remind the viewer that despite their wandering, many of the characters seem inexorably sucked back into *xiancheng* life. And if labor itself moves, it is primarily in circles. Yet the films themselves have been made in part because of Jia's departure and in his subsequent features and documentaries he delves deeper into the substance of that dynamic.

Beginning with *The World* (*Shijie*, 2004), Jia officially submitted his projects for government approval; this is not selling out exactly but represents another level of "realism." *The World* meets the globalization of the PRC head on in the form of a phantasm it projects to its people. The story, such as it is, is set at World Park in Beijing where one can tour major landmarks of human endeavor, in miniature (some of the filming was done at Window of the World in Shenzhen, which is similar in design and decay).[18] Here involution is scalar in a process of simultaneous dis- and de-orientation. Riffing on global Disneyfication ("it's a small world") World Park provides a local tour of the Earth for those who cannot afford transnational travel (a parked plane emphasizes this affect). It is a phantasmagoria of desire and global integration. If the workers of the world cannot unite, perhaps in *The World* they might? Jia's film suggests cultural workers can perform integration but that the very idea is hamstrung by the everyday for which theme parks themselves are respite. Jia constantly plays with the surreal contradictions of capitalist integration for the Chinese. As the film title is announced, an old worker collecting trash moves across the screen with the Eiffel Tower and global city architecture as background. It is a planet of slums image, a lived relation for the dagong surrounding China's mirror glass cities.

But how do the Shanxi characters get to Beijing? Simple, says one, "I bought a ticket." If the state had actively encouraged immobility in the early stages of modernization, now it wants workers to move, and quickly. Although residency, with variations on the old hukou permit, still restrict where you can live (subject to donations for local officials), the government needs its labor pool strategically fluid, especially with something as labor intensive as infrastructural expansion or export-driven industries. For instance, as the USA struggles to create a commuter rail in the Northeast that would average greater than 43 miles an hour, the Chinese, with 300,000 laborers, built 1,200 miles of high-speed line from Beijing to Shanghai in four years and cut the travel time to 5 hours. The maglev train from Pudong to downtown Shanghai has a top speed twice that of the Acela in the USA (which because of a paucity of high-speed track, rarely ever reaches it). True, in the shift from "serve the people" to "serve business" migrant labor does not have the money or time to save money or time which constitutes an immobility all of its own. Jia's film is not about this founding contradiction of China's emergence but, just as young couples flock to World Park to image a transnational honeymoon they cannot take, so Jia foregrounds a sense of this disparity by reversing modernity's symbolic and questioning what makes worldliness as such. When a character notes, "I see the world every day without leaving Beijing" one appreciates the pun or trope as a new ideology of differentiation: be happy with this stasis, or would you prefer Fenyang? Of course, this is one of the contemporary meanings of mediatization: the problem of labor immobility is dissolved by Wi-Fi connectivity which is now the electronic version of World Park's simulacra. After a spat with her boyfriend (Taisheng, who is a guard at the park and a conduit for other Shanxi dagong), Tao then takes a bus through Beijing. Just as she passes in front of Mao's famous visage in Tiananmen Square her cell phone rings and Jia renders the bus in animation. The text on the phone reads, "How far can you go?" At first the animation seems as tacky as the park. It is an easy cinematic trick, but then perhaps that is the point. Kinesis is convenience by degrees and the real question is who creates it and for whom? Again, Jia is in no way nostalgic for China's socialism (or the peremptory and dismissive "let's be poor together") but even with the convenience of state approval he questions the logic of convenience, the counterpoint in the dialectic of dereliction. "Paris in a Beijing suburb," a caption announces. What is all this movement for?

Taisheng takes Tao to see a friend he has helped out at the building site where he now works. He notes "Little Sister" now speaks Putonghua rather than his dialect. Little Sister comments, "We're from everywhere in China so we speak Putonghua" (there are Russian migrant workers at the World who try to use English in this way—one, Anna, will eventually become a prostitute). Not long after, "Little Sister" is gravely injured at the building site when a cable breaks—he had been working a day and night shift back to back (he dies in hospital). It is worth noting the death payment to his parents is significantly more than 500 yuan, but perhaps this is because it comes from the Fenyang boys in Beijing like Taisheng, rather than from the construction company itself. *The World*'s social commentary is largely muted, but while this permits greater emphasis on visual style, including the sometimes literal flights of fantasy provided by animation (a punctum for illusion and reality evident in other Jia films), it tends to foreground the weakness of a more conventional romance narrative. The latter leads Jia's denouement to a dead end, again somewhat literally. Taisheng and Tao are found gassed to death. Their bodies are laid out, the screen fades to black and in a voiceover we hear them whisper, "Are we dead? No. This is just the beginning." In this moment the film's wish-fulfillment seems to mesh with that of the park itself, "You give us a day, we'll show you the world."

There are two further provocations in *The World* that address Jia's confrontation with the meaning of Chinese modernity. First, by bringing migrant labor from Fenyang to Beijing Jia underlines the limits of *xiancheng* are not overcome merely by movement and that outsideness is mediated by economic logic as much as if not more than geographic location. One might think of this in terms of the vigorously contested concept of the people. "Renmin," the state or essentially Maoist notion of the people, is banalized and held in deep suspicion. "Putongren" connotes something of ordinary people, while "xiaorenwu," or small folk, might still allow for the difference in dialect of the peasantry. The "below" are filmed but this is not filming from below in the sense Jia's own ordinariness is overdetermined by the structures of China's film industry and the conditions of global image circuits. Nevertheless, Jia intimates the reproduction of migrant outsideness precisely because of their ambivalent relationship to state notions of people. This obviously extends to the problem of the worker ("gongren"). What was central in communist China was actually marginalized in terms of labor power. Yet what is visualized by Jia as marginalized in Chinese modernity is actually central to modernization itself. This is not the key to moving labor or Jia's depiction of it but it does set the terms for the some of the visual quandaries Jia's creativity seeks to undo.

Second, however, the World Park cannot bear the weight of its own worldliness. Its concept is wedded to an immobility that is increasingly economically and technologically transgressed. Part of this is indicated in Jia's film through the enlightened networking of walkie-talkies and mobile phones, but obviously the Internet and the expansion of an urban middle class (who can fly all over the place) has dented the allure of an actual world in miniature. Indeed, the park is quite run down now—many of the tiny reproductions (including Red Square, with its Lenin Mausoleum) are crumbling, the gardens are unkempt, and the airplane now doubles as a dorm for some of the workers (the security guards on horseback and "flight attendants" are long gone if they were ever there in the first place). World Park, like many other parts of Beijing, is haunted by the specter of creative destruction and near instant redevelopment. Perhaps this makes it still more a crucible of kitsch in Benjamin's sense: "the last mask of the banal... to take in the energies of an outlived world of things."[19] Significantly, World Park has been overwritten by the full force of globalization and the effulgence of an intricately networked transnational worldliness exemplified most obviously by the opening of Shanghai Disneyland in 2016. One ride in particular, "Soarin' Over the Horizon," captures the inverted aura of experiencing the world by having you glide across a digital reality, drone like in its ability to detail from afar. Now you only have to give four minutes to see the world (it's an even smaller world than Disney's most famous ride). There is still the Eiffel Tower, the Pyramids, and the Taj Mahal, but no more reminders of the Twin Towers, and certainly no Lenin! With an entrance fee ten times that of the decrepit World Park, Shanghai's world of Disney may be beyond the dagong, including those who make up its workforce of 10,000. China's new urban bourgeoisie will no doubt compensate for this discrepancy.

The temporal problem of uneven development in daily life is often assuaged by a discourse of efficiency. *Still Life* (*Sanxia Haoren*—"the good people of the Three Gorges"), an HD DV drama shot against the building of the Three Gorges Dam, is Jia's return to this disjunction in time, one for which long takes, long shots, slow pans, and silence appear apposite if not integral to a critique of economic rationality, the steady thrumming of capital on the move. These compositional elements are perhaps more important than the narrative thread, which hinges on the journey from Fenyang to Fengjie, two people (unconnected) from Fenyang searching for their spouses in Fengjie, a town in the process of demolition as the dam reservoir rises. True, the themes once more include the trials of labor migration and the ways in which it can divide families and decimate communities; the pitfalls of modernization which in this case means an alternative to coal power produces the displacement of over a million people (the government admits that over the years its dam projects have displaced over 23 million people); and the production of a kind of cultural disinterestedness whereby the region's inspiration to classical art, its importance to archaeology, and its complex biodiversity is seen to be irrelevant before the prestige that comes with building one of the world's largest man-made structures (sixty-six Eiffel Towers just in steel alone, to recall another monument in World Park).

Critics of *Still Life* appear impatient with its companion piece *Dong* (shot simultaneously), a documentary on the artist Liu Xiaodong, but while *Dong* is cinematically loose it offers an interesting resonance. First, it contains footage that Jia uses in *Still Life*, including some shots of its non-professional lead actor, Han Sanming, Jia's cousin, who has appeared in other films (he is the miner in *Platform* and the construction worker in *The World*, for instance). In case this question of realism is not registered, the documentary also includes a sequence of Liu painting Sanming in character (Jia shoots a painter painting an amateur actor playing a worker, a representational drama of labor in culture). While it is clear Jia and Liu do not agree on the status of realism here besides being "on the scene" (Liu insists on the importance of site painting), whatever the social and aesthetic truth of the worker, it does not exist in the fact of representation itself. This is not a Lukacsian moment, especially given Jia's resistance to realism as state objectivity, but it does accentuate a theoretical, political, and aesthetic interrogation of realism's remains and what remains for realism beyond recapitulating various discourses on worker subjectivity. Once more, it would be incorrect to ascribe this project to Jia, but it seems to me it speaks to the schism between the worker of actual existence and the actual existence of the worker that no state, and particularly not the PRC, has been able to resolve. One of the reasons Zizek is read in China is because much of his dialectical daring comes out of a direct experience of the failure of actually existing socialism. Zizek's argument is that much of the socialist experiment of the twentieth century was born from capitalism rather than its subsumption and it failed not because it was not socialist enough but because it was not capitalist enough (thinking the negative and the counterintuitive is writ particularly large in Zizekian dialectics). Maoist modernization, like the Great Leap Forward or the Cultural Revolution, failed spectacularly and sometimes horrifically because it disengaged from the processes that were its very possibility. Socialist realism is problematized by this genealogy and, although it would be unfair to classify Liu as a capitalist realist, he has nevertheless been commoditized in this way so that, coincidentally, his Three Gorges painting broke the record for the sale of a work by a living Chinese artist at that time ($2.75 million).

The second echo between *Dong* and *Still Life* follows from the first which is to say if Jia explores the space between fact and fiction it is because he wants to document beyond the official story and deeply appreciates any unofficial attempt to do this. The more relevant companion piece to *Still Life* is Li Yifan and Yan Yu's documentary, *Before the Flood* from 2005 which Jia had judged in competition earlier that year.[20] Its intimate, naturalistic, and direct style spoke to the quotidian critique of Jia's art. Yet Jia's signature tone, his "red detachment" (a term I use to describe his difference from socialist realism as well as a kind of resolute distancing through stillness—another version of this will appear below) pervades *Still Life*. In its intricate formal structure and its matter of fact magic (a touch of science fiction), Jia's film does not aestheticize its subject but asks whether art can be as determined as Sanming and Shen Hong even as progress dismantles alternative viability (a slogan among the ruins says "Try Hard"). These are complex relations not binaries or alibis. Recall the earlier reference to the availability of electricity. China's hydroelectric projects provide 17 percent of its power supply and another option to the yellow skies of Beijing or Chongqing. Rather than moralize about this dilemma, *Still Life* suggests living is more than a set of amenities, however much they facilitate subsistence in general. The poignancy and difficulty of expressing desires from needs comes through the film in several ways, and two in particular are noteworthy.

The opening title sequence with its slow pan of a boatload of ordinary Chinese, many of them on their way to work on the Three Gorges project or on their way out of Fengjie, in its destruction and creation, is not necessarily about the essence of China (like the Pequod in US culture, for instance) but a condition of its reality, its people, its masses, their number. What links them? One swift answer comes immediately afterwards at a show for the boat passengers. "All you need to float is U.S. dollars," the trickster proclaims and just like that he turns paper into cash, then euros into Renminbi (there is a joke here that is largely lost on the passengers but not necessarily on Jia's audience about trade flows in globalization). Nevertheless, to float above the destruction wrought by the dam the peasants must learn the meaning of money in modernization. Yes, places in China are celebrated on its banknotes, and there is a scene where Sanming makes friends through the identification of place on currency, but to make more money means that such places may come to exist only on the banknotes but not in China itself. Just to further this point, Sanming goes to the gorge imaged on the banknote and one can see the change already in Jia's depiction. Then, in close up, the note is flipped and there is the Great Leader himself, Mao, whose poem "Swimming" had imagined a great concrete wall across the Yangtze. The banknote makes the basic point about the differences between abstract value and what is represented, between what persists in the present, and what, in visualization, is made to disappear. This is the great conundrum of labor in culture.

The work framed in *Still Life* is mostly demolition, the work of destruction, erasure. To earn his keep Sanming does this too, breaking concrete with a sledgehammer. There are several shots of sweating bodies but given the amount of buildings to be destroyed their efforts seem relatively futile, gestural, and theatrical. Everywhere Sanming goes we see the character for "chai"—to be demolished—as the residents of Fengjie are asked to participate in their town's effacement. Jia offers still lives of the town's decay—at a factory being taken apart we see rusted pipes and machinery, a solitary work glove, the detritus of a broken past (here are the stirrings of Jia's next project, *24 City*). A self-styled gangster, Brother Mark warns Sanming about being nostalgic (based on the latter's cellphone's ringtone) but since he quotes Chow Yun-Fat from John Woo's *A Better Tomorrow* (1986), clearly nostalgia is relative. There are other hints of labor's quandary within the Three Gorges transformation. A sixteen-year-old girl asks Shen Hong if they need maids in Shanxi. Workers seek compensation for their factory closure; others seek confirmation of their relocation. Those managing the redevelopment, however, are doing much better. An entrepreneur boasts to a VIP of his new bridge then orders its lighting switched on. No electrical problems here.

Other than a plot device (i.e., that Sanming needs to work to support himself while searching for his wife and child), is the work of dismantling Fengjie merely a background device as picturesque and stylized as Liu's Three Gorges paintings? It is true the demolition work depicted is compositional rather than practical. Workers are seen bashing random pieces of concrete but in positions that "compose" the act itself. Yet if this seems like "learning from Liu" Jia offers another layer of tableaux by repeating the slow pan of the first sequence discussed above and by bonding Sanming to the group of workers with whom he has been demolishing buildings. Pans are painterly (although not quite as much as tracking shots, as the work of Peter Greenaway reminds us) but in the final meal scene, where the workers decide to leave with Sanming to work in the mines ($25 a day rather than $5 for demolition) the scene is all about the intensity of gesture, the rituals of toasting and smoking and eating. Although this could be read as a celebration of masculinity, if not masculinism, Jia suggests both in Shen Hong's story and Sanming's interactions with his wife alternative grounds of companionship and interaction. There is a vitality that can be abused but it is not by the camera in this instance. The workers together are far from the idealistic perfectability of endless state campaigns. If Jia himself always seems to seek first a zero degree of humanist dignity, the expressive elements of worker interaction in these scenes are less certain of their credentials, less tied to an individualist ontology. At the end of the film Sanming and the other workers move on together to the coalmines of Shanxi. Sanming stops to look at the ruins they are leaving. Again, just like the building earlier that turns into a rocket, Jia disturbs the field of vision, or comments on its surreality, by presenting us with a tightrope walker perched between two partially demolished buildings. If this means either balance or harmony then even postmodern ironizing would not save it from cliché. Yet it is not its symbolic consistency with Chinese cultural traditions that is important but its visual refusal to endorse the implications of the workers leaving demolition for digging. The aesthetic tightrope is the one Jia walks between state workerism and the role of work in the modernization he images. Like the state, he can no longer celebrate the worker left behind, but neither can Jia fully endorse the new ideology that says the labor of the present needs no labor representation, no complex cultural presence. The identification processes of Eisenstein's *Strike* are gone for all kinds of legitimate reasons (some of which I have discussed in the workers' inquiry) but the Chinese worker in her profundity and profusion troubles the field of vision as the image disturbs all of those service industry economies that depend on its largesse. It is not just Chinese labor history but the present of worker aphanisis that Jia finds visually provocative if insoluble in the new China.

When workers "appear" then, they are primarily situated by their stasis, by their dead objectivity (irrespective of whether they represent "dead labor"). When they move, or are seen moving, the promise of objectification is not simply subvented or subverted but is figured by the time/space in which the image is condensed. Deleuze, whose relationship to popular film is the cause of his theorization (absent causes, non-said, as Macherey puts it, like the economic and political), nevertheless offers a rhetoric of the image, a grammar of distinction, that reveals why the many (or the multitude in a Spinozist key) do not distill in the tension between time/image and image/movement. It is as if, in the collapse of the actual existence of socialism in Dengist China, the worker has fallen into an "any space whatever," an *espace quelconque* that Deleuze for his part reads into Bresson's *Pickpocket*.[21] The cinematic difficulty of the worker exists in how work takes place, the image of its duration and thus the worker persists as symbol more than substance, labor itself, affective or otherwise. The workers may have left the factory in the political unconscious of the West, but factories also move (sometimes quite literally) and for capital never occupy any space whatever, even the most virtual. The workers move to labor at the end of *Still Life* but what if labor moves from them? This is, in part, the unknown or unacknowledged pleasure of *24 City* (*Er shi si Cheng ji*, 2008).

Jia's *24 City* (co-written with the poet Zhai Yongming) begins with an establishing shot of the front of a factory, of the Chengfa Group as its workers sing "Welcoming the sun of the new century, we workers at Chengfa raise our voices." In the new century, paradoxically, workers are not leaving the factory on celluloid but entering it on DV (for me, this is the visual bookend of labor in culture: it is how the representation of the worker disrupts the world of globalization). This is followed by a close up of the hands of two workers in tandem using a hydraulic press to shape hot steel rivets. While this making occurs, Jia's making occurs and he rolls the credits of those who have financed his making. I find this image one of the most powerful representations of the antinomies of modernized China. It is not because it ties the privatization of the film industry to steel (although China has been the world's largest producer of steel by far for some time now) but because it presents such relations as highly volatile and bound to other agendas, real or imagined. Strangely, the Maoist refrain ("the five star red flag flutters in the wind" goes the song) is part of the economic realism, and Jia marks the duration of a specific asynchronicity. Of course, this factory, 420, in Chengdu is closing. It cannot be sustained by the simple fact that rivets, for instance, are needed. Its system of production is grossly inefficient. The machines are old and require too much labor. Margins mean marginalization. Chinese workers are cheap, but the transnational steel and arms industries do not need so many of them, and the land itself is worth more (perhaps for a five star hotel or high-rise residential buildings, the development that gives the film its title—this is World Park's future). And so we have Chinese workers who have labor power but less power to exercise it. Or maybe not, which is why Jia in this film plays with their memories of what may be a false attachment to the worker state.

There is a cinematic density to *24 City* and again many elements that need not be explicitly tied to moving labor, or its falling/failing. But obviously, a major question is what do we do with this factory's history; how can cinema examine what 420 represents? Is it essentially beyond documentary? Is it beyond the sense of document? What does *24 City* share with other documentaries of Chinese labor that have proliferated in direct proportion to the explosion of transnational joint ventures and special economic zones in the New China (films like *Mardi Gras–Made in China, China Blue,* and *Manufactured Landscapes*[22])? What is the visual connection, explored most deeply by Wang Bing in his film *Tie Xi Qu, West of the Tracks,* between duration and endurance, between an image of time and labor's persistence?[23] Do interviews ever seek truth from facts, or is all that bunkum as dead as Mao, as dead as the 420 factory?

Many of the workers of 420 came from Shenyang when military production was shifted from factory 111 (itself built to support Korea's military effort against American imperialism). Labor migration is not just practical but often strategic, as in the formation of special economic zones themselves. The older workers in the film are mostly retired and are often simply recorded in "still life"—posed shots where they remain immobile and carefully lit. For now they live in the old factory's dormitories, alongside the decrepit MIGs and missiles left over from the early years of the People's Republic. As the film continues, however, we witness once again demolition's demand, and in moments the narrative ponders dereliction as a concept in a derelict factory and its dream. Yet Jia rightly refuses to indulge in such decay even as he shows once more buildings being pulled down and some broken memories in their ruins. An hour into the film he introduces Little Flower (xiao hua), a worker played by Joan Chen who references a film in which she has played and then notes that workers have compared her to herself (light humor with a theoretical comment on the power of reflexivity in cinema). Soon Jia presents us with Su Na played by Zhao Tao, a mainstay of Jia's films (and now his wife). These subtle interventions (four of the interviewees are played by actors) are formally brilliant but simultaneously suspect. On the one hand, it represents a long-standing technique for questioning what we mean by veracity, memory, and belief. Should we believe more in the workers' recollections from the first part of the film or are these no less invented than those that are scripted? Is the problem that worker interviews are boring but acted ones are aesthetic? Is it more important to make 420 incidental to the life stories that emerge from it? The deciding factor here is not so much the worker herself but the film's dialogue with its audience. This is part of "the coming of wisdom with time" (a poem by Yeats Jia quotes within the film), and a temporal dimension that tempers both anger and knowing satisfaction with the implications of Jia's conceit. If I have less of a problem with Jia's acted interviews it probably reflects a sense that this is no different from his representations of Fenyang in earlier films—from heartfelt memories that do not suture authentic selves. When Su Na is given the last dialogue of the film, "I am the daughter of a worker," Jia might be said to have pushed not just generational differences but labor differentiation itself to the fore. Without simply confirming a Zizekian aesthetic for paradox within paradox (the rise of the truly proletarian in a communism holding up capitalism), several theoretical issues emerge in Jia's moving labor.

If proletarian being is always a becoming, not the "is" of capital but the relation in its attenuation, then we should not be surprised that the Chinese worker is, in essence, invisible but always seen. Labor as relation is the Lacanian Real of modernization. Yet by now we are steeped in the representational aesthetics of the Chinese worker who, apparently free from the posterism and monumentalism of yesteryear, is intricately documented at every turn. To continue our sense of paradox, cinematic theory needs less sociology and more abstraction to come to terms with the (sur) reality of the Chinese worker onscreen. Unfortunately, such abstraction, which must be differentiated from the abstraction of abstract labor, comes close to being a global currency since the visual field it offers or complicates is always someone else's problem, and does not trouble globalization's gaze, except around a counter-discourse with sometimes vague notions of human rights. Despite the outpouring of documentation of the undocumented, the Dagong sans papiers, the presence this new archive provides is little more than a quotidian effect (not a special one) and the abstruse connections of, for instance, mining and data mining remain cinematic sediment, not a contradiction for its language (palpable in the following section on Jia's *A Touch of Sin*). As Jia reflects on the pure fictions of Maoism the aestheticized facts of ordinary people are a formal challenge that he has met more insistently than any other contemporary Chinese director. It is a Chinese neo-realism shot through with imperfection that, rather than wish away its contradictions, attempts to grapple with the visual economy of this shortfall. Although such a discourse of imperfectability is a break from the idealistic pastness indicated in the Fifth Generation, it remains enmeshed in the continuing vexed relationship of the artist and intellectual to the state. Jia's rigorously unaffiliated vision is a precise symptom of an acute political dilemma. It may be that the false populism of the Party has driven Jia's passionate explorations of the people to the critical "to-see" list of film festivals and cinema studies and not to those who, nominally within the frame, might learn from or question his affective embrace of their contemporary predicaments. Moving labor may not be moved by Jia Zhangke but neither are workers waiting on their image. A more elusive Jia, like the Bazin Dudley Andrew extols, picks away at the doxa of worker realism as the worker falls. What then happens to the politics of aesthetics? What recomposes realism as the worker stands up?

A Touch of Sin brings us eerily to a present, one of obscene economic inequality and a seething cauldron of corruption and violence, in China. Like Jia's other films, it is not really about labor or the fate of workers in contemporary China. It does share something of Berger's inquiry "into their labors" as a sense of a whole way of life, one marked by disjunction, dislocation, and an existential question, "who are we?" under the sign of globalization. Yet even this perception falls short of Jia's cultural problematic on China in the world, and the question of cinema and visuality per se. Deeply committed to cinema as art, Jia reads the social as a challenge of representationality, for which labor in culture is our modest shorthand. While Jia revisits some of the locations he has detailed in previous films (and uses characters from those films as artful transitions or notation devices, like Sanming from *Still Life*) this film (and the more recent *Mountains May Depart*) is a leap ahead in production values. Much of this shift is a tribute to Jia's sustained entrepreneurialism and the way he has navigated the transformation from state run to private and independent studio possibilities (the latter including his own production company, XStream Pictures, long-time supporters like Office Kitano, and the entity that replaced the old Shanghai Studios, the Shanghai Group). For a filmmaker who has often depicted the quandary of the new for the old, his own career seems to have overcome it.[24] This does not detract from Jia's aesthetic commitments, which have also benefitted from a close knit group of actors and, for instance, the cinematography of Yu Lik-wai and the music of Lim Giong. Yet *A Touch of Sin* in particular highlights the contradiction between its polemical surfaces and the infrastructural conditions of its production, the skein of labor representation.

A Touch of Sin (*Tian Zhuding*, or "ill-fated") is split into four interlocking stories that are based on reports circulating through the microblogging network, Weibo, of which Jia has been an avid user. Given the difficulties of official accounts of social contradiction, Weibo has sometimes provided an alternative source for assessing the state of the People's Republic (subject, of course, to censorship). Whatever the actual events on which the film is based, Jia's reflections on violence and despair have a strong resonance in figuring the dilemmas of labor in contemporary globalization. As with all of the examples I have offered, representing labor is not the quintessence of the artist's Weltanschauung, yet here again Jia's film elaborates a political and cultural unconscious that shapes how the worker may be understood in globalization and the challenge she poses to it.[25]

The first story focuses on the moral outrage of an ex-miner, Hu Dahai, who has taken on the task of exposing the corruption of local officials as state industries become privatized. His ire is particularly directed at Jiao Shengli who, through bribes and connections, took over the local mine in Wujinshan, Shanxi, and now counts among his assets a private plane. Shengli is a bigger man than Mao, whose forlorn statue sits abandoned in the center of town, and Shengli expects deep appreciation for his massive accumulation of wealth (he pays for appreciation by giving each worker a bag of flour for showing up to greet him at the airport). Hu, who knows Shengli from their school days, tells him that he is going to file a report about his corruption with the government and bring him down (there is no direct suggestion either the state or the Party has indulged in any foul play by producing millionaires and billionaires but once again the pseudo slogan, "To get rich is glorious" hangs over the core of the narrative). After being beaten up by Shengli's security Hu decides to take up the fight more literally by loading a shotgun and attempting to wipe out corrupt elements of the ruling class. There is no sense this is an allusion to Mao's quip "Political power grows out of the barrel of a gun." Rather, Hu drapes a picture of a tiger over his gun (Tony Rayns, who also did the English subtitling for this film, has suggested this is a reference to Wu Song, the tiger killer of *Water Margin* fame, and there is even a tiger growl in the soundtrack[26]) and simply sets off on a killing spree. The violence is graphic and features copious amounts of blood and brain splatter (Shengli is dispatched sitting in his Maserati Quattroporte, and the use of a car interior for this event of righteous excess has a strong air of Tarantino). Does Jia appeal to the ethical Id of China's lower orders that might harbor the justifiable strands of a new Chinese revenge tragedy (that also extends to references to King Hu [*A Touch of Zen*] and the *wuxia* tradition)? The depiction of violence itself might be seen to expand the possibilities of viewership across a popular base but clearly Jia is drawing on the incidence of increased violence and social wrongs that go unmediated. While it is undeniable significant want has been greatly remedied in China's modernization, it is the unevenness and inequality of this process that is insufficiently addressed. At the aesthetic level, Jia's depiction of violence, like those long existential moments of silence, is symptomatic of a conditional limit in imaging the Chinese migrant worker: there is no language of class available to this representation, no pointed visual syntax for its articulation. Moral outrage and violence eventually come to fill this void in an intricate play of parable and the parabolic.

Hu does not just kill the rich—he also kills the wife of a corrupt accountant and a farmer who is senselessly beating his horse—so the justice of the vigilante is just diffuse enough to be read as its own singular outbreak, a touch of lawlessness in a world touched by lawlessness in general. The second story, prefigured by the opening sequence of the film, suspends any moral question in foregrounding Zhou San, whose adventure in killing appears premised only by boredom and the possession of a gun. True, he is an equal opportunity psychopath (he kills in order to rob but also kills those attempting to rob him) but the story remains unconvinced about any connection between killing and supporting his family. He moves not to find work but to substitute for it. In the third story, Xiaoyu works at a sauna as a receptionist but is assumed to be a sex worker like the other people at the establishment (the imbrication of migrant labor and sex trafficking hovers at the edge of this segment). Despite her insistence, Xiaoyu is harassed and beaten by a customer who repeatedly hits her with a wad of 100 yuan notes. Xiaoyu responds by stabbing him to death with a knife that belonged to her former lover. If the image of money as a weapon is not subtle, the sequence nevertheless draws attention to the patriarchal privileges that wealth assumes and the rapid resurgence of sex work itself in Mainland modernity. Xiaoyu's self-defense stands in sharp contrast to Zhou San's practiced disaffection, but justifiable homicide is not seen as an answer to the abuses of power money emboldens.

If the sauna is in many ways a conventional brothel, The Golden Age, the Dongguan club featured in the fourth story, takes sex work up market by appealing to wealthy men from Hong Kong and Taiwan. One fantasy includes renting a room that evokes a special railway carriage from the Mao era so patrons can play communist cadres "correctly handling contradictions" (as in *Platform*, we are taking the train to Shaoshan).

Indeed, the Golden Age is a pastiche of privilege that yet pivots on it (it reminds one of the old China Club in Hong Kong that featured a Long March Bar, a capitalist joke about who has marched longer). At one point we see the "honored guests" pondering potential women escorts at the club who are marching before them as a scantily clad Red Detachment. If Jia's films offer a politics of the worker it is primarily at the level of showing rather than telling which is hardly unusual but is always given a visual twist. In this part of the film it is provided by the main character, Xiaohuai, a young man who will move anywhere to support himself, and to be able to send money to his mother (a standard but significant narrative of Chinese migrant labor). We see Xiaohuai working at a clothing factory, at the Golden Age, and at a large electronics factory (where the FSK hats link it to Foxconn, the major subcontractor for Apple among other tech giants). His friend at the latter explains the salary structure (approximately $1,200 a month plus meals and dorm space, rising to $2,400 a month after a probationary period) which is not bad in relation to the past but hints at the large margins companies like Apple are able to secure within China's rapid proletarianization. The Weibo story from which Jia draws and one which has come to symbolize the predicament of the worker under global capitalism is the incidence of worker suicide at Foxconn's massive Shenzhen factory. Although statistically the suicides (fourteen in 2010) were lower than the national average, the point was the connection between forms and conditions of employment and the kinds of despair that would lead young people to take their lives (the age range of the dead was 17–24). With debt obligations rising and not enough working hours in the day to cover them, Xiaohuai leaps to his death off one of the dorm buildings. Here the shot length and lighting is much more restrained as if the fact of this death itself is more impactful than its representation. For the most part, of course, the above are sociological markers, but what makes labor moving in Jia's understanding of change in China's globalization?

Jia is always addressing the quality of memory in his art and labor on the move is more than a theme in that regard. Part of this has to do with the conditions of abstraction in memory itself (which, not surprisingly, is often drawn from Jia's personal recollections) and part with how change is experienced, felt more generally. Rich in cultural traditions and deeply embedded modes of identification, China, like countries across globalization, is never simply a template for proletarianization even if contemporary capitalism often interpellates it as such. Yet, as Jia visualizes change in what becomes of lives moving from the land to the new megacities of Chinese modernity, the abstraction of labor speaks to memory's ability to abstract. On the one hand, elements of the social division of labor are relatively easy to represent—reveal the workplace or the conditions it shapes from Fenyang to Shenzhen (even as idea of *xiancheng* in the latter has been demonstrably overreached). On the other hand, how these places are recalled entails all kinds of associative effects that include but are not limited to the experience of labor from one place to another. Jia marks this movement as affect, how a character feels in this moment of movement, and as a tonal dissociation, as if change unpins the reality of the image and permit puncta of surreality in the everyday (for instance, after Hu kills the brutal farmer the horse and cart speed off behind two nuns in the foreground).

The final juxtaposition in the film accentuates the difficulty of capturing what has been done and lost in making the new China. Jia shoots part of a Beijing Opera, "The Woman Prisoner," whose main character, Su San, a prostitute then concubine, has been accused of killing her master and is being taken to a place of judicial review and execution. On the way she pleads her case with one of the guards and then again before a tribunal. Traditional culture permits the consideration of injustice but what performs this function in the present? Using one of Jia's favorite shots, of an audience of ordinary Chinese, workers and peasants, staring directly at the viewers as if they were being seen seeing this quandary, Su intones, "Do you understand your sin?" There is a deep sense of ambivalence in the use of the second person here. Within the frame the question can be addressed to Su's guards, the system of justice they represent, and the audience before her. For the film viewer the question comes not just from Su, but from the workers and peasants looking off screen. This can be just as much the sin of ignorance as willfulness and depends in part on the extent to which one connects the force of globalization to the production of violence in the workforce. The Chinese audience shares this link but it is also clearly meant to reflect upon the longue durée of the question within China's cultural traditions. What of class composition?[27] Are well-off urban Chinese meant to think what grounds the possibility of their new car, apartment, or trips abroad? Are the dagong being asked to consider the consequences of their migration for their sense of self, family, and community? And what of the state? Can culture broach the question of abject inequality without falling victim to the very power which permits it? Sin, of course, teeters on melodramatic moralism and the formal rectitude of ethical decision. It makes of "moving labor" more an emotional response rather than a knowledge of the material conditions of change in Chinese modernity, some of which I have tried to emphasize in "dereliction" and "involution." Yet, even from the fleeting news cycle and meme-ridden presentism of Weibo, Jia has drawn a picture of Chinese change that exceeds the first circle of its existential aura. This does not mean it is really about Chinese migrant workers (the denouement of Su San's story offers a much happier ending than that faced by most workers, and women workers in particular) but the dagong are hardly incidental to its storytelling possibilities. What worlds could be made if their wrongs were righted?

NOTES

1. The special issue of *Chinese Studies in History* 43(1) (Fall 2009) is particularly useful in tracking Chinese modernization while being careful not to simply collapse back this narrative into a theoretical model that is primarily Western and Eurocentric.
2. See Spivak's "Finding Feminist Readings," *Social Text* 3 (Autumn 1980): 73–87 (Spivak 1980). The idea here is both to find feminist readings in worker narratives, as Grace Lee Boggs shows in her critique of Romano's "An American Worker," and also to find worker narratives within other possible interpretations. It is globalization itself that puts pressure on this twin imperative.
3. See, again, Marx's reading of the commodity in the opening chapter of *Capital*. Karl Marx, *Capital, (Vol. One)*. Ed. Ernest Mandel, trans. Ben Fowkes. London: Penguin, 1992.
4. Karl Marx, "Economic and Philosophic Manuscripts of 1844" in *The Marx-Engels Reader*, Robert Tucker (ed.) New York: Norton, 1978: 70–91 (Marx 1978). Marx, "The forming of the five senses is a labor of the entire history of the world down to the present."
5. Walter Benjamin, *The Arcades Project*. Trans. Howard Eiland and Kevin McLaughlin. Cambridge, MA: Harvard University Press, 1999: 462 (Benjamin 1999).
6. I tend to use this term restrictively to signal the migrancy and proletarianization of Chinese peasants, although it can obviously be extended to mark the kinds of precarity and exploitation in the labor market associated with Chinese modernization in general.
7. There is an expanding literature on labor migration in China for which the following may prove useful, especially with their further references. See, for instance, Hsiao-Hung Pai, *Scattered Sand: The Story of China's Rural Migrants*. New York: Verso, 2013 (Pai 2013); Lü Guoguang, *Behind the Chinese Miracle: Migrant Workers Tell Their Stories*. San Francisco: Long

River Press, 2012 (Lü Guoguang 2012); and Han Changfu, *Migrant Workers in China*. Singapore: Cengage Learning Asia, 2011 (Changfu 2011). The work of Pun Ngai is particularly polemical around the formation of a new Chinese proletariat and the key role of women workers in that process. See *Made in China: Women Factory Workers in a Global Workplace*. Durham, NC: Duke University Press, 2005 (Pun Ngai 2005); and *Migrant Labor in China*. London: Polity, 2016 (Pun Ngai 2016). But see also the excellent analysis of C.K. Lee. *Gender and the South China Miracle: Two Worlds of Factory Women*. California: University of California Press, 1998 (Lee 1998); and *Against the Law: Labor Protests in China's Rustbelt and Sunbelt*. California: University of California Press, 2007 (Lee 2007). Like Jia's films, not all of this work constitutes workers' inquiry (and some even engages in official mystification) but it does accentuate the massive impact of China's entry into worlds of labor.

8. As a leading director in China and frequent contributor to international film festivals Jia's career has been well documented. This now includes a film documentary, *Jia Zhangke, A Guy from Fenyang* (2014), by the Brazilian director Walter Salles (*Motorcycle Diaries, Central Station*). I will refer to specific contributions as the argument develops.

9. An up-to-date filmography on Jia Zhangke can be found on IMDB at http://www.imdb.com/name/nm0422605/.

10. For more on the impact of this mode of inquiry, see Chris Berry, Lu Xinyu and Lisa Rofel, Eds., *The New Chinese Documentary Film Movement*. Hong Kong: Hong Kong University Press, 2011 (Berry et al. 2011); and Chiu Kui-fen and Zhang Yingjin, *New Chinese-Language Documentaries*. London: Routledge, 2014 (Kui-fen and Yingjin 2014). The latter also includes work on Taiwanese documentaries as well as including a chapter on Jia.

11. For more on Jia's filmic influences, see Evan Osnos, "The Long Shot," *New Yorker*, May 11, 2009 (Osnos 2009); and Kevin Lee, "Jia Zhangke," *Senses of Cinema* 25 (March 2003), http://sensesofcinema.com/2003/great-directors/jia/ (Lee 2003). The Bresson quote is from Robert Bresson, *Notes on Cinematography*. Trans. Jonathan Griffin. New York: Urizen, 1977: 5 (Bresson 1977).

12. See Wang Xiaodong, "Lun Jia Zhangke dianying zhong de guxiang" ["Hometown in Jia Zhangke's Films"], in *Dianying wenxue* [*Film Literature*], 5 (2009) (Xiaodong 2009); and Zhang Xudong, "Poetics of Vanishing," *New Left Review* 63 (May/June 2010): 71–88 (Xudong 2010). A revised version of this essay appears as "Market Socialism and Its Discontent: Jia Zhangke's Cinematic Narrative of China's Transition in the Age of Global Capital" in *Neoliberalism and Global Cinema: Capital, Culture, and Marxist Critique*, Jyotsna Kapur and Keith B. Wagner (eds.)

London: Routledge, 2011: 135–156 (Xudong 2011). Wagner's contribution to this collection, "Fragments of Labor," also offers a pertinent Gramscian interpretation of the effects of neoliberalism in South Korea in the films of Park Chan-wook that focuses on the re-purposing of worker tools and the prospect of vengeance. This critique is not unrelated to my later discussion of *A Touch of Sin*.
13. Jia has argued that without the market for bootleg dvds in China much of his early film career would have remained unseen. Up to *The World*, Jia's independence made distribution and exhibition in China almost impossible.
14. See Philip Levine, *What Work Is: Poems*. New York: Knopf, 1991 (Levine 1991). Although we can think of many different examples of what work is, in social reproduction, in IT, in the knowledge industry, in all kinds of immateriality, Levine is particularly insightful about the deracination of post-industrialism and the new forms of precarity it has presaged.
15. Jacques Rancière, *Film Fables*. Trans. Emiliano Battista. London: Bloomsbury, 2006: 143 (Rancière 2006).
16. See Jason McGrath, *Postsocialist Modernity: Chinese Cinema, Literature, and Criticism in the Market Age*. Palo Alto: Stanford University Press, 2010 (McGrath 2010).
17. See, for instance, Wang Hui, "Jia Zhangke's World and China's Great Transformation," Trans. Nathaniel Proctor. *Positions* 19(1) (Spring 2011): 217–228 (Hui 2011).
18. Bianca Bosker's intriguing book, *Original Copies: Architectural Mimicry in Contemporary China*. Honolulu: University of Hawaii Press, 2013 (Bosker 2013), looks at the more general phenomenon of China's "fascination with faux."
19. Walter Benjamin, "Dream Kitsch" in *Walter Benjamin—Selected Writings, 1927–1930*, Howard Eiland and Gary Smith (eds.) Cambridge, MA: Belknap, 2005: 4 (Benjamin 2005).
20. *Before the Flood* Dir. Li Yifan and Yan Yu, Fan and Yu Documentary Studio, 2005.
21. See Gilles Deleuze, *Cinema 1: The Movement Image*. Trans. Hugh Tomlinson and Barbara Haberjam. Minneapolis: University of Minnesota Press, 1985 (Deleuze 1985).
22. *Mardi Gras: Made in China*. Dir. David Redmon. Carnivalesque Films, 2005; *China Blue*. Dir. Micha X. Peled. Teddy Bear Films, 2005; and *Manufactured Landscapes*. Dir. Jennifer Baichwal. Zeitgeist Films, 2006. The latter is especially impressive and features photographs and video by Ed. Burtynsky. Like Salgado, Burtynsky captures the scale of global labor but pays particular attention to what humans have made in addition to the workers themselves. The use of color photography seems to accentuate the capacity of manufacture itself.

23. *Tie Xi Qu*, (*West of the Tracks*). Dir. Wang Bing. Wang Bing Film Workshop, 2002 (Tie Xi Qu 2002). A film divided into three parts: "Rust" (240 Minutes), "Remnants" (176 Minutes), and "Rails" (135 Minutes) with a total running time over 9 hours, the film's rhythms can be hypnotic, as if you can feel the entropy it documents. For an article that places Wang's work within the new documentary movement see Lu Xinyu, "Ruins of the Future: Class and History in Wang Bing's Tiexi District," *New Left Review* 31 (January/February 2005): 125–136 (Xinyu 2005). See also, Ying Qian, "Power in the Frame: China's Independent Documentary Movement," *New Left Review* 74 (March/April 2012): 105–123 (Qian 2012).

24. This is a complicated question but the collaborative documentary that Jia put together, *Yulu* (2011) intensified criticism of Jia's strategic alliances. Funded by Johnny Walker, the film in general celebrates the new faces of China's "can-do" spirit. Jia's opening segment on Cao Fei, who develops a grocery shopping website, is typical in this regard, but his last segment, on Pan Shiyi, founder and chairman of SOHO China is the most galling. If Jia's work has often criticized the ways in which property in China gets privatized and "developed," providing a hagiography of Pan and the work of SOHO, that has been central to this process, appears more than mildly contradictory. Is the modernity Jia depicts merely a problem of a few "bad apples"? Is there a right way to throw people off their land under globalization?

25. It should be stressed, however, that if any opposition is represented within these vignettes, it is individual rather than collective, although the final shot suggests otherwise, perhaps. There is a good deal of research into Chinese labor protests. In addition to the work of C.K. Lee already mentioned, see Eli Friedman, *Insurgency Trap: Labor Politics in Postsocialist China*. Ithaca: Cornell ILR, 2014 (Friedman 2014); Lu Zhang, *Inside China's Automobile Factories: The Politics of Labor and Worker Resistance*. Cambridge: Cambridge University Press, 2014 (Lu Zhang 2014); and Immanuel Ness, *Southern Insurgency: The Coming of the Global Working Class*. London: Pluto, 2016 (Ness 2016).

26. See Tony Rayns, "Heard It Through the Grapevine," *Film Comment*, September/October 2013 (Rayns 2013).

27. I have been thinking of this in terms of aesthetic composition but clearly the problem of class is an intense arena of contestation in China studies. Despite all of the capital flowing into and out of China over the last thirty years David Goodman, for instance, is adamant what we are witnessing is a "reforming socialist market economy" (178) that clings to a strong sense of redistributive logic. Again, there can be no doubt that the quality of life in general for workers has improved within modernization but the evidence of class relations place significant pressure on the idea of socialist

reform. Indeed, Goodman's closing comments on inequality cast a pall over the Communist Party's Plenum pronouncements on redistribution. Nevertheless, the differentiation within the working class Goodman identifies helps to understand the tensions between established urban workers and the dagong. See David S.G. Goodman, *Class in Contemporary China*. Cambridge: Polity Press, 2014 (Goodman 2014). For a critique of the fate of class as a discourse in China see Lin Chun, "The Language of Class in China" in *Transforming Classes—Socialist Register 2015*, Leo Panitch and Greg Albo (eds.) London: Merlin Press, 2014: 24–53 (Chun 2014).

Bibliography

24 City (Er shi si cheng ji). Dir. Jia Zhangke. Xstream Pictures, Office Kitano and Shanghai Film Group et al. 2008.

Adorno, T. W., and Max Horkheimer. *Dialectic of Enlightenment*. Trans. Edmund Jephcott Stanford: Stanford University Press, 2002.

Agamben, Giorgio. *The Coming Community*. Trans. Michael Hardt Minneapolis: University of Minnesota, 1993.

Albert, Eric. "La vie dans une usine" *Les Temps Modernes* 81 (Juillet 1952): 95–130.

Ali, Tariq. *The Idea of Communism*. London: Seagull, 2009.

Althusser, Louis, and Etienne Balibar. *Reading Capital*. Trans. Ben Brewster London: NLB, [1970] 1998.

Althusser, Louis, and Etienne Balibar eds. *Reading Capital: The Complete Edition*. New York: Verso, 2016.

Althusser, Louis et al. *Lire le Capital*. 1st edn. Paris: Maspero, 1965. 3rd edn. Paris: Presses Universitaires de France/Quadrige, 1996.

Appadurai, Arjun. *Modernity at Large*. Minneapolis: University of Minnesota Press, 1996.

Aronowitz, Stanley, and William DiFazio. *The Jobless Future*. Minneapolis: University of Minnesota Press, 2010.

Auerbach, Erik. *Mimesis: The Representation of Reality in Western Literature*. Intro. Edward Said. Trans. Willard R. Trask. Princeton: Princeton University Press, 2003.

Badiou, Alain. "The Lessons of Jacques Rancière: Knowledge and Power after the Storm" in *Jacques Rancière: History, Politics, Aesthetics*. Gabriel Rockhill and Philip Watts eds. Durham: Duke University Press, 2009: 30–54.

Badiou, Alain. *The Communist Hypothesis.* Trans. David Macey and Steve Corcoran. London: Verso, 2010.
Badiou, Alain. *The Rebirth of History.* Trans. Gregory Elliott. New York: Verso, 2012.
Badiou, Alain. *Being and Event.* Trans. Oliver Feltham. London: Bloomsbury, 2013.
Bakhtin, M.M. *Art and Answerability.* Intro. Michael Holquist. Trans. Vadim Liapunov and Kenneth Brostrom. Austin: University of Texas Press, 1990.
Bakhtin, M.M. *Toward a Philosophy of the Act.* Michael Holquist and Vadim Liapunov eds. Trans. Vadim Liapunov. Austin: University of Texas Press, 1993.
Balibar, Etienne. "Sujets ou citoyens? (Pour l'égalité)" *Les Temps Modernes* 40 (March–April–May 1984): 1726–1753.
Balibar, Etienne. *Masses, Classes, Ideas.* Trans. James Swenson. New York: Routledge, 1994.
Balibar, Etienne. *Nous, citoyens d'Europe?: Les Frontières, l'Etat, le peuple.* Paris: Editions la Decouverte, 2001.
Balibar, Etienne. *We, the People of Europe?.* Trans. James Swenson. Princeton: Princeton University Press, 2003.
Balibar, Etienne. *The Philosophy of Marx.* Trans. Chris Turner. New York: Verso, 2014.
Balibar, Etienne. "Citizen Subject" in Cadava et al.: 33–57.
Balibar, Etienne, and Immanuel Wallerstein. *Race, Nation, Class.* 2nd Edition. New York: Verso, 2011.
Balibar, Etienne et al. *Sans-papiers: l'archaïsme fatal.* Paris: La Découverte, 1999.
Barthes, Roland. *Camera Lucida.* Trans. Richard Howard. New York: Hill and Wang, 1982.
Before the Flood. Dir. Li Yifan and Yan Yu, Fan and Yu Documentary Studio, 2005.
Benjamin, Walter. "On the Mimetic Faculty" in *Reflections: Essays, Aphorisms, Autobiographical Writings.* Peter Demetz ed. Trans. Edmund Jephcott. New York: Schocken, 1978: 333–336.
Benjamin, Walter. "Little History of Photography" in *Selected Writings Volume Two, 1927–1934.* Michael W. Jennings ed. Cambridge MA: Harvard University Press, 1999.
Benjamin, Walter. *The Arcades Project.* Trans. Howard Eiland and Kevin McLaughlin. Cambridge, MA: Harvard University Press, 1999.
Benjamin, Walter. *Selected Writings: 1913–1926, Volume 1.* Marcus Bullock and Michael W. Jennings eds. Cambridge, MA: Harvard University Press, 2004.
Benjamin, Walter. "Dream Kitsch" in *Walter Benjamin—Selected Writings, 1927–1930.* Michael William Jennings et al. eds. Cambridge, MA: Belknap, 2005.
Benjamin, Walter. *The Work of Art in the Age of its Technological Reproducibility, and Other Writings on Media.* W. Michael, Brigid Doherty Jennings, Thomas Y. Levin eds. Trans. Edmund Jephcott, Rodney Livingstone, Howard Eiland. et al. Cambridge MA: Harvard University Press, 2008.

Benjamin, Walter. *The Work of Art in the Age of its Technological Reproducibility*. W. Michael, Brigid Doherty Jennings eds. Trans. Thomas Y. Levin, Edmund Jephcott, Rodney Livingstone, Howard Eiland et al. Cambridge, MA: Belknap Press, 2008.
Berger, John. *Permanent Red: Essays in Seeing*. London: Methuen, 1960.
Berger, John. *The Success and Failure of Picasso*. London: Penguin, 1965.
Berger, John. *The Look of Things*. Nikos Stangos ed. London: Penguin, 1972.
Berger, John. *About Looking*. London: Writers and Readers, 1980.
Berger, John. *And Our Faces, My Heart, Brief as Photos*. New York: Pantheon, 1984.
Berger, John. "Imagine Paris" Harper's (January 1987a): 72–74.
Berger, John. *Once in Europa*. New York: Pantheon, 1987b.
Berger, John. *Pig Earth*. New York: Pantheon, 1988.
Berger, John. *Keeping a Rendezvous*. New York: Pantheon, 1990a.
Berger, John. *Lilac and Flag*. New York: Pantheon, 1990b.
Berger, John. "John Berger: An Interview" Interview with Nikos Papstergiadis. *The American Poetry Review* 22 (1993): 9–12.
Berger, John, and Jean Mohr. *Another Way of Telling*. London: Writers and Readers, 1982.
Berger, John, and Jean Mohr. *A Seventh Man*. London: Verso, 2010.
Berger, John, and Patricia Macdonald. *Once in Europa*. London: Bloomsbury, 1999.
Berger, John et al. *Ways of Seeing*. London: Penguin, 1972.
Berry, Chris, Lu Xinyu, and Lisa Rofel eds. *The New Chinese Documentary Film Movement*. Hong Kong: Hong Kong University Press, 2011.
Bogre, Michelle. *Photography as Activism: Images for Social Change*. Burlington MA: Focal Press, 2012.
Bosker, Bianca. *Original Copies: Architectural Mimicry in Contemporary China*. Honolulu: University of Hawaii Press, 2013.
Bosteels, Bruno. *The Actuality of Communism*. London: Verso, 2011.
Bourdieu, Pierre. *Distinction*. Trans. Richard Nice. Cambridge, MA: Harvard University Press, 1984.
Bresson, Robert. *Notes on Cinematography*. Trans. Jonathan Griffin. New York: Urizen, 1977.
Buhle, Paul. *C.L.R. James: The Artist as Revolutionary*. New York: Verso, 1989.
Buhle, Paul. *Marxism in the United States*. 3rd Edition. New York: Verso, 2013.
Cadava, Eduardo., Peter Connor., and Jean-Luc Nancy eds. *Who Comes After the Subject?* New York: Routledge, 1991.
Caffentzis, Georges. "An Essay on Marx's Legacy" in *Reading Negri*. Pierre Lamarche, Max Rosenkrantz, and David Sherman eds. Chicago: Carus, 2011: 101–126.
Caffentzis, Georges. *In Letters of Blood and Fire*. Oakland: PM Press, 2013.

Castoriadis, Cornelius. "Proletarian Leadership" in *Political and Social Writings* (Volume One, 1946–1955: "From the Critique of Bureaucracy to the Positive Content of Socialism"). Ed. and Trans David Ames Curtis. Minneapolis: University of Minnesota Press, 1988: 198–206.

China Blue. Dir. Micha X. Peled. Teddy Bear Films, 2005.

Chiu, Kui-fen, and Yingjin Zhang. *New Chinese-Language Documentaries*. London: Routledge, 2014.

Chun, Lin. "The Language of Class in China" in *Transforming Classes—Socialist Register 2015*. Leo Panitch and Greg Albo eds. London: Merlin Press, 2014: 24–53.

Cott, Jonathan. "Sebastião Salgado's Visionary Light" *Rolling Stone*, 619 (December 12, 1991).

Crary, Jonathan. *Techniques of the Observer: On Vision and Modernity in the Nineteenth Century*. Cambridge, MA: MIT Press, 1992.

Dalla Costa, Mariarosa, and Selma James. *The Power of Women and the Subversion of the Community*. Bristol: Falling Wall Press, 1972.

Dalla Costa, Mariarosa, F. Giovanna, and Dalla Costa eds. *Women, Development, and Labor of Reproduction: Struggles and Movements*. London: Africa World Press, 1999.

De Goncourt, Edmond Jules. *Germenie Lacerteux*. New York: Book Jungle, 2010.

Dean, Jodi. *The Communist Horizon*. London: Verso, 2012.

Del Valle Alcalá, Roberto. *British Working-Class Fiction*. London: Bloomsbury, 2016.

Deleuze, Gilles. *Cinema 1: The Movement Image*. Trans. Hugh Tomlinson and Barbara Haberjam. Minneapolis: University of Minnesota Press, 1985.

Denby, Charles. *Indignant Heart: A Black Worker's Journal*. Boston: South End Press, 1978.

Deranty, Jean-Phillippe ed. *Jacques Rancière: Key Concepts*. Durham, UK: Acumen, 2010.

Derrida, Jacques. *The Truth in Painting*. Trans. Geoff Bennington and McLeod Ian. Chicago: University of Chicago Press, 1987.

Derrida, Jacques. *Specters of Marx*. Trans. Peggy Kamuf. New York: Routledge, 1993.

Derrida, Jacques. *Given Time: 1. Counterfeit Money*. Trans. Peggy Kamuf. Chicago: University of Chicago Press, 1994.

Derrida, Jacques. *The Gift of Death*. Trans. David Wills. Chicago: University of Chicago Press, 1997.

Derrida, Jacques. *Right of Inspection*. New York: Monacelli Press, 1998.

Descartes, René. *Meditations on First Philosophy*. John Cottingham ed. Cambridge: Cambridge University Press, 1996.

Dick, Philip K. *Do Androids Dream of Electric Sheep?* New York: Del Ray, 1968.

Dong. Dir. Jia Zhangke. Xstream Pictures, 2006.

Dunayevskaya, Raya. *Marxism and Freedom: From 1776 to Today.* New York: Humanity Books, 2000.
Dyer, Geoff. *Ways of Telling: The Work of John Berger.* London: Pluto, 1986.
Eagleton, Terry. *The Ideology of the Aesthetic.* Blackwell: Oxford, 1990.
Elson, Diane ed. *Value: The Representation of Labor in Capitalism.* New York: Verso, 1998.
Engels, Friedrich. *Anti-Dühring.* Karl Marx, Frederick Engels: Collected Works, Vol. 25. New York: International Publishers, 1987.
Federici, Silvia. *Revolution at Point Zero.* New York: PM Press, 2012.
Feltes, N.N. *Modes of Production of Victorian Novels.* Chicago: University of Chicago Press, 1989.
Figiel, Joanna, Stevphen Shukaitis, and Abe Walker. "Editorial" *ephemera: Theory and Politics in Organization* 14: 3: 308, 2014.
Foley, Barbara. *Radical Representations: Politics and Form in U.S. Proletarian Fiction, 1929–1941.* Durham: Duke University Press, 1993.
Fortunati, Leopoldina. *The Arcane of Reproduction: Housework, Prostitution, Labor and Capital.* New York: Autonomedia, 1996.
Friedman, Eli. *Insurgency Trap: Labor Politics in Postsocialist China.* Ithaca: Cornell ILR, 2014.
Gadamer, Hans-Georg. *Truth and Method.* 2nd rev Edition. Trans. Joel Weinsheimer and Donald G. Marshall. New York: Continuum, 1993.
Galeano, Eduardo. "Salgado, Seventeen Times" in *An Uncertain Grace.* Sebastião Salgado ed. New York: Aperture, 1990.
Gasiorek, Andrzej. *Postwar British Fiction: Realism and After.* London: Hodder, 1995.
Gauny, Gabriel. *Le philosophe plébéien.* Rancière Jacques ed. Paris: La découverte-Maspéro, 1983.
Gold Lust Dir. Neil Hollander. Adventure Film Productions, 1985.
Goodman, David S.G. *Class in Contemporary China.* Cambridge: Polity Press, 2014.
Gorz, Andre. *Farewell to the Working Class.* London: Pluto, 2001.
Grogan, Susan. *Flora Tristan: Life Stories.* London: Routledge, 1998.
Guenoun, Solange, and James H. Kavanagh. "Jacques Rancière, Literature, Politics, Aesthetics: Approaches to Democratic Disagreement" Interview with Jacques Rancière. *SubStance* 92 (2000): 3–24.
Haider, Asad, and Salar Mohandesi. "Workers' Inquiry: A Genealogy" Available at: https://viewpointmag.com/2013/09/27/workers-inquiry-a-genealogy/.
Han, Changfu. *Migrant Workers in China.* Singapore: Cengage Learning Asia, 2011.
Hannerz, Ulf. *Transnational Connections.* London: Routledge, 1996.
Hardt, Michael, and Antonio Negri. *Labor of Dionysus.* Minneapolis: University of Minnesota Press, 1994.

Hardt, Michael, and Antonio Negri. *Commonwealth*. Cambridge: Harvard University Press, 2009.
Harvey, David. *Limits to Capital*. New York: Verso, 2006.
Harvey, David. *A Brief History of Neoliberalism*. Oxford: Oxford University Press, 2007.
Harvey, David. *A Companion to Marx's Capital*. New York: Verso, 2010.
Harvey, David. *The Enigma of Capital*. London: Profile, 2010.
Hastings-King, Stephen. *Looking for the Proletariat: Socialisme ou Barbarie and the Problem of Worker Writing*. Chicago: Haymarket Books, 2015.
Haywood, Ian. *Working-Class Fiction: From Chartism to Trainspotting*. London: Northcote, 1997.
Heidegger, Martin. *Being and Time*. Trans. John Macquarrie and Edward Robinson. New York: Harper Perennial, 1962.
Henderson, George. *Value in Marx*. Minneapolis: University of Minnesota Press, 2013.
Heron, Liz, and Val Williams. eds. *Illuminations: Women Writing on Photography from the 1850s to the Present*. London: Tauris, 1996.
Herrán, Eric. *What is (the) Political? Notes on the Work of Claude Lefort*. Shelbyville, KY: Wasteland Press, 2013.
Hitchcock, Peter. *Working-Class Fiction in Theory and Practice: A Reading of Alan Sillitoe*. Ann Arbor: UMI Research Press, 1989.
Hitchcock, Peter. *Dialogics of the Oppressed*. Minneapolis: University of Minnesota Press, 1993a.
Hitchcock, Peter. *"Exotopy and Feminist Critique"*. David Shepherd ed. Bakhtin: Carnival and Other Subjects. Amsterdam: Rodopi Press, 1993b: 196–209.
Hitchcock, Peter. "Passing: Henry Green and Working-Class Identity" *Modern Fiction Studies* 40: 1 (Spring 1994): 1–31.
Hitchcock, Peter. *Oscillate Wildly: Space, Body, and Spirit of Millennial Materialism*. Minneapolis: University of Minnesota Press, 1999.
Hitchcock, Peter. "They Must be Represented?: Problems in Theories of Working-Class Representation" *PMLA* 115: 1 (January 2000): 20–32.
Hitchcock, Peter. *Imaginary States: Studies in Cultural Transnationalism*. Urbana/Champaign: University of Illinois Press, 2003.
Hitchcock, Peter. "Women, Men, and Exotopy: On the Politics of Scale in Nuruddin Farah's Maps" in *Masculinities in African Literary and Cultural Contexts*. Helen Nabasuta Mugambi and Tuzyline Jita Allan eds. Boulder: Lynne Reinner, 2010.
Hitchcock, Peter. "Defining the World" in *Literary Materialisms*. Mathias Nilges and Emilio Sauri eds. New York: Palgrave, 2013: 125–144.
Hitchcock, Peter. "Slumming" in *Passing: Essays in Identity and Interpretation*. Maria Sanchez and Linda Schlossberg eds. New York: New York University Press, 160–186, 2001.

Hopkinson, Amanda. "Interview with Salgado" *British Journal of Photography* 6762: 29 (March 1990): 11–12.
Irigaray, Luce. *This Sex Which is Not One*. Trans. Catherine Porter and Carolyn Burke. Ithaca: Cornell University Press, 1985.
James, C.L.R., Freddie Forest, and Ria Stone *The Invading Socialist Society*. 2nd Edition. Detroit: Bedwick Editions, 1972.
James, Selma. "A Woman's Place" in *The Power of Women and the Subversion of the Community*. Mariarosa Dalla Costa and Selma James co-authors. London: Falling Wall Press, 1972: 57–79.
Jameson, Fredric. *The Political Unconscious: Narrative as a Socially Symbolic Act*. Ithaca: Cornell University Press, 1981.
Jameson, Fredric. *Signatures of the Visible*. New York: Verso, 2007.
Jameson, Fredric. *Representing Capital*. New York: Verso, 2013.
Jameson, Fredric. *The Antinomies of Realism*. New York: Verso, 2013.
Jeffries, Hasan Kwame. *Bloody Lowndes: Civil Rights and Black Power in Alabama's Black Belt*. New York: New York University Press, 2009.
John, Woo. *A Better Tomorrow*. Starz/Anchor Bay, 1986.
Kirk, John. *Twentieth Century Writing and the British Working Class*. Cardiff: University of Wales Press, 2003.
Klaus, H. Gustav. *The Literature of Labor*. New York: St. Martin's Press, 1984.
Lacan, Jacques. *Four Fundamental Concepts of Psychoanalysis*. Trans. Alan Sheridan. New York: Norton, 1998.
Lacan, Jacques. *Écrits: A Selection*. Trans. Alan Sheridan. New York: Routledge, 2001.
Larsen, Neil, Mathias Nilges, Josh Robinson, and Nicholas Brown eds. *Marxism and the Critique of Value*. Chicago: MCM', 2014.
Lee, C.K. *Gender and the South China Miracle: Two Worlds of Factory Women*. California: University of California Press, 1998.
Lee, C.K. *Against the Law: Labor Protests in China's Rustbelt and Sunbelt*. California: University of California Press, 2007.
Lee, Kevin. "Jia Zhang-ke" *Senses of Cinema*, 25 (March 2003). Available at: http://sensesofcinema.com/2003/great-directors/jia/.
Lefort, Claude. "L'experience prolétarienne" *Socialisme ou Barbarie* 11 (novembre/decembre 1952): 1–19.
Lefort, Claude. *Éléments d'une critique de la bureaucratie*. Paris: Gallimard, 1971.
Lefort, Claude. *"Proletarian Experience"*. Trans. Stephen Hastings-King. Available at: http://viewpointmag.com/2013/09/26/proletarian-experience/.
Les Revoltes Logiques No.1. Hiver 1975.
Levine, Philip. *What Work is*. New York: Knopf, 1991.
Lippincott, Robin. "One Big Canvas: The Work of John Berger" *The Literary Review* 35 (Fall 1991): 134–142.
Looking Back at You. Dir. Snell, Andrew. BBC, 1993.

Lotringer, Sylvere, and Christian Marazzi eds. *Autonomia: Post-Political Politics.* New York: Semiotext(e), 2007.

Lü, Guoguang. *Behind the Chinese Miracle: Migrant Workers Tell their Stories.* San Francisco: Long River Press, 2012.

Lukacs, Georg. *Toward the Ontology of Social Being: Labor.* Trans. David Fernbach. London: Merlin Press, 1980.

Lukacs, Georg. *The Historical Novel.* Trans. Hannah Mitchell and Stanley Mitchell. Lincoln: University of Nebraska Press, 1983.

Lukacs, Georg. *History and Class Consciousness: Studies in Marxist Dialectics.* Trans. Rodney Livingstone. Cambridge, MA: The MIT Press, 2000.

Lu, Xinyu. "Ruins of the Future: Class and History in Wang Bing's Tiexi District" *New Left Review 31* (January/February 2005): 125–136.

Macherey, Pierre. *A Theory of Literary Production.* Trans. Geoffrey Wall. New York: Routledge, 2006.

Makreel, Rudolph A. *Dilthey, Philosopher of the Human Studies.* Princeton: Princeton University Press, 1975.

Mantel, Hilary. *A Place of Greater Safety.* London: Picador, 2006.

Manufactured Landscapes. Dir. Jennifer Baichwal. Zeitgeist Films, 2006.

Mardi Gras: Made in China Dir. David Redmon. Carnivalesque Films, 2005.

Marx, Karl. "Economic and Philosophic Manuscripts of 1844" in *The Marx-Engels Reader.* Robert Tucker ed. New York: Norton, 1978: 70–91.

Marx, Karl. *Capital*, Three Vols. Ernest Mandel ed. London: Penguin, 1990.

Marx, Karl, and Friedrich Engels. *The German Ideology.* New York: Martino Fine Books, 2011.

Marx, Karl, and Friedrich Engels. *The Communist Manifesto.* Intro. Eric Hobsbawm. New York: Verso, 2012.

Mauss, Marcel. *The Gift.* Trans. W. D. Halls. New York: W.W. Norton, 2000.

McGrath, Jason. *Postsocialist Modernity: Chinese Cinema, Literature, and Criticism in the Market Age.* Palo Alto: Stanford University Press, 2010.

Medvedev, P.N. *The Formal Method in Literary Scholarship: A Critical Introduction to Sociological Poetics.* Trans. Albert J. Wehrle. Cambridge MA: Harvard University Press, 1985.

Merrifield, Andy. *John Berger.* London: Reaktion, 2012.

Mezzadro, Sandro, and Brett Neilson. *Border as Method, or, the Multiplication of Labor.* Durham: Duke University Press, 2013.

Mitchell, David. *Cloud Atlas.* New York: Random House, 2004.

Montag, Warren. "Rancière's Lost Object" *Cultural Critique* 83 (Winter 2013): 139–155.

Mountains May Depart (Shan he gu ren). Dir. Jia Zhangke. Office Kitano, Xstream Pictures et al., 2015.

Nair, Parvati. *A Different Light: The Photography of Sebastião Salgado.* Durham, NC: Duke University Press, 2012.

Nederveen Pieterse, Jan. *Globalization and Culture.* London: Rowman and Littlefield, 2008.
Negri, Antonio. *Marx Beyond Marx.* Trans. Harry Cleaver. New York: Autonomedia, 1992.
Negri, Antonio. *Goodbye, Mr. Socialism.* New York: Seven Stories Press, 2008.
Ness, Immanuel. *Southern Insurgency: The Coming of the Global Working Class.* London: Pluto, 2016.
Orvell, Miles. *After the Machine.* Jackson, MI: University Press of Mississippi, 1995.
Osnos, Evan. "The Long Shot" *New Yorker*, 11 May (2009).
Pai, Hsiao-Hung. *Scattered Sand: The Story of China's Rural Migrants.* New York: Verso, 2013.
Panzieri, Raniero. *Socialist Uses of Workers' Inquiry.* Trans. Arianna Bove. Available at: http://eipcp.net/transversal/0406/panzieri/en.
Papstergiadis, Nikos. "John Berger: An Interview" *The American Poetry Review* 22 (July/August 1993a): 9–12.
Papstergiadis, Nikos. *Modernity as Exile: The Stranger in John Berger's Writing.* Manchester: Manchester University Press, 1993b.
Serra Pelada. Dir. Heitor Dhalia. Paranoid, 2013.
Perera, Sonali. *No Country: Working-Class Writing in the Age of Globalization.* New York: Columbia University Press, 2014.
Pfeil, Fred. "Between Salvage and Silvershades: John Berger and What's Left" *TriQuarterly* 88 (Fall 1993): 230–243.
Piketty, Thomas. *Capital in the Twenty-First Century.* Trans. Arthur Goldhammer. Cambridge, MA: Harvard University Press, 2014.
Pizzolato, Nicola. *Challenging Global Capitalism: Labor Migration, Radical Struggle, and Urban Change in Detroit and Turin.* London: Palgrave, 2013a.
Pizzolato, Nicola. "The American Worker and the Forze Nuove: Turin and Detroit at the Twilight of Fordism" *Viewpoint*, 3 (2013b). Available at: https://viewpointmag.com/2013/09/25/the-american-worker-and-the-forze-nuove-turin-and-detroit-at-the-twilight-of-fordism/.
Platform (Zhantai). Dir. Jia Zhangke. Office Kitano et al., 2000.
Plato. *The Republic.* Ed. and trans. Allan Bloom. New York: Basic Books, 1991.
Pun, Ngai. *Made in China: Women Factory Workers in a Global Workplace.* Durham: Duke University Press, 2005.
Pun, Ngai. *Migrant Labor in China.* London: Polity, 2016.
Qian, Ying. "Power in the Frame: China's Independent Documentary Movement" *New Left Review* 74 (March/April 2012): 105–123.
Rabinowitz, Paula. *Labor and Desire: Women's Revolutionary Fiction in Depression America.* Chapel Hill: University of North Carolina Press, 1991.
Rancière, Jacques. "On the Theory of Ideology" *Radical Philosophy* 7 (Spring 1974a): 1–14.

Rancière, Jacques. *La Leçon d'Althusser*. Paris: Gallimard, 1974b.
Rancière, Jacques. *La Nuit des prolétaires: Archives du rêve ouvrier*. Paris: Fayard, 1981.
Rancière, Jacques. *Le Philosophe et ses pauvres*. 1st Edition. Paris: Fayard, 1983; 2nd edn, Paris: Flammarion, 2007.
Rancière, Jacques. *The Nights of Labor: The Workers' Dream in Nineteenth-Century France*. Trans. John Drury. Introduced by Donald Reid. Philadelphia: Temple University Press, 1989.
Rancière, Jacques. *Disagreement*. Trans. Julie Rose. Minneapolis: University of Minnesota Press, 1999.
Rancière, Jacques. *The Philosopher and His Poor*. Trans. Andrew Parker Durham: Duke University Press, 2004.
Rancière, Jacques. *Film Fables*. Trans. Emiliano Battista. London: Bloomsbury, 2006.
Rancière, Jacques. *Dissensus: On Politics and Aesthetics*. Ed. and Trans. Steven Corcoran London: Continuum, 2009.
Rancière, Jacques. "Communists Without Communism?" in *The Idea of Communism*. Costas Douzinas and Slavoj Zizek eds. New York: Verso, 2010: 167–177.
Rancière, Jacques. *Althusser's Lesson*. Trans. Emiliano Battista. New York: Continuum, 2011a.
Rancière, Jacques. *Staging the People*. Trans. David Fernbach. New York: Verso, 2011b.
Rancière, Jacques. *Proletarian Nights: The Workers' Dream in Nineteenth-Century France*. Edition with New Preface by Rancière. Trans. David Fernbach. New York: Verso, 2012a.
Rancière, Jacques. *The Intellectual and His People*. Trans. David Fernbach New York: Verso, 2012b.
Rayns, Tony. "Heard it Through the Grapevine" *Film Comment*, September/October 2013.
Read, Jason. "Politics as Subjectification: Rethinking the Figure of the Worker in the Thought of Badiou and Rancière" *Philosophy Today*, SPEP Supplement (2007): 125–132.
Rifkin, Jeremy. *The End of Work*. New York: Putnam, 1996.
Ritchin, Fred. "The Lyric Documentarian" in *An Uncertain Grace*. Sebastião Salgado ed. New York: Aperture, 1990.
Robbins, Bruce. "Feeling Global: John Berger and Experience" in *Postmodernism and Politics*. Jonathan Arac ed. Minneapolis: University of Minnesota Press, 1986: 145–161.
Robbins, Bruce. "John Berger's Disappearing Peasants" *Minnesota Review* 28 (Spring 1987): 63–67.
Robbins, Bruce. *The Servant's Hand: English Fiction from Below*. Durham: Duke University Press, 1993.

Roberts, Bruce. "The Visible and the Measurable" in *Postmodern Materialism and the Future of Marxist Theory*. Antonio Callari and David Ruccio eds. Middletown, CT: Wesleyan University Press, 1996: 193–211.
Robertson, Roland. *Globalization*. London: Sage, 1992.
Robinson, Cedric J. *Black Marxism: The Making of the Black Radical Tradition*. London: Zed Press, 1983.
Romano, Paul, and Ria Stone. "The American Worker" 1947. Available at: https://libcom.org/history/american-worker-paul-romano-ria-stone.
Roy, Arundhati. *Power Politics*. Cambridge MA: South End Press, 2001.
Said, Edward. *Beginnings: Intention and Method*. New York: Columbia University Press, 1985.
Salgado, Sebastião. *An Uncertain Grace*. New York: Aperture, 1990.
Salgado, Sebastião. "A Lecture" in *The Photo Review 16*. Stephen Perloff ed. (Fall 1993a): 10.
Salgado, Sebastião. *Workers: An Archaeology of the Industrial Age*. New York: Phaidon, 1993b.
Salgado, Sebastião. *Migrations: Humanity in Transition*. New York: Aperture, 2000a.
Salgado, Sebastião. *The Children*. New York: Aperture, 2000b.
Salgado, Sebastião. *Sahel: The End of the Road*. Berkeley: University of California Press, 2004.
Salgado, Sebastião. *Africa*. Cologne: Taschen, 2007.
Salgado, Sebastião. *Genesis*. New York: Taschen, 2013.
Salgado, Sebastião. *Sebastião Salgado: Other Americas*. With Claude Nori, Gonzalo Ballester, and Alan Riding New York: Aperture, 2015a.
Salgado, Sebastião. *The Scent of a Dream: Travels in the World of Coffee*. New York: Abrams, 2015b.
The Salt of the Earth, Dir. Juliano Ribeiro Salgado and Wim Wenders. Sony, 2014.
Shukaitis, Stevphen, Joanna Figiel, and Abe Walker. "A Workers' Inquiry Reader" Available at: http://www.ephemerajournal.org/events/politics-workers-inquiry.
Silverman, Kaja. *The Miracle of Analogy, or, the History of Photography*. Palo Alto: Stanford University Press, 2015.
Simon, Henri. "Workers' Inquiry in Socialisme ou Barbarie" *Special Issue of Viewpoint Magazine on the Workers' Inquiry*, available at https://libcom.org/library/workers'-inquiry-socialisme-ou-barbarie.
Sischy, Ingrid. "Good Intentions" *New Yorker*, September 9th (1991): 89–95.
Smith, Neil. *The Endgame of Globalization*. New York: Routledge, 2004.
Soar, Matthew. "The Advertising Photography of Richard Avedon and Sebastião Salgado" in *Image Ethics in the Digital Age*. Larry Gross, John Stuart Katz, and Jay Ruby eds. Minneapolis: University of Minnesota Press, 2003: 269–294.
Sontag, Susan. *Regarding the Pain of Others*. New York: Picador, 2003.

The Spectre of Hope. Dir. Paul Carlin. Netherlands: Minerva Picture Company, 2002.
Spivak, Gayatri Chakravorty. "Finding Feminist Readings" *Social Text* 3 (Autumn 1980): 73–87.
Spivak, Gayatri Chakravorty. "Scattered Speculations on the Question of Value" *Diacritics* 15: 4 (Winter 1984): 73–93.
Stallabrass, Julian. "Sebastião Salgado and Fine Art Photojournalism" *New Left Review* 223 (1997): 131–162.
Still Life (Sanxia haoren) Dir. Jia Zhangke. Xstream Pictures and Shanghai Film Group, 2006.
Tie Xi Qu (West of the Tracks). Dir. Wang Bing. Wang Bing Film Workshop, 2002.
Tomlinson, John. *Globalization and Culture*. Chicago: University of Chicago Press, 1999.
A Touch of Sin (Tian zhu ding). Dir. Jia Zhangke. Xstream Pictures, Office Kitano and Shanghai Film Group et al. 2013.
Tristan, Flora. *The London Journal of Flora Tristan 1842: The Aristocracy and the Working Class of England*. Trans. Jean Hawkes London: Virago, 1989.
Tronti, Mario. *Operai e Capitale*. Roma: DeriveApprodi, 2006.
Tronti, Mario. "Our Operaismo" *New Left Review* 73 (January–February 2012): 119–139.
Tucker, Robert C. ed. *The Marx/Engels Reader*. Norton: New York, 1978.
Unknown Pleasures (Ren Xiao Yao). Dir. Jia Zhangke. Office Kitano et al., 2002.
Wald, Matthew L. "Sebastião Salgado: The Eye of the Photojournalist" *New York Times Magazine*, June 9th (1991).
Wang, Hui. "Jia Zhangke's World and China's Great Transformation" Trans. Nathaniel Proctor. *Positions* 19: 1 (Spring 2011): 217–228.
Wang, Xiaodong. "'Lun Jia Zhangke dianying zhong de guxiang' ['Hometown in Jia Zhangke's Films']" *Dianying wenxue [Film Literature]* 5 (2009): 53–82.
Weeks, Kathi. *The Problem with Work*. Durham: Duke University Press, 2011.
Weil, Simone. "Human Personality" in *Simone Weil: An Anthology*. Ed. and Introduced by SianMiles. New York: Grove Press, 2000.
Williams, Raymond. *Marxism and Literature*. Oxford: Oxford University Press, 1978.
Williams, Raymond. *Resources of Hope: Culture, Democracy, Socialism*. New York: Verso, 1989.
Wolff, Richard D., B. Roberts Bruce, and Antonio Callari "Marx's (not Ricardo's) 'TransformationProblem': A Radical Reconceptualization" *History of Political Economy* 14: 4 (1982): 564–582.
The World (Shijie). Dir. Jia Zhangke. Office Kitano and Shanghai Film Group et al., 2004.

Wright Mills, C. "Letter to the New Left" *New Left Review*, 5 (September–October 1960).
Wright, Steve. *Storming Heaven: Class Composition and Struggle in Italian Autonomist Marxism*. London: Pluto, 2002.
Yulu. Dir. Jia Zhangke. Xstream Pictures, 2011.
Zandy, Janet. *Hands: Physical Labor, Class, and Cultural Work*. New Brunswick: Rutgers University Press, 2004.
Zhang, Lu. *Inside China's Automobile Factories: The Politics of Labor and Worker Resistance*. Cambridge: Cambridge University Press, 2014.
Zhang, Xudong. "Poetics of Vanishing" *New Left Review* 63 (May/June 2010): 71–88.
Zhang, Xudong. "Market Socialism and its Discontent: Jia Zhangke's Cinematic Narrative of China's Transition in the Age of Global Capital" in *Neoliberalism and Global Cinema: Capital, Culture, and Marxist Critique*. Jyotsna Kapur and Keith B. Wagner eds. London: Routledge, 2011: 135–156.
Zizek, Slavoj. "The Lesson of Rancière" in *Jacques Rancière, The Politics of Aesthetics*. Trans. Gabriel Rockhill. London: Continuum, 2004.
Zizek, Slavoj. *Revolution at the Gates*. New York: Verso, 2004.

INDEX

A

Accumulation, vi–ix, 12, 62, 66, 77, 88, 169, 189n47, 200, 215
Adams, Ansell, 137
Adorno, T. W., 16, 41n23, 183
Aesthetics, 6, 13, 24, 51, 61, 64, 70n8, 72n26, 73n27, 84, 86, 89, 98n18, 109, 131n14, 134, 157, 183, 186n17, 217, 214
Affect, 30, 31, 35, 62, 64, 70n6, 76, 90, 99n26, 99n27, 113, 139, 196, 203, 218
Agamben, Giorgio, vii, xiin2, xiiin7
Albert, Eric, 26, 43n39
Algren, Nelson, 19
Ali, Tariq, 73n29
Althusser, Louis, 51, 58, 59, 61, 67–68, 70n8, 72n21, 78–80, 85, 87, 96n6, 97n11, 97n16
The American Worker, 10, 11, 14, 15, 17–20, 31, 40n16, 40n17, 181
Another Way of Telling, 108, 119, 130n6, 131n8, 131n11, 138, 147, 185n8, 185n12
Answerability, 84, 114, 118, 120, 124, 128, 129, 136

Antinomy, v, 12, 15, 26, 34, 50, 52, 54–55, 57, 58, 60, 65, 77, 90, 92, 99n26, 106, 174, 183, 198, 200
Aphanisis, 49, 52, 134, 135, 194, 210
Appadurai, Arjun, xiiin5
Aronowitz, Stanley, 96n8
Artisan, 3, 37n2, 58, 61, 62, 71n9
Auerbach, Erich, ix, 6, 7, 9, 10, 12, 15, 18, 21, 36, 37n5, 38n9, 39n15, 41n22, 89, 110
Austen, Jane, 83
Autonomia (operaismo), 32, 44n47, 45n49, 69n4

B

Badiou, Alain, 64, 70n8, 71n11, 73n29, 91, 97n11, 99n31
Bakhtin, M. M., 70n7, 109, 131n14, 135, 143, 159, 167, 175, 185n7, 185n17, 186n19, 187n33, 188n42
Balibar, Étienne, 53–60, 63, 66, 68, 72n14, 72n16, 72n17, 72n18, 72n19, 72n21, 96n6, 97n11, 105, 130n3
Balzac, Honoré de, 61, 83, 90

Barthes, Roland, 139, 162, 165, 185n15, 188n36
Benjamin, Walter, 5, 29, 35, 38n8, 43n40, 45n52, 55, 180, 183, 185n13, 188n39, 190n57, 193, 206, 219n5, 221n19
Before the Flood, 208, 221n20
Berger, John, Chapter Four, 98–131, *passim*, viii, x, xi, xivn11, xvi, 80, 103–132, 136, 138–139, 141–149, 151, 154, 159, 161, 168, 177–179, 182–183, 185n8, 185n12, 189n49, 192, 214
Berry, Chris, 220n10
Bogre, Michelle, 187n32
Bosker, Bianca, 221n18
Bosteels, Bruno, 73n29
Bourdieu, Pierre, 5, 38n7
Bourgeoisie, 55, 104, 206
Brant, Marie (Selma James), 20, 42n28
Bresson, Robert, 133, 195, 198, 211, 220n11
Buhle, Paul, 40n20, 41n26

C

Cadava, Eduardo, 71n12
Caffentzis, Georges, 97n16, 97n17
Caillebotte, Gustave, 90, 91, 93
Capital, vii–ix, xi, 5, 8, 11, 16–18, 22, 25, 29, 32, 34, 39n13, 48, 50–53, 57–59, 62–69, 69n1, 74n34, 75–91, 93–94, 97n11, 97n13, 97n15, 98n18, 106, 109, 130n2, 136, 139, 153, 156, 159, 160, 164, 165, 167, 169, 176, 182, 183, 187n31, 188n40, 189n47, 191–194, 199, 206, 211, 213, 222n27
Capital and labor (relation), 8, 52, 80, 86, 191
Capital (cultural), 38n7, 182

Capital, Marx, 8, 29, 39n13, 45n49, 52, 53, 57–59, 63, 65, 69n1, 69n3, 71n13, 79, 81, 82, 85–88, 96n9, 104–105, 130n2, 161, 219n3
Capitalism, vi, ix, x, xiiin8, 8, 11, 12, 14–15, 17, 29, 34, 35, 40n20, 44n48, 51–52, 58, 59, 61, 63, 65–67, 69n1, 73n31, 75, 77, 78, 84–86, 88, 89, 109, 134, 137, 139, 152, 156, 157, 167, 171, 174, 176, 185n11, 187n31, 188n40, 191, 193, 195, 198, 207, 213, 217
Capitalism, racial, x, 15, 157, 187n31
Capitalist, viii, xiiin6, xiiin7, 17, 25–27, 32, 33, 35, 41n23, 45n49, 53, 57, 76, 78, 80, 82, 84, 87–89, 91, 94, 95, 98n18, 104, 105, 111, 134, 137, 161, 165–167, 169, 171, 184n1, 192, 203, 207, 217
Castoriadis, Cornelius, 26, 27, 43n33, 43n38
Chen, Joan, 212
China, 49, 77, 88, 154, 192, 194, 195, 200, 201, 204, 205, 207, 208, 210–212, 214, 217, 218, *passim*, 218n7, 220n8, 221n13, 222n24, 222n27
China Blue, 212, 221n22
Chiu Kui-fen, 220n10
Chow Yun-Fat, 209
Class, architectonics of, 106
Class composition, xi, 24, 31–33, 35, 44n45, 218
Class consciousness, 60, 62, 70n6, 80, 97n15, 98n24, 131n16, 161
Class struggle, vii, 13, 39, 69n4, 77, 80, 81, 87, 89, 105
Cloud Atlas (novel and film), 93, 100n33

Commodity, viii, xiiin7, 28, 48, 53, 57, 63, 69n1, 69n3, 75, 77, 79, 81–82, 85–87, 89, 91, 98n21, 199n26, 153, 168, 180–183, 184n6, 186n25, 219n3
Common, the, 66, 73n32
Communism, xiiin7, 10, 15, 30, 54, 57, 61, 63, 64, 72n24, 73n29, 83, 173, 184n6, 213
Communist Manifesto, 6, 25, 38n10, 52, 57, 71n9, 187n31
Comportment (Lefort), 24, 25, 27, 43n35
Correspondence (group), 13, 14, 20
Cott, Jonathan, 187n32
Crary, Jonathan, 184n4
cultural materialism, v

D

Dagong, 194, 203, 204, 206, 213, 218–219
Dalla Costa, Mariarosa, 35, 45n51
Alighieri, Dante, 6, 7
Dean, Jodi, xi, 73n29
Debs, Eugene, 19
de Goncourt, Edmond and Jules, 9, 39n14
Deleuze, Gilles xiin2, 210–211, 221n21
del Valle Alcalá, Roberto, xiin2
Denby, Charles, 21–22, 31, 42n47, 42n30
Deranty, Jean-Phillippe, 37n4, 71n11
Dereliction, 198–199, 204, 212, 219
Derrida, Jacques, 135, 139, 141, 159–161, 164–167, 170, 171, 184n6, 185n14, 188n35, 188n40, 189n45, 193
Descartes, René, 54–55

Dialectic, vii, ix, xii, 4, 6, 9, 12, 14, 16, 18, 28, 29, 35, 36, 41n22, 41n23, 43n37, 45n49, 48, 50, 52, 55, 59, 60, 65, 67, 69, 76, 86–88, 90, 91, 95, 98n18, 98n24, 99n30, 105–107, 178, 183, 187n27, 189n49, 191, 193, 196, 200, 204, 207
Dialogic, xiin3, 12, 33, 39n13, 52, 163, 187n33
Dick, Philip K., 93, 99n27
DiFazio, William, 96n8
Disneyland, 206
Documentary, 18, 24, 25, 27, 29, 134–136, 151, 167, 172, 177–178, 181, 184n3, 186n26, 186n27, 190n54, 195, 196, 200, 207, 208, 212, 220n8, 220n10, 222n23, 222n24
Dong, 207, 208
Dunayevskaya, Raya, 10, 18, 22, 40n18, 41n24, 42n30
Dyer, Geoff, 130n4

E

Eagleton, Terry, xiiin10, 73n26
Eisenstein, Sergei, 92, 210
Elson, Diane, 94
Engels, Friedrich, vi, 38n10, 52
Erlebnis, 5, 37n6
Evans, Walker, 137
Eventness, 50, 70n7
Exotopy, 158, 167, 187n33

F

Falling labor, 200
Federici, Silvia, 23, 42n31, 45n51, 189n47
Feltes, N.N., 84, 97n14
Figiel, Joanna, 19, 41n25, 43n34

Figura, ix, 6, 7, 9, 17, 30, 89
Foley, Barbara, 90, 99n29
Fortunati, Leopoldina, 35, 45n51
Foucault, Michel, 135
Friedman, Eli, 222n25

G

Gadamer, Hans-Georg, 37n6
Galeano, Eduardo, 152
Gasiorek, Andrzej, 130n4
Gauny, Gabriel, 61–62, 70n5, 72n25
Gift, 50, 116, 126, 134–136, 141, 143, 152, 157, 159–172, 175, 183, 188n34, 188n40, 189n47
Globalization, vi–ix, xi, xiin1, xiin2, xiin5, xiiin7, xivn11, 68, 76, 82, 106, 129, 134, 136–138, 140, 142, 146, 149, 150, 155, 157, 172–174, 177, 179–181, 183, 186n23, 186n25, 189n47, 190n53, 191–192, 202, 203, 206, 208, 211, 213–215, 217, 218, 219n2, 222n24
Gödel, Kurt, 92
Goethe, Johann Wolfgang von, 6, 38n10
Gold Lust, 169, 188n43
Goodman, David S.G., 222n27
Gorz, Andre, xi, 96n8
Grace, 134, 152, 159, 162, 164, 166–172, 180
Granel, Gerard, 54
Grogan, Susan, 39n13
Grundrisse, Marx, 34, 85, 94

H

Haider, Asad, 10, 19, 20, 31, 39n12, 42n27
Hammershoi, Vilhelm, 90
Han Changfu, 220n7
Hannerz, Ulf, xiiin5
Hardt, Michael, xiiin7, 66, 73n32, 78, 96n5, 98n18
Harvey, David, xvi, 59, 68, 72n23, 74n34, 84, 88, 95n1, 97n10
Hastings-King, Stephen, 11, 20, 27, 29–31, 40n19, 43n41, 44n43, 97n15
Haywood, Ian, 90, 99n29
Hegel, G.W.F., 6, 42n30, 55, 79, 85, 89, 97n16
Heidegger, Martin, 24, 43n35, 112, 113, 123, 135, 145, 184n6
Henderson, George, 82, 95n1, 97n12
Heron, Liz, 189n52
Herrán, Eric, 43n33
Hinckley, John, 133
Hine, Lewis, 137
Hitchcock, Peter, xiin1, 38n10, 70n7, 96n6, 130n1, 131n17, 187n33
Hopkinson, Amanda, 187n32
Horkheimer, Max, 16, 41n23
Hu, King, 215

I

Ideology, 21, 30, 50, 56–58, 61, 63, 67–68, 77, 105, 106, 130n8, 131n16, 133, 149, 161, 167, 168, 169, 172, 173, 179, 204, 210
Involution, 197, 203, 219
Irigaray, Luce, 70n6

J

James, C.L.R., 10, 41n24, 41n26
Jameson, Fredric, 15, 41n22, 87–94, 96n7, 99n26, 99n30
James, Selma, 20, 35, 42n28, 45n51
Jeffries, Hasan Kwame, 42n29

Johnson-Forest Tendency, 10, 13, 17, 19, 40n18, 42n30
Joy Division, 198

K
Kirk, John, xi, 90, 99n29
Klaus, H. Gustav, 90, 99n29

L
Labor, cultural representation of, v, vi, ix–xi, xiiin10, xivn11, xvi, 28, 32, 65, 76, 81, 86, 88, 89, 130n4, 187n27, 189n53, 193
Labor in culture, v, viii, xi, xivn11, 11, 16, 29, 30, 35, 36, 38n9, 39n13, 40n16, 43n36, 72n15, 106, 109, 119, 187n27, 188n34, 191, 192, 207, 209, 211, 214
Labor, vii–ix, 3–36, 37n5, 45n51, 50, 59, 71n9, 75–95, 95n1, 96n5, 98n24, 99n29, 165, 185n16, 191–219, 220n7, 221n12, 222n25
Labor, migration, 32, 206, 212, 219n7
Labor mimesis, 29–30, 34, 71n13, 190n53
Labor power, 15, 63, 64, 75, 77–80, 83, 85, 86, 88, 92, 94, 95, 114, 174, 194, 196, 205, 211
Labor, as relation, 28–30, 33, 35, 48, 50–52, 65–68, 69n4, 76, 81, 84, 86, 90, 91, 92, 98n18, 109, 136, 165, 179, 191, 193, 213
Labor value, 64, 75, 76, 80, 81, 85, 86, 89
Lacan, Jacques, 30, 60, 86, 162, 163, 176, 188n37, 188n38, 213
Larsen, Neil, 95n1
Lee, C.K., 220n7, 222n25
Lee, Kevin, 220n11
Lefort, Claude, 11, 23–29, 40n19, 42n32, 43n33, 43n35
Lenin, V.I., 42n30, 77, 86, 89, 165, 206
Levine, Philip, 48, 69n2, 197, 221n14
Lilac and Flag, (Berger), 123–127, 142
Lim Giong, 214
Lin Chun, 223n27
Lippincott, Robin, 118, 131n9
Liu Xiaodong, 207
Lotringer, Sylvere, 44n47
Lü Guoguang, 219n7
Lukacs, Attila Richard, 92
Lukacs, Georg, 84, 89, 97n14, 98n24, 99n30
Lumière, 193
Lu Xinyu, 220n10, 222n23

M
Macdonald, Patricia, 106, 130n6, 131n16
Macherey, Pierre, 72n21, 83, 84, 96n6, 97n13, 210
Makreel, Rudolph A, 37n6
Mantel, Hilary, 91, 100n32
Manufactured Landscapes, 212, 221n22
Maoism, 51, 194, 199, 200, 213
Mao Zedong, 195, 196, 199, 201, 209, 212, 215, 216
Marikana massacre, xi
Marazzi, Christian, 44n47, 45n49, 45n50
Mardi Gras: Made in China, 212, 221n22

244 INDEX

Marxism, xvi, 11, 20, 27, 37n4, 40n18, 40n20, 42n30, 44n48, 52, 57, 59, 60, 70n5, 75, 78, 80, 83, 85–86, 89, 95n1, 97n11, 98n24, 161, 199, 200
Marx, Karl, vi, viii, 7, 8, 11, 15, 21, 25, 28, 31, 34, 38n10, 52, 55, 58, 61, 63, 69n1, 69n3, 71n13, 75, 76, 78–83, 85–90, 94, 95, 95n1, 98n21, 104–106, 109, 115, 130n2, 130n7, 132n18, 150, 161, 183, 184n6, 193, 219n3, 219n4
Mauss, Marcel, 159, 188n34
McGrath, Jason, 200, 221n16
Medvedev,P.N., 186n17
Memory, 50, 93, 108, 116, 121, 124, 125, 127, 139–141, 144–147, 150, 154, 168, 212, 217–218
Merrifield, Andy, 130n4
Mezzadro, Sandro, xivn12
Migrant, 56, 58, 67, 127, 128, 178, 194, 195, 204, 205, 216, 217, 219, 220n7
Mimesis, ix, 5–6, 9–11, 15, 18, 19, 23, 27–30, 34, 37n5, 38n9, 39n15, 41n22, 43n40, 89, 110, 190n53
Mitchell, David, 93
Mohandesi, Salar, 10, 19, 20, 31, 39n12, 42n27, 44n44, 44n46, 45n50
Mohr, Jean, 106, 119, 130n6, 131n8, 131n11, 138, 141–147, 149, 151, 154, 178, 185n8, 185n12
Montag, Warren, 59, 72n22
Montaldi, Danilo, 31, 32, 44n46
Mothé, Daniel (Jacques Gautrat), 29–31, 43n41, 44n44
Mountains May Depart, 197, 214
Moving labor, 191–219
Multiculturalism, vii
Multitude, xi, 210

N
Nair, Parvati, 148, 184n1
Nancy, Jean-Luc, 53–56, 58, 71n12, 208
Nederveen Pieterse, Jan, xiiin5
Negri, Antonio, xi, 66, 73n32, 78, 85, 96n5, 96n8, 97n16
Neilson, Brett Neilson, xii, xivn12
Neoliberalism, xiiin5, 106, 189n47, 220n12
Ness, Immanuel, 222n25
Nolan, Christopher, 92

O
Occupy Wall Street, 67
Once in Europa, (Berger), 110, 111, 113, 114, 121, 125, 128
Orvell, Miles, 151, 179–181, 190n54
Oscillate Wildly, xiin3
Osnos, Evan, 220n11
Other, the, 83, 89, 90, 104, 109, 118–120, 124, 128, 135, 141, 143, 147, 149, 152, 156–160, 163, 166, 202
Out-of-timeness, 50, 51, 137, 145, 161, 164, 185n11, 193, 194

P
Pai, Hsiao-Hung, 219n7
Panzieri, Raniero, 32, 33, 45n49
Papstergiadis, Nikos, 131n12
Parker, Andrew, 71n10
Peasant, xi, 104, 106–111, 113, 115–122, 124–126, 128, 141–146, 172, 179, 196, 197, 200
Perera, Sonali, xiin2
Pfeil, Fred, 107, 124

Pig Earth, (Berger), 113, 114, 117–119
Piketty, Thomas, 76, 77, 82–87, 92, 96n3, 97n11
Pimenov, Yuri, 87
Pizzolato, Nicola, 40n17
Platform (Jia Zhangke), 194, 198–202, 207, 216
Plato, 3–6, 36n1, 38n7, 38n9, 93
Postcolonialism, 28, 153, 160
Postsocialism, 198, 199, 200, 201
Production, social, viii, ix, 23, 52, 75
Proletarian being, 36n2, 38n10, 81, 103–106, 134, 161, 213
Proletarianization, 10, 19, 49, 77, 82, 103–106, 108–110, 113, 140, 177, 192, 194, 217, 219n6
Proletarian, x, 3, 4, 8, 16, 18, 19, 23–28, 30–33, 36n2, 38n10, 42n32, 43n35, 43n40, 49–51, 53, 57–68, 69n1, 71n9, 81, 85, 91, 97n15, 103–106, 134, 136, 161, 179, 185n11, 196, 201, 213
Proletariat, x, 24, 26, 56–58, 60, 63, 66, 69n5, 71n12, 97n15, 98n24, 103, 105, 220n7
Punctum, 162, 165, 166, 168, 170, 200, 205
Pun Ngai, 220n7

Q
Quin, Mike, 28
Quin, Mike, 19

R
Rabinowitz, Paula, 90, 99n29
Rana Plaza, xi

Rancière, Jacques, x, xi, 3, 4, 8, 25, 36n2, 37n5, 49–53, 58–68, 69n5, 71n9, 71n10, 72n21, 72n24, 72n25, 72n26, 73n28, 73n30, 73n33, 96n6
Rayns, Tony, 215
Read, Jason, 71n11
Reagan, Ronald, 133
Realism, 6, 9, 10, 18, 24, 41n22, 54, 78, 83, 89–91, 94, 99n26, 99n29, 110, 130n4, 134, 142, 181, 198, 200, 201, 203, 207, 208, 211, 214
Representation, v, vi, viii–xi, xiin1, xiin2, xiiin10, xivn11, xvi, 5–19, 21, 24, 27–30, 32, 34, 36, 37n6, 38n9, 43n37, 43n40, 48, 54, 65, 67, 69n1, 70n5, 76, 78, 79, 81, 84–92, 94, 98n18, 109, 122, 125, 130n4, 134, 136, 137, 142, 148–149, 151, 159, 161, 164, 166, 169, 172, 176, 183, 184n2, 186n19, 187n27, 188n40, 189n53, 191, 193, 194, 200, 207, 210, 211, 214, 216, 217
Reproduction, social, vii, ix, 4–5, 17, 23, 82, 174, 221n14
Revoltes Logiques, Les, 4
Revolution, 15, 23–26, 41n23, 42n30, 48, 55, 57, 94, 100n32, 105, 140, 161, 195, 207
Ricardo, David, 61, 75, 78, 95n1
Rifkin, Jeremy, 140
Ritchin, Fred, 167, 168
Robbins, Bruce, 9, 39n15, 118
Roberts, Bruce, 97n17
Robertson, Roland, xiiin5
Robinson, Cedric J., 40n21, 187n31
Romano, Paul (Phil Singer), 10, 12–21, 24, 26, 27, 40n16, 41n23, 41n26, 42n32, 219n2
Roy, Arundhati, 174

S

Said, Edward, v
Salgado, Sebastião, x, xii, xvi,
    133–183, *passim*, 184n1, 184n2,
    185n9, 186n25, 186n27,
    187n28, 187n31, 188n34,
    189n47, 189n53, 191, *Africa*
    (Salgado), 133, *An Uncertain
    Grace* (Salgado) 133, 152,
    Genesis (Salgado), 148, 182,
    186n25, *Migrations* (Salgado),
    149, 154, 177, 178, *Sahel*
    (Salgado), 133, 158, 163, 169,
    The Scent of a Dream (Salgado),
    152, 187n28, *Terra* (Salgado),
    172, *Workers* (Salgado),
    133–190, passim, 191
Salles, Walter, 220n8
The Salt of the Earth, 179
Santori, Ellen (Filomena
    D'Addario), 20
Selfie, 188n40
Serra Pelada, 159, 169, 170, 174,
    176, 182
Shukaitis, Stevphen, 19
Silverman, Kaja, 136, 165
Simon, Henri, 44n42
Singularity, vii, ix, xiiin7, 31,
    37n2, 40n15, 59, 98n18,
    127, 129, 146, 172,
    178, 189n47
Sischy, Ingrid, 180–181, 189n53
Smith, Adam, 64, 75, 78–80, 95n1
Smith, Neil, xiiin5, xvi
Smith, W. Eugene, 137, 180
Soar, Matthew, 181
Socialism, 10, 24, 54, 80, 89, 92,
    105, 173, 196, 204, 207,
    211, 220n12
Socialisme ou Barbarie, 18, 26–29, 31,
    40n19, 42n32, 43n41

Sontag, Susan, 148
Specters, 135
The Spectre of Hope, 185n10,
    189n48
Spinoza, Baruch, 54, 90
Spivak, Gayatri Chakravorty, 95n1,
    193, 219n2
Stallabrass, Julian, 148, 159, 168
Still Life (Jia Zhangke), 194, 196,
    206–209, 214
Stone, Ria (Grace Lee Boggs), 10,
    14–19, 40n16, 41n24
Subject, vi–vii, x, xi, xiin5, 3, 4, 7–12,
    15–17, 20, 25, 28, 29, 31, 33, 34,
    37n5, 47–69, *passim*, 69n1,
    69n5, 70n6, 71n10, 71n11,
    73n27, 76, 78, 81, 84, 89, 90,
    91, 95n1, 96n7, 105, 108, 109,
    113, 114, 118–120, 124, 129,
    133–140, 142–148, 150–153,
    157–159, 162, 163, 167, 169,
    176, 178–182, 191, 192, 200,
    203, 208, 215
Subjectification, 51, 52, 62, 65, 66,
    68, 71n11, 81, 89, 184n6
Subjectivity, 8, 30, 38n9, 39n13,
    43n35, 52, 56–58, 60, 76–77,
    104, 105, 107, 109, 135–139,
    142, 159, 161, 162, 176,
    182, 207
Synecdoche, 20, 92, 142

T

Thereness, 94, 112–113, 128, 135,
    146, 151, 184n6
Tie Xi Qu, 212
Tomkins, Sylvan, 90
Tomlinson, John, xiiin5
A Touch of Sin (Jia Zhang-ke), 194,
    196, 202, 213, 214, 221n12

Transformation problem, 75–76, 86, 87, 92
Translation xivn11
Tristan, Flora, 8, 39n13
Tronti, Mario, vii, 33, 45n50
24 City (Jia Zhang-ke), 194, 196, 209, 211, 212

U

Universality, 3, 15, 16, 55, 78, 107, 164, 192
Unknown Pleasures (Jia Zhangke), 194, 197–199
Useless (Jia Zhangke), 196

V

value, aesthetic, 28, 63, 84, 86
value, economic, 51, 63, 64, 66, 75, 76, *passim*, 79, 84, 85, 87, 96n3
Value, exchange, xiin6, 63, 81, 85
Value, vi, viii, x, xi, 7, 26, 34, 49, 63, 64, 66, 73n27, 75–95, *passim*, 95n1, 103, 125, 128, 161, 193, 209, 214
Value, labor theory of, 61, 63, 75–95, *passim*, 95n1
value, social, 63
Visuality, 92, 96n7, 134, 137, 175, 176, 193, 214

W

Wallerstein, Immanuel, 56
Wang Bing, 212, 222n23
Wang Hui, 200
Wang Xiaodong, 195
Ways of Seeing, 106, 143, 182, 183
Webb, Constance, 20–22
Weeks, Kathi, xiin8
Weibo, 95, 214, 215, 217, 219
Weil, Simone, 178
Williams, Raymond, 3, 7
Williams, Val, 189n52
Wolff, Richard D., 96n2
Woo, John, 209
worker inquiry, v–vi, ix, 8, 10, 21, 24–29, 31, 36, 44n44, 150
worker of the world(s), vi, xii, 31, 98n18, 107, 142, 162, 172, 185n11, 192
worker, as subject, vi, 9, 12, 29, 37n5, 47, 52, 62, 64–67, 70n5, 81, 99n24, 136
Workerism, 10, 13, 24, 29, 32, 44n47, 49, 56, 69n4, 181, 201, 210
Workers of the world, ix–x, 25, 36, 38n10, 134, 135, 161, 163, 172, 185n11, 189n53, 191, 192, 203
Workers' Inquiry (Marx), 7, 10, 11, 18, 19, 21, 24, 31, 181
Working class, viii, x, xi, xiin1, 4, 7, 8, 11, 13, 14, 15, 17, 18, 25, 28, 40n19, 44n48, 50, 60–62, 66, 68, 69n5, 85, 90, 97n15, 103–107
Work, ontology of, 49, 72n15, 103
The World (Jia Zhangke), 194, 196, 203, 205, 207
World Literature, 38n10
Wright Mills, C., 32, 44n48
Wright, Steve, 44n45

X

Xiancheng, 195–196, 203, 205, 218

Y

Yeats, W.B., 213
Ying Qian, 222n23
Yulu (Jia Zhangke), 222n24

Z

Zandy, Janet, 99n29
Zhang, Lu, 222n25
Zhang Xudong, 195
Zhang Yingjin, 220n10
Zhao Tao, 212
Zizek, Slavoj, 64, 70n8, 72n24, 97n16, 207
Zola, Émile, 81, 92